ADOLPHE APPIA, *Prophet of the Modern Theatre: A Profile*

Figure 1. Adolphe Appia, ca. 1890. *Jean Mercier.*

ADOLPHE APPIA

Prophet of the Modern Theatre:
A Profile

By WALTHER R. VOLBACH

WESLEYAN UNIVERSITY PRESS, *Middletown, Connecticut*

Library of Congress Catalog Card Number: 68–27547
Manufactured in the United States of America

FIRST EDITION

To my wife Claire
and
Edmond Appia

To be what we are, and to become what we are capable of becoming, is the only end of life.

—Robert Louis Stevenson

When you come in contact with a man . . . fix your attention upon his suffering, needs, anxieties, pains. Then you will always feel kinship with him.

—Arthur Schopenhauer

CONTENTS

LIST OF ILLUSTRATIONS

PREFACE

My deep interest in Adolphe Appia and his prophetic ideas reaches back to my student days in Munich. In late fall, 1918, I, a neophyte actor, was privileged to observe the rehearsals of Dietrich Christian Grabbe's *Hannibal* in the Bavarian National Theater. Albert Steinrueck, who played Hannibal, directed the production; Emil Pirchan, then an almost unknown young artist, designed the settings. When these were mounted for the first time, an older colleague sitting next to me in the house analyzed the spatial picture and concluded that it looked as if it were devised by Appia. I had never heard his name before, but my tutor told me where I could discover more about this unique artist. Soon I had read *Die Musik und die Inscenierung* and *La Mise en scène du drame wagnérien*; they were a revelation, and I must add that I was even more absorbed in Appia's strange theories and dreams about staging in general than in his magnificent sketches, notwithstanding the spell they had on me and still have. I have never ceased to be fascinated with Appia's artistic concept; reading one of his essays or visiting an exhibition of his most impressive designs has always been a thrilling experience. When I became a stage director I noticed that unconsciously I tried to apply his principles in both play and opera productions.

It was not until the middle fifties that I was given the chance to do something worthwhile for this Swiss genius. As chairman of the Rare Books Project, American Educational Theatre Association, I had the task to set up a list of books that were to be translated and published. Appia's writings were indeed included in my selection which was enthusiastically approved by my colleagues. I had a fair knowledge of his writings, but I did not know their scope until Donald Oenslager, the distinguished designer, showed me his treasure of unknown Appia essays. Through him I got in touch with Edmond Appia, a distant cousin of Adolphe and the director of the Fondation Adolphe Appia in Geneva. Monsieur Appia, an internationally known musician and conductor, was agreeable to my project and authorized me to publish all of Appia's writings in English and French.

The present book is an outgrowth of my contact with Edmond Appia. During a visit to his home in 1959, he showed me not only many of Adolphe's manuscripts and sketches but also interesting mementoes, such as letters written to Appia by Edward Gordon Craig and Emile Jaques-Dalcroze. The great number of Dalcroze letters led to a discussion about the possibility of making them the centerpiece of a book about Appia and Dalcroze. This idea was later expanded into the plan of a full biography of Adolphe. I urged M. Appia to write this biography, and promised that I would help with the research and writing of some chapters, particularly the Prologue and the Epilogue, as they were to be called. He, on the other hand, suggested that I take on this demanding task, and offered his full collaboration which would include making available the entire material of the foundation. M. Appia's persuasive power was stronger than mine, and I agreed to start work on the biography. An admirable collaborator, Edmond Appia never tired of answering my many inquiries and of doing the spade work for me in Europe. His untimely death early in 1961 was a dreadful shock to me, for I lost a friend, whose confidence I highly valued, and an irreplaceable collaborator. After several months of soul searching, I vowed to finish the task alone.

As this book was to be the first full-fledged study devoted to Adolphe Appia, I eliminated, from the beginning, the thought of a complete biography. No attempt was made to follow the artist from city to city from day to day, not even from year to year, since such a purely chronological method can contribute little to our understanding of his genius; nor are all data known at present sufficient to close many gaps; much material has been lost or is unavailable as yet. My intention was, therefore, to sketch a profile of the eminent designer, the philosopher, and the complex man. It seemed important to destroy some of the prevailing notions about him and to delineate the depth and variety of his prophetic ideas, few of which he was able to materialize during his life. The over-all organization did not offer any particular problems; on the contrary, the book developed in a natural manner, each chapter dealing with a major period of his work; only one, Chapter IV, devoted to his complicated personality.

In my research I pursued every hint, every clue, and of course some led to a dead end. My experience during these years taught me that most people are willing, even anxious, to help in such a venture. Very few of those I approached did not answer or declined to give any information. In several cases I received the same facts and opinions about Appia from two or three of his friends and relatives. Rarely was it necessary to choose between somewhat contradictory data. The information from his friends and relatives has been inserted without footnotes; the context of a passage makes my source or sources clear. No specific references have been added to quotations from Appia's writings; they can be found in the articles I wrote about his art and life.

It is rather easy to make mistakes. Unconsciously I might have misunderstood or misinterpreted explanations given me or data I discovered myself. As Appia rarely talked about his past or his work, not even those closest to him were positive that they always had the right answer. They all emphasized his utter truthfulness, but this does not mean that he revealed his innermost thoughts. Consequently, the conclusions drawn are my responsibility alone; I am prepared that, in later years, another writer will consider some of my statements untenable and correct them, although I hopefully expect my errors to be of a minor nature. I shall be satisfied if this labor of love will help create a better and more comprehensive knowledge and understanding of one of the great theatre artists.

ACKNOWLEDGEMENTS

T HE basic research was made possible through a grant from the Faculty Research Committee of Texas Christian University, and the final form through one from the Faculty Research Council of the University of Massachusetts. I express my sincere thanks to both institutions for the financial support of this study. I was able to visit several collections and libraries and to talk to friends and relatives of Adolphe Appia in Europe and the United States. Most gratifying was the wonderful support I received from almost everyone and every office. Again Edmond Appia must be mentioned first. Of immeasurable value have been Mrs. Blanche Bingham and Dr. Raymond Penel; these cousins of Appia made available much interesting material and never hesitated to answer my many questions. Equally essential has been the cooperation of Jean Mercier, Appia's friend and pupil, who gladly supplied much pertinent material and information, and, in addition, graciously acceded to my request to check the entire manuscript. Oskar Waelterlin, Appia's other pupil, kindly granted me a long interview and permission to make use of material he sent me. The extended explanations provided by Dr. Oscar Forel, Appia's friend and physician, have been of immense value. I am deeply indebted to Karl Reyle for his help in solving manifold problems and in sharing with me his memories of the great artist. The University of Miami Press was kind enough to permit the insertion of longer quotations from two Appia books, *Music and the Art of the Theatre* and *The Work of Living Art*. I am obliged, moreover, to *Die Musikforschung*, *Educational Theatre Journal*, and *Players' Magazine* for allowing me to use essays of mine published in these periodicals, and to the College of Fine Arts of The University of Texas for permission to use my article which appeared in *Paul A. Pisk Essays in his Honor*.

There are not enough words to express my admiration for, and my thanks to, Lois Atkinson who, in her editorial capacity, worked with great skill and delicate empathy on the preparation of the final version of my manuscript. I would like to explain what each of those mentioned below contributed to this book, but all I can say is that I am grateful to each person and each institution for the consideration given to my sometimes complicated inquiries and requests.

AUSTRIA
Miss Liselotte Kitzwegerer
Miss Trudl Kukula

FRANCE
Bibliothèque Nationale
Mrs. Beatrice Appia Blacher
Mrs. Ilse Caspari
Jean Daré
André Veinstein, Bibliothèque de l'Arsenal

FEDERAL REPUBLIC OF GERMANY
Rolf Badenhausen, Institut für
  Theaterwissenschaft, Cologne
Wolfgang Baumgart, Institut für
  Theaterwissenschaft, Berlin
Joachim Berghoff, Richard Wagner
  Museum, Bayreuth
Alfred Bruckmann
Hans Fellerer
Miss Elfriede Feudel
Count G. Gravina
Max Eduard von Liehburg
Carl Niessen
Chr. Peters, Institut fuer
  Zeitungswissenschaft, Munich
Guenther Schoene, Theatermuseum,
  Munich

DEMOCRATIC REPUBLIC
OF GERMANY
Mrs. Gertrud Rudloff-Hille

GREAT BRITAIN
Miss Annie Beck
British Museum
Miss Hilde Manassee

ITALY
Ferruccio Marotti
Gianni Mezzanotte
Nicolo Picella
Miss Emma Pirassi, Biblioteca
  Nazionale, Milan
Stefano Vittadini, Museo Teatrale
  alla Scala

Roland von Weber

THE NETHERLANDS
Joh. M. Coffeng, Vereniging Het
  Toneel Museum

SWITZERLAND
Mr. Germaine Appia
Mrs. Elsa Bonifas
Jacques Chenevière
Tibor Denès
G. Gueldenstein
Mrs. Charlotte MacJannet
Neue Zürcher Zeitung
Victor Ravizza
Kurt Reichel
Oliver Reverdin, *Journal de Genève*
Adolf Zinsstag

U.S.A.
Paul A. Bonifas
Miss Billie Bozone
Mrs. Ursula Chen
Ernest T. Ferand
Miss Elsa Findley
George Freedley, Library of the
  Performing Arts, New York
John Gaston
Barnard Hewitt
Mrs. Elizabeth Reynolds Hapgood
René Martin
University of Massachusetts, Library
Donald Oenslager
Hans Pusch
Lee Simonson
Texas Christian University, Library
Miss Zina Tillona
Mrs. Marisa Volbach
Terry H. Wells
Miss Helen D. Willard, Harvard Library

U.S.S.R.
Mrs. R. D. Shurinova, Pushkin Museum
A. Solodovnikov

Amherst, Massachusetts
June 1, 1968

W.R.V.

ADOLPHE APPIA, *Prophet of the Modern Theatre: A Profile*

PROLOGUE

During the decades prior to Adolphe Appia's entrance into the world of the theatre, Western civilization was in a rare state of serene tranquillity; no signs of sudden political, economic, or social upheavals threatened to disturb the peace, and a seemingly carefree society in most European countries lived in affluence. It was the time when in the British Empire, the Victorian period reached its zenith. In France another *belle époque* flowered during the Republic which followed the fall of Emperor Napoleon III. In Central Europe, Makart, a painter of huge over-loaded canvases, put his name and stamp on that period.

Victorian period, Makart style, *la belle époque* immediately evoke an atmosphere of superficiality, of abundance; a title, a high position, and money were the dominant factors in those circles which, under the effect of industrial expansion, played an all-important role in the cultural life of the day. Toward the end of the nineteenth century the imprint of this culture became increasingly noticeable. Theatre flourished particularly when it consisted of light entertainment or sumptuous productions of grand operas, operettas, drawing-room comedies, or shallow dramas. The new upper class of merchants and industrialists, joined by many members of nobility, were fascinated by the merry-go-round of diversions in which this kind of theatre fitted very well. To meet at performances, to dabble in the arts, to arrange artistic events in their spacious salons was a pleasant pastime. Theatre managers who wished to succeed without taking any risk had to cater to the taste of this society.

Among the favorite playwrights were Eugène Scribe, Victorien Sardou, and later Oscar Wilde, who for many years drew crowds into the theatres in Central and Western Europe. True, Henrik Ibsen's greatness was recognized by a small group of the intelligentsia, but he was certainly not appreciated by the public at large; nor were his disciples the naturalists very popular. The darling of the operetta audiences was Jacques Offenbach; the protagonist of grand opera, Giacomo Meyer-beer. Richard Wagner was as yet a rather controversial composer, more the idol of the young generation than a success among the ruling class. Not even Bizet was then generally acclaimed, and Claude Debussy was a name known only to a comparatively few cognoscenti. Among the painters, Karl von Piloty, Jacques Louis David, Eugène Delacroix, and their followers were still in vogue although the leaders of a new movement—Claude Monet, Pierre Auguste Renoir, Edouard Manet, Vincent van Gogh, and others—began to challenge their predominance. The style of both the historical and later the impressionistic artists was, to a high degree, reflected in the designs of stage settings.

Historic Realism

TECHNICALLY, the *décorateurs* merely elaborated on a style they inherited from the great masters of the eighteenth century. They adhered to the perspective designs developed to an admirable climax by the Bibienas and Burnacinis. The only real change, made early in the nineteenth century, was that, for interior settings, legs were replaced by flats on both sides of the acting area with the rear still often masked by a backdrop; doors and windows were not yet three-dimensional, and borders masked the fly system. Later, when a ceiling was placed on the setting, and doors as well as windows acquired plasticity, the way was open for complete realism. The first stage director who consistently followed this new style was André Antoine. Outdoor settings passed through a similar transition, though at a slower pace. For a long time arches remained essential; backdrops provided the forest, the hill, the seashore, or whatever the text called for. Since most stages were adequately equipped with fly galleries, slits, traps, and grooves, all these legs and backdrops could easily be shifted even before the eyes of the audience.

After the middle of the century a new method of treating the upstage area came into use by means of a blue skydrop in front of which ground-row pieces were placed to indicate the required location. However, the development of plasticity had to overcome two distinctive obstacles. One was the realistic painting applied to the "romantic" scenery; the other was expense: money was spent rather lavishly on musical works which were usually produced according to tradition with no desire for, or even thought of, innovation. As operas and plays were, as a rule, performed in the same theatre, the directors of the spoken drama had to use whatever was available in the scene docks. Thus many theatres were slow to introduce new technical media.

A word must be said about lighting. Gaslight had been installed in all leading theatres in the middle of the nineteenth century, while a new invention, the arc light, offered interesting opportunities to create special effects, such as sun rays or moonlight, thrown from a fly gallery. Before the end of the century the transition to electric light brought about an incisive change in the technique of scene painting. Under the stronger illumination it became customary to apply ever more subtle details to the setting.

Platforms and set pieces had been known for decades; in dozens of productions pillars and columns, even trees were being executed three-dimensionally; they were placed in front of painted backdrops and juxtaposed with painted legs in halls, churches, and forests. Eventually platforms were employed to indicate a corridor in the rear of a hall, the entrance to a castle or a church, the upstage part of a hill or a forest; and naturally stairs or ramps connecting the different levels were also available. Some theatres made wider use of dollies and wagons wherever feasible in order to shorten the time for shifting between acts and scenes. Others added revolving and elevator stages to handle the increasingly more complicated settings. All these innovations, however, remained purely technical; they were not based on any artistic conception. Possibly in one or another case there was an aim toward greater verisimilitude, but in general, the plastic pieces were separate units haphazardly lumped together by the head carpenter or the stage director. Indeed the new techniques were rarely applied for the purpose of achieving an integrated picture devised by a designer. Some felicitous exceptions occurred in Paris where the Opéra offered impressive settings as, for instance, in Meyerbeer's *L'Africaine*, and in London where equally splendid pictures were designed particularly for some Christmas pantomimes.

Gradually the wider use of three-dimensional pieces seemed to endanger the powerful position of the scene painter. An argument was in the offing: should the setting be painted more realistically with little emphasis on practical pieces, or, vice versa, should it consist of more practical pieces with less concern about painting? This problem had already arisen with Count Moritz von Bruehl in Berlin early in the century. He might be called the godfather of historic realism on the stage. The movement became more pronounced in the productions of Franz von Dingelstedt between 1850 and 1870 and culminated in those of George, Duke of Meiningen, whose production style prevailed beyond the turn of the century. This great showman and director transferred the style of historic painting onto the flats and backdrops of his settings. The use of platforms and their different levels was limited to a minimum. His conception being aped and emulated, especially in its weak aspects, gave the scenic painter a new lease on life, one could almost say with greater influence than before.

In connection with the revived stress on painting, a particular development contributed to the uniformity found on so many stages. Formerly, a designer had his own studio or was engaged by a leading theatre for a production or a longer term. Now in the wake of industrialization and commercialism, his place was taken over by business managers rather than by artists. The entire situation changed from that of a personal artistic endeavor to a rather large-scale commercial enterprise. This new type of studio would accept orders to design and make settings for a theatre; in addition, it executed settings from sketches submitted by a theatre. The principal result of the system was that a setting devised for one theatre could, with slight changes, be readily duplicated for another; sometimes no changes were needed at all. Thus a regrettable trend away from individual artistry developed. German theatres were, in a large measure, subjected to that system; the French less so. Whatever was devised by firms like Hartwig in Berlin, Kautzky in Vienna, especially Brueckner in Koburg, and Rublé et Chaperon in Paris became standard not alone in the theatre which gave the original order but in many others as well. The "creations" were seen and admired in dozens of cities. An entire "package" could be delivered within a brief period of time; all that any of those firms basically expected to know was the measurements of the stage, possibly some sketches, and of course the amount a theatre was willing to spend. Consequently, a production of *Faust, Aida, Oberon, Tannhäuser,* and all the other standard works in one of the leading opera houses was essentially like its production in a middling provincial theatre; the difference was only in size and splendor, not in style which although positively romantic was realistically executed.

These conditions prevailed for about a generation, and if they are viewed somewhat disparagingly, criticism should be concentrated on the inartistic attitude in general, which in turn can be understood only against its historical background. Besides, it must be emphasized that, technically, many of these settings were usually excellent. Many facets of staging widely accepted today were introduced and developed during this period.

Attempts at a Reform

THROUGHOUT the nineteenth century, currents of production style ran in opposite directions. The main stream moved toward ever more realism in scenery, costumes, properties, and acting in spite of a romantic foundation. This style left little freedom for variations; these concerned almost exclusively details of the setting which was sometimes more realistic, sometimes less so. The argument of whether ornamental pieces were to be painted on flats and backdrop or whether real ones were to be hung on the walls became more important and more significant than the overall conception. This exaggerated realism actually dominated the stage. Yet, sporadic attempts were made to simplify the scenic picture while adhering to the romantic school of acting; other currents, submerged rather than in the open, drifted in toward a modernized version of the Renaissance or the Elizabethan stage. Common to all reformers was their opposition to the realistic trend, to the resplendence and extravagance of the traditional Baroque staging. Some limited their reform plans

Figure 2. The Valkyrie, Act III, as staged by Richard Wagner in Bayreuth in 1876. *Richard Wagner Gedenkstaette, Bayreuth.*

to the scenic picture, others extended their experiments to the field of acting, but none of them thought of a new approach to the production as a whole.

True, Wolfgang von Goethe advanced principles of modern staging even before any realistic trend could be noticed. As the *Intendant* of the Court Theatre in Weimar for twenty-five years, Goethe did not try to alter the neo-classic style he favored nor the budding romanticism which invaded many theatres early in the nineteenth century; but in his writings he set forth ideas which were to bear fruit later. In his *Wilhelm Meister* Goethe discussed the art of the theatre in several chapters indicating he could win an audience with the most primitive stage, simply boards laid across some barrels, provided he had Shakespeare as playwright. In the same work he delineated the common roots of acting and dancing. Thus, although Goethe himself did not put these ideas into practice, they found response in the proclamations and experiments of the succeeding reformers, all of whom concentrated, however, on a single aspect; not one of them tried to understand the entire esthetics of a new theatre.

Karl Friedrich Schinkel, an excellent architect and designer in Berlin, was the first scenic artist of the century anxious to develop a simplified scenery. Just as he stressed "usefulness" in buildings,[1] so he searched for a more functional stage. He was in favor of a large forestage and a neutral proscenium. Some of his plans reveal that he also kept the wings in a neutral color thus leaving only the backdrop to be painted and to indicate the location. Yet he was not averse to set pieces placed in front of that backdrop or to an arch with painted trees simulating a forest. Since Schinkel's backdrops were often executed in the prevailing romantic style—an excursion into neo-classicism notwithstanding—and since he never arrived at a definite solution for his reform dreams, his attempts have been of minor consequence. The honor to be called a real reformer is due Karl Leberecht Immermann who threw out the conventional arrangement and instead devised a unit setting based on ideas propagated during the Renaissance. The downstage area of his setting jutted into the auditorium like a wide apron; the upstage was raised to form a special acting area. On this wide platform he erected a wall with a large center opening, two entrances left and right of it and one each left and right in the false proscenium. Set pieces were used particularly behind the large center opening. This type of setting was primarily devised for the dramas of Shakespeare and the German classics. But in the 1830's the citizens of Düsseldorf did not appreciate his new way of staging, and Immermann found little artistic encouragement and even less financial success. After a few years he had to give up the management of his theatre.

In 1843 an interesting experiment was prepared by Ludwig Tieck, one of the most sensitive and cultured romanticists. He was as acquainted with the English theatre and the Elizabethan stage as any German of that time could be. His concept of a reform was definitely influenced by Goethe whose plans he elaborated. Counseled by the architect Gottfried Semper, he devised a spatial arrangement showing, stage center, a rather high platform to which a set of stairs led from left and right; underneath the platform a door was located. Tieck's production of *A Midsummer Night's Dream* at the Royal Palace in Potsdam was, however, not performed in this simple setting; he added backdrops and set pieces, designed by J. C. J. Gerst, and thus destroyed the basic simplicity of the scenery. Several years later he made plans for a production of *Henry V* on a stylized stage, but the revolutionary tensions of 1848 prevented their realization.

Gottfried Semper, the architect of the new Opera House in Dresden, developed further the staging principles he had discussed with Tieck. While Schinkel somehow accepted the Greek ideal itself, Semper followed the Greek arrangement as the Renaissance had interpreted it, and consequently his designs emphasized the width rather than the depth of the stage. His wish was to simplify the oppressive proscenium frame and the complex romantic scenery. Recognizing the actor's need for a light source independent of the one which illuminates the setting, Semper also intended to install special lighting effects for the performer downstage.

In England the first break in the growing realistic trend came in the 1840's when Benjamin Webster staged, in London's Haymarket Theatre, *The Taming of the Shrew*, against drapes arranged between screens. This nonrealistic *mise en scène* remained an isolated venture. England, under the impact of Kean's productions, was already leading in complicated scenic effects and strove toward ever greater perfection in this field. No other attempt to modify the scenery was made until 1881 when William Poel also used only drapes for his production of *Hamlet* in Oxford's St. George's Hall. Like other admirers of Shakespeare he sought to take advantage of the growing knowledge of Elizabethan customs and to produce the great plays as they were presented by the author himself. Twelve years later he built an Elizabethan stage in a conventional theatre for *Measure for Measure*. During the following twenty years Poel produced at least twelve more plays by Shakespeare in a similar manner. These experiments earned high praise even from the sharp pen of George Bernard Shaw. Indeed, in spite of their "scholarly dryness" they had some effect on the next generation. Poel proved that simplified scenery benefits the Shakespearean drama and that a faster pace of delivery can be used for it.[2] At the turn of the nineteenth century Ben Greet followed the same concept but with little artistic success, as his purpose was too deeply involved in "education."[3] Across the Atlantic Ocean this trend was taken up, not in the professional field, of course, but in a university. At Harvard, Ben Johnson's *The Silent Woman (Epicoene)* was presented on a kind of Elizabethan stage in 1895, and nine years later, a further experiment was made with *Hamlet*. These few examples remained the exceptions as only a small number ventured against the prevailing realistic movement which had its climax in the productions of Henry Irving.

To include Franz Dingelstedt among the reformers is somewhat daring since

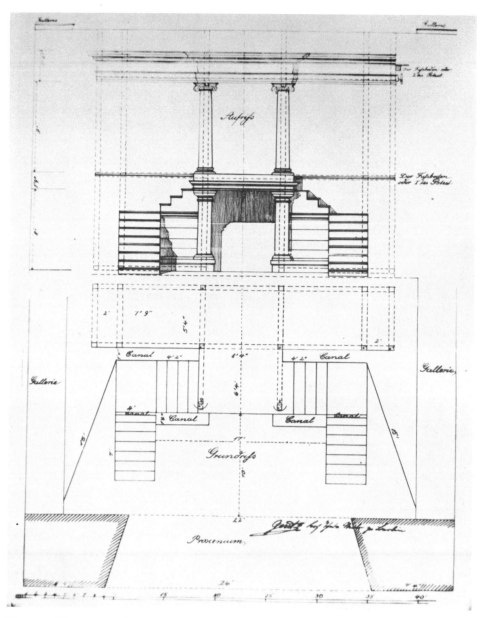

Figure 3. Elevation and floorplan of *A Midsummer Night's Dream* in Tieck's production.
Institut fuer Theaterwissenschaft, Cologne.

he is usually termed a predecessor of the Duke of Meiningen. An excellent manager and showman, he was responsible for several innovations, though not always fortunate ones. His treatment of supernumeraries was expanded in Meiningen and his *Mustervorstellungen* (model performances), as he called the special performances of classic dramas with a galaxy of stars, were the precursers of the modern festivals. In connection with this study it is vital to remember Dingelstedt's production of Schiller's *The Bride of Messina* in the Bavarian Court Theatre in the early fifties, for it demonstrated an adherence to a classical style of staging out of fashion at that time. For his unit setting Dingelstedt foreswore all traditional trappings; instead, he confined himself to an elaborate arrangement of platforms and stairs surrounded by neutral flats and doors. However critically we may today view the Meiningers' historic realism we must acknowledge that the Duke had an amazing sense of space and, a few times, made excellent use of levels in the upstage area. His unique arrangement of a leading character placed on a platform in the rear, with the extras—their backs to the audience—scattered in front of him, left a tremendous impact on succeeding stage directors.

A production of *King Lear* in Munich on June 1, 1889, was mounted with a simplified setting which became known as the Shakespeare Stage and remained in use for almost thirty years; it even affected the designs of some new theatres. Actually this stage form had little in common with the original Elizabethan type and the name given to it probably refers more to the fact that it served the presentation of Shakespearean tragedies, although several demanding German classical dramas were also performed on it. It consisted of three parts: (1) the wide apron filling half of the orchestra pit, a broad staircase leading down into the pit and footlights installed in the outer rim (years later spotlights installed in a box illuminated the forestage); (2) the rather shallow middle area framed by a false proscenium with doors left and right; (3) the raised upstage area which was fairly deep but only about half as wide as the proscenium opening. Curtains could be drawn between the areas which made it possible to play either on the apron, in the middle area, in the upstage area, or in any combination desired. Set pieces were at first limited to the third area; behind the upstage platform, backdrops and even a diorama were used.[4] Jocza Savits, the stage director, had suggested the new arrangement and Karl Lautenschlaeger, the technical director, solved its manifold problems; Karl von Perfall, the general manager of the Court and National Theatre, supervised the venture which was consciously based on the spade work done by Immermann and Tieck.

Before this chapter on stage reform in the nineteenth century can be closed, one more dreamer must be mentioned. His deeds include no productions, merely three books; but some of the ideas expressed by George Fuchs were fruitful indeed and, interesting to note, a few resemble those brought forth by Adolphe Appia before and during the same period. In 1891 Fuchs published his treatise *Von der stilistischen Belebung der Schaubuehne (Stimulating the Style of Staging)* which was followed by *Die Schaubuehne der Zukunft (The Stage of the Future)* (1904) and then *Die Revolution des Theaters* (1909). In his books Fuchs did not recommend radical surgery on the existing theatre; like some of his predecessors he was in favor of a wide apron flanked by two permanent towers behind the proscenium frame; like others before him, he was dissatisfied with the bad effects of the footlights. Footlights had been damned by several sensitive artists before, among them August Strindberg who in his Preface to *Miss Julie* (1888) took a sharp position against their adverse effect. Fuchs advised that their role be cut down and that they never be used at full volume. In his opinion strong light from above and the rear should strike the actor in order to throw him into focus. Equally remarkable is his principle that "dramatic art is . . . dancing, that is, rhythmic movement of the human body in space."[5]

With George Fuchs ends this brief survey of nonrealistic theories and experiments in Central Europe. In France, which had contributed so much to the development of theatre arts, no true reformer, alas, arose to preach against the ever-growing scenic realism. For all the bitter complaints about the conventionality of the theatre uttered by several outstanding authors beginning with J. J. Rousseau, a researcher must go far to discover a genuine reform. After 1860 Théophile Gautier pondered how the *mise en scène* could be reformed. Before the end of the century the only artistic experiment was initiated by Paul Fort and Aurélien-Marie Lugné-Poë who in 1891 opened the Théâtre d'Art, where a helping hand was extended to the young symbolists. After Fort left, Lugné-Poë showed more interest in experimenting with a new approach away from the realistic staging method of André Antoine. This was particularly noticeable when he founded the Théâtre de l'Oeuvre in 1893, yet he did not become completely imbued with the nonrealistic style until several years later. Particularly interesting was his production of *Measure for Measure* in 1898 less because of the simplified shallow setting than because of the facts that the audience surrounded the forestage on three sides and that steps connected the acting area with the auditorium. In general, opposition to the predominant staging concept was restricted to a few authors of whom Stephen Mallarmé and Louis Becq de Fouquières were the outstanding representatives.

In evaluating these sundry experiments we come to the conclusion that they all served the same purpose: to eliminate the exaggerations of scenic realism, to do away with the many faked trappings, to de-emphasize historic details, and to return to a fundamental concept of dramatic art derived from the classic Greek theatre in its renaissance in the sixteenth century, or from the Elizabethan stage. Some reformers shared the impression that the theatre had lost contact with the audience; hence they experimented with arrangements that would bring the performer closer to the theatregoer seated in front of him. A few were puzzled by the opportunities offered by the newly invented electric light; others even considered a change in the acting style.

Unfortunately, though by no means surprisingly, all these sincere attempts to bring that powerful realistic movement to a halt had no immediate practical result. Except for the Shakespeare Stage in Munich, not a single experiment lasted to gain many followers; the public at large remained unmoved, and thus the various experiments made hardly a ripple in the main stream of events. As often happens, though, in the long run none of the endeavors was made in vain. In general, reformers are well acquainted with the work of their predecessors and contemporaries, and they draw upon that knowledge to bring their own ideas to fruition. Eventually the timid voices become stronger and are heard more widely until the time is ripe for a change.

This favorable condition, the climax of realism, occurred between 1880 and 1890 when the pendulum had reached an extreme point and was ready to swing in the opposite direction. Realism could push no further. A new style appeared, away from exaggerated illusion, accurateness, and verisimilitude. The avant-garde of symbolism aspired to poetic transformation, and the leaders of impressionism discarded the style of yesteryear. Light received a new role; it began to create new dimensions in painting. Chiaroscuro became a term applicable to poems and dramas, to paintings and compositions. It was inevitable that some day this trend would affect the theatre too. Even the average theatre patron eventually grew tired of the traditional staging. Anselm Feuerbach expressed this mood: "I hate the modern theatre because my sharp eye always sees through the cardboard. . . . The true work of art has enough power within itself to make its situations visible and real without unworthy artificial means, which violate all the canons of art. Unobtrusive suggestion is what is needed, not bewildering effects."[6] About the time when this statement was made, Adolphe Appia, then a young musician in his formative years, studied and observed the theatre in several countries. Toward the end of the 1880's he decided to advance a new revolutionary concept of the art of the theatre.

Figure 4. Adolphe Appia, 16 years old. *Blanche Bingham.*

I

Geneva, 1881

ONE evening in 1881 Adolphe Appia, nineteen years old, went to the new Grand Théâtre in Geneva to attend a performance of Gounod's *Faust*. The young man was excited, full of expectations. He had dreamed about performances from the days of his childhood; he had imagined what the scenic picture had looked like— or *should* look like. Now at last, thanks to an invitation from his mother's sister, Mademoiselle Emilie Lasserre, his parents were allowing him to hear and see an opera for the first time. Theatre and everything related to it was fundamentally against their religious belief, but since it was agreed he was to study music, they had finally given their consent. They could not suspect that their younger son was obsessed by theatre; that his primary wish was to choose a theatrical career, that it was thus less the music than the opera—the lyric drama on a stage—that had such a hold on his imagination.

A few hours after the final curtain had fallen Adolphe was disenchanted and depressed. The performance of *Faust* was by no means what he had expected. He had paid scant attention to the orchestra, the singing, or the music in general, rather he had concentrated on the acting of the singers and on the settings in which they moved. What he witnessed had nothing in common with his vision of this opera. He had thought the stage settings would be three-dimensional, with platforms to add to the positions and movements of the characters. Instead there were merely a flat stage floor and flimsy painted wings and backdrops bearing no relation to the singers. So disappointing was this experience that the young Appia suffered "a moral and artistic let-down," as he confessed many years later.

To find it incredible that a young man so preoccupied with the theatre did not attend any performance until he was nearly twenty years old is to overlook the compelling influences of staid Geneva and the Victorian era. In Appia's youth, life in his native city was quiet and well regulated, offering few opportunities, at least officially, to enjoy the good and merry things of life. Geneva was then a city of about 50,000 or, including a few suburbs, 70,000. Its disciplined citizens were proud of Geneva's historical background and all its traditions and personalities. Jean Calvin, the great religious reformer, was especially held in esteem; in opposite regard was another native son, Jean-Jacques Rousseau, whose valuable writings were never enough of an excuse for his having been a libertine.

In the 1880's Geneva had none of its present-day international flavor. Despite the facts that its center is just a few miles from the French border and that it is surrounded on three sides by foreign territory, strangers had no part in its civic life a hundred years ago. Even then the city was a center for education, business, and tourism, but the outsiders, lured by its attractions, had little opportunity to meet the natives who, considering themselves morally above the crowds, preferred to remain among their own kind. Provincialism was so extreme that when Geneva finally joined the Swiss Federation in 1814—more than six hundred years after its founding—it did not do so as a canton like all the other regions, but as the Republic of Geneva. Its old leading families, culturally oriented toward France, were slow in accepting their German and Italian compatriots despite their numerous business connections with them. Outsiders, including Geneva's own middle class, rarely succeeded in breaking into that upper circle, which was probably the most impenetrable in Europe. Marriages as a rule were exclusively among members of the elite; few ventured elsewhere to find a spouse.

In such an atmosphere new ideas, reforms, let alone adventures, were not welcome. Good citizens were expected to conform and to execute a traditional job in a reliable manner. To be good and well behaved was more than a slogan—it was a way of life; almost a law.

Appia's Family

Dr. Louis Paul Amédée Appia, Adolphe's father, was highly respected in Geneva, although the Appias were not one of the old native families. As their name indicates they are of Italian stock. In the Vallées Vaudoises of Piedmont the Appia tree can be retraced several hundred years, definitely to the fifteenth century, vaguely as far back as the seventh. Appias were known as nonconformists when, in a Catholic country, some of them joined the fundamentalist movement of the Vaudois which based its faith exclusively on the teachings of the Bible. It thus came as no surprise that people in Piedmont, located in the Southwestern part of the Alps, were strongly attracted by Calvin's doctrines; a good many crossed the mountains to hear Calvin and later to study the new theology in Geneva more thoroughly. Even in modern times contact was quite lively between Geneva and Piedmont where some families still speak French.

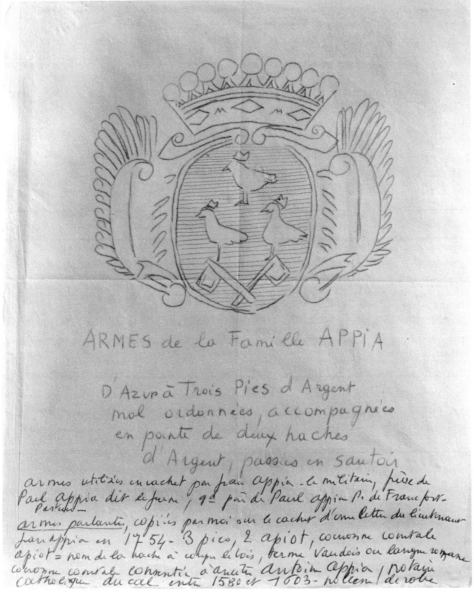

Figure 5. The Appia coat of arms. It shows three silver magpies above two hatchets. Mrs. Blacher, the unofficial historian of the family, copied it from a seal of the year 1751. *Béatrice Appia Blacher.*

The name Appia likely derives from the word *hâppia;* in modern French it appears as *hâche* (hatchet). The *h* of hâppia disappeared in the Italian (or Italianized) name Appia.

Paul Joseph Appia (1782–1849) decided to leave that Protestant enclave, and in 1811 accepted a pastorate in Hanau near Frankfurt am Main, moving, a few years later, to the French Church in Frankfurt proper. With his wife, née Caroline Develay (1786–1867), he had six children: Pauline (1815–1872), married to Louis Vallette (1800–1872); Marie (1816–1886), married to Jacques Claparède (1809–1879); Louis (1818–1896), married to Anna Caroline Lasserre (1824–1886); Cécile (1822–1858), married to Gabriel Bouthillier Beaumont (1811–1887); Louise (1825–1904; and George (1827–1910), married to Hélène Sturge (1831–1928).

Pastor Paul Appia intended to retire to Switzerland in his later years but he passed away before he was able to carry out his plan. His son Louis went to school and college in Frankfurt. For two years he stayed with some cousins in Geneva, then in 1838 moved to Heidelberg to study medicine. At the university Louis devoted considerable time to the humanities, acquiring a good knowledge of the authors and composers of the German classic era. At the age of twenty-five he passed his medical examination and several years later he obtained a second doctorate from the University of Paris. Louis' first years as a physician were divided between Geneva and Paris. After his father's death in 1849 he made his home in Geneva where his sisters Marie and Louise were living. The doctor practiced first in Jussy; later in Geneva itself. He and his wife Anna, whom he married in 1853, lived at 5, Rue Calvin, an old street close to the famous Cathédrale de Saint-Pierre. He was soon known as an excellent surgeon and his good standing among his colleagues led to his nomination and election as president of the Medical Society in 1861. In the preceding year he had been accepted as citizen of the Republic of Geneva, an honor not easily conferred upon an immigrant.

In 1863 he was the driving power behind the founding of the Red Cross. Joined by four other physicians he initiated the original association, *Commission des Cinq*, with the aim of alleviating the suffering of the wounded in any war. His talent for organization, his untiring energy, and his idealism won him numerous admirers in many countries. One of these was Clara Barton, often referred to as "the American Nightingale," who collaborated with him through many years. Dr. Appia also made a name for himself as the author of several essays and books. Success, however, did not spoil him. On the contrary, he remained a modest man, a true follower of his faith who coveted no glory in this world; typically, he requested that his burial place have no stone.

These facts provide the public image of Adolphe's father. In the privacy of his home Dr. Appia created a different impression, especially to his children. It may already be guessed that his religious background and zeal, his drive and capacity for work, his perfectionism made him a stern disciplinarian, strict even by the rigid standards of the day. The severe rules he made for himself were likewise applied to his children's upbringing and education—making him greatly respected but little loved. Life in the Appia home was never relaxed nor happy.

The doctor was seldom communicative except when annoyed. He tried to control his frequent outbursts of irritation, but often could do so only by leaving the room abruptly. His unpredictable behavior created tensions within the family circle; because it seemed safer to avoid close contact with their father, the children learned to live their own lives separately, to form no close relationships even with their brothers and sisters. This apartness seemed to have worried Dr. Louis for he talked to outsiders about it, even to strangers. His unhappiness grew with the knowledge that he made his family suffer.

There is one clue to how the doctor's extreme puritanism shaped his character and eroded his emotions to a point that he was unable even to express simple parental love. Calvinistic dogma had created within him an overwhelming fear of damnation. When the anxiety seized him, he had to flee to one of his sisters who alone could console and reassure him.

Apart from his religion and his profession he had few interests. In his spare hours he would read in his large library at home, and he would occasionally go to a concert, but theatre and all that was connected with it was banned: in his presence the word "theatre" was not to be uttered. Adolphe may have had his father in mind when he stated in an essay that "persons who despise the theatre satisfy their taste through reading." In his so-called memoirs he included a characteristic quote of his father's: "Men have written quite interesting things, they have created sublime pieces of art . . . but getting out of bed and into my slippers is of greater interest to me." And, in his son's words, another example of his practicality: "When Dr. Louis was asked one day why he took an interest in the Salvation Army he laconically answered, 'If you want to know the camel, go to Africa.'" In spite of his suspicion of the arts, he liked to draw. Those who saw sketches Dr. Appia brought from his many trips had high praise for their artistic conception and technical execution.

Dr. Louis was a handsome and impressive man; even at a ripe age he was beautiful, according to his son. He had a magnificent head; his piercing eyes now and then showed irony or a suppressed tenderness. Some relatives thought he resembled Friedrich Nietzsche; they wondered if, under the extreme severity, there did not lurk a very human being with interests and passions suppressed with all energy. After the death of his wife he was a very lonely man. His daughter Hélène, who occupied an apartment above his, looked after him, but only his work and his church provided him with social contacts; in his apartment he was alone. At his death bed in 1898 his children assembled dutifully, but he left this world without being missed by any of them.

Although Adolphe was twenty-four when his mother died, she seemed to have left no imprint on his life. After her early death little remained of her memory; no visible mementoes such as photographs and the like were to be seen in the home. She was kind, insignificant perhaps, and unable to mitigate the disturbing influences of her dominant husband, but she was a loyal wife who did her duty as she interpreted it. Like her husband she enjoyed traveling and she also helped him in his work for the Red Cross. She loved Switzerland, particularly the wonderful countryside. In all of his writings Adolphe referred to her only in a brief passage: "she raised her children for heaven, not for this world. . . . Religious compassion dominated her life."

The couple had four children: Paul (1856–1925), who married Olympe Laugt (1852–1916); Hélène (1858–1944); Marie (1860–1914); and Adolphe François (1862–1928).

Marie, never conspicuous, was a pious child who decided at an early age to devote her life to her church and eventually to missionary work. In her twenties she became a kind of evangelist, spending many years in Syria teaching school and attempting to read the Scriptures in the houses of the Arabian population. Adolphe had no contact with her and never mentioned her even to friends.

Paul was a banker engrossed in his business; his only other interest was his church. An aunt of his called him "a man of one dimension." A greater contrast than that between the two brothers can hardly be imagined, and it is easy to understand why they ignored each other as much as possible. Once in a while Adolphe chatted with Geneviève, Paul's only child, or told her exciting tales. She would then run to her father and ask whether all that was true. Paul would merely answer, "We know nothing about it. We know for sure only what is found in the Bible." Geneviève was, mildly speaking, retarded; although sweet, gentle, and harmless, she was apt to run away from home. Several times police found her in other cities and her parents had to fetch her back to Geneva. Paul's wife, Olympe, was unstable, particularly after reaching middle age, and at times had to be sent to an asylum. This sad situation surely added much to the fact that Paul, like his father, was uncommunicative. He had neither friends nor friendly relations with colleagues or other people in the city.

Hélène, a remarkable woman, gave Adolphe moral and financial support throughout his adult life. Although she was attractive when young, she never married. For reasons of her own, she decided to take care of her father—Dr. Appia in his egocentricity may even have requested this care—and she always made her home at 5, Rue Calvin, where she was born. Her main occupation was her lifelong interest in and work for the Red Cross. Hélène was a cultured woman, a fine musician, well versed in literature, an able translator; she and Adolphe were thoroughly congenial. Of all the family members she alone had close contact with her artistic brother whom she admired and adored. With deep sympathy she tried to understand him and his work and was always ready to help. A few times the two made arrangements to live together but, outspoken individualists and strong-willed as were many of the Appias, they found it more convenient to separate again.

It is significant for the Appias that in addition to Adolphe's grandfather, four uncles and several cousins were pastors of Calvinist and Lutheran churches; one of them had some artistic talent and loved to draw, but his sketches are considered academic next to those by Adolphe's father. Adolphe paid little attention to his numerous relatives with the exception of his mother's sister Emilie and some distant cousins who also shared a spiritual kinship with him.

Young Adolphe

THE salient elements of Adolphe's environment were exaggerated piety, strict discipline, monotony, and contempt for what most interested the boy. His father had apparently no inkling of his son's great sensitivity nor his curiosity about the arts—in particular, the theatre—traits which Adolphe showed at an early age. Thus his interests and latent talents received no encouragement, and the "frustration" of which Appia later wrote began when he was quite small. Evidently there was never an open clash between father and son; the father dictated and the son withdrew, becoming more and more an introvert. Repeatedly Adolphe tried, consciously or unconsciously, to protest and fight against everything his parents stood for. He succeeded in concentrating on his innate gifts in spite of the atmosphere that depressed and intimidated him, but his childhood experience left its mark. The stress so affected the boy that he began to stutter; nobody seemed to know how to take corrective steps or even to care about it, and the defect grew worse with the years. In fact, this impediment compelled him to change his theatrical ambitions. As a young man he dreamed of productions under his direction. When he first studied music seriously he may have aspired to be a conductor, but his later aim was definitely to become a director and designer. However, his stuttering made him so self-conscious—he even withdrew from the presence of strangers—that the eminently sensitive artist had to turn theorist and use writing to expound his visions of a new approach to the theatre.

A youth so different from other boys that he shared none of the interests and activities common to childhood, and so little understood by his parents had to seek his own way to pursue his intense interests. His father's large library provided young Adolphe with some means to satisfy his passion for the theatre. He was barely able to read when he began to spend hours and hours scanning the volumes of dramatic works. At about ten years of age he was completely absorbed in reading the great plays of the past, and the term "theatre" began to exercise an ever-growing fascination which it never lost. Among his father's books he found the classic French and German authors like Corneille, Racine, Molière, Hugo, Lessing, Goethe, and Schiller, most of whom he admired the rest of his life. Probably many of these editions were illustrated as was often the case in that period. This then could give a clue to the origin of his peculiar interest in stage scenery. As young

Adolphe started, so he proceeded later on, namely to seek knowledge and to train himself. He would have readily agreed with Oscar Wilde's ironic remark, "Education is an admirable thing, but it is well to remember from time to time that nothing that is worth knowing can be taught."

When we look for impressions of a dramatic nature which might have stimulated Adolphe's imagination we should consider the popular pageants he surely witnessed as a boy. For all his parents' opposition to the theatre, they could have hardly objected to his watching some of the traditional festivities seen in the streets of Geneva. Two of them in particular are still held annually—*Escalade* on December 12, celebrating the repulse of an unexpected attack on Geneva by the Duke of Savoie in 1602, has groups of people in seventeenth-century costumes wandering and "performing" in the streets. In the *Feuille,* a spring festival, winter is chased off and its last vestiges are driven away; this event takes place on a large open square close to the lake. Both pageants demonstrate the intimate contact between performers and spectators, a feature recurring again and again in Appia's esthetics. It is further not impossible that Adolphe had as a schoolboy attended one of the large regional or national folk festivals, for instance *La Fête des Vignerons* at Vevey, which combine dancing, singing, and sometimes acrobatics. In these presentations staged outdoors or in simple auditoriums he would have noticed the same intimacy between audience and performers. He himself does not mention any of those events until in his later years.

Altogether Appia tells us very little about his boyhood; indeed with the years he grew increasingly reluctant to talk about it even to friends and relatives. In his writings he scarcely refers to observations and experiences at home, in school, or with young friends. In dealing with the topic "theatre" as it relates to children he tells only one personal anecdote. Yet as his writings contain much autobiographical material, the conclusion may be drawn that he wrote about his own experience in *Notes sur le théâtre* when he described the attitude of adults toward a boy attending a performance for the first time. To be sure his story cannot be literally true—he himself was no longer a boy when he saw *Faust,* and certainly the ladies' conversation is exaggerated; nevertheless, a core of truth remains. The story goes like this: Two ladies taking a boy along to an opera try to explain everything to the child. "You see, this is the curtain! Actually it is not a curtain but a painted canvas. This is the forestage, there are the boxes," and so on and so forth. All this chatter disturbs the young fellow who is really excited. When the house darkens and the orchestra plays he has to hear that "this is the overture," while he simply wants to listen to music. When the curtain opens he is told, " . . . you see the scenery! There, on both sides are the wings; the backdrop is painted. It is night because the lights are blue. This is the tenor. Now comes the duet of Act One." And so on and on it went. Appia despised the idleness and superficiality of adults who would destroy child's illusion. The boy suffered throughout the evening; he could not understand how adults could remain so indifferent when confronted with the wonders of the stage. There was the real world, not in the house; it was the audience that appeared unreal to him. Theatre meant beautiful and amazing things to live through. Appia then concluded that the ladies should have explained to the boy the workings of a production in a different vein and well before the performance proper. His empathy would then not have been crudely interrupted "and it is only in the tumult of intense excitement that the child must try to find himself."

In two articles written in the early 1920's Appia returned to the problem of the child's relation to the theatre. One (*L'Enfant et l'art dramatique*) deals with a child's born talent and inclination for acting "in the sense that for him imitating is inseparable from learning" although for such imitations no audience is needed. Indeed as soon as the child knows he is imitating he wants to be alone or at least unobserved. Children performing among themselves do not consider other children spectators. With the growing awareness of life around him the child turns to make-believe; fiction becomes more precious than reality. In Appia's opinion this propensity for fiction must be respected; it should neither be approved nor disapproved, stimulated nor repressed. He stipulates that, in order to keep the child's "feelings pure," he should never be exposed to an audience, not even to that of his parents. Consequently, arranged performances, especially in costume, should be excluded from the child's activities. He recommends introducing boys and girls to the teaching of dramatics as late as possible.

The other article, similarly entitled, is the only one in which Appia inserts a personal experience to prove his point. It is significant in that it reveals how impressionable he was as a very young boy and also where his aversion to costuming children originated. Young Appia and some other boys—probably in their preschool days or during their first school year—were left for several afternoons a week in the care of a somewhat elderly woman. The lady, an exceptionally gifted educator, understood the great importance of fiction in a child's life, but at the same time was painfully aware of the dilemma in which the child, vacillating between dream and reality, finds himself. She strove to take the sting out of this difficulty. She let the boys have a marvelous time indulging in their fantasies, but although they also passionately loved to masquerade, they were not allowed to do so. Of course they were only too eager to taste what is forbidden and once, when the lady left the room for a while, they hastily dressed up with all the odd pieces they could grab. Catching them by surprise, the lady gave them a sobering look and in a few words asked them to examine their actions realistically. "She made us feel individually that we had defiled divine fiction," continued Appia, and he emphatically demanded that children not use costumes no matter whether their fictional activities take place with or without an audience, with or without a curtain.

Young Adolphe went to grade school in Geneva until he was eleven years old.

He was then sent to a boarding school, Collège de Vevey, where he remained from fall, 1873, until spring, 1879. So little is preserved about his life and studies at this school that no valid conclusion can be drawn. Friends report that he showed more interest in art and music than in the so-called academic courses. But under the stern system then prevailing it is unlikely that the headmaster gave special consideration to a pupil who demonstrated an interest in subjects of minor importance to the school program. One or another teacher may have counseled Adolphe and stimulated his still-dormant talents. Outside the school he was initiated in great music when at the age of fifteen, he heard J. S. Bach's *The Passion According to St. Matthew* which made an everlasting impression upon him. Shortly thereafter he was similarly affected in a concert at which Beethoven's *Symphony No. 9* was played; its last movement seemed to express the "heart of the human drama."[1]

The taboo on theatre at home only increased Adolphe's attention to it. At the boarding school he did not experience this totally negative attitude. The boys were permitted, for instance, to build small cardboard stages, and Appia described a significant experience he had when he was fourteen. With a friend he constructed a model stage, but the two had very different views about the type of scenery they wished to mount. His friend wanted to crowd the small space with conventional painted flat pieces while Appia insisted on plastic set pieces so vehemently that a sharp argument ensued. The hot controversy ended in a joint decision to burn the model stage. Even then Appia's vision of three-dimensional settings was manifest. He was also definite about his conception that in staging, the performer is the decisive factor. When he talked to a friend who had seen a performance of *Tannhäuser*, Appia pressed for a description of the setting; he insisted above all on knowing what the stage floor looked like. When his friend failed to grasp his questions he finally exclaimed, "Where were the singers' feet?" Indeed a strange question for a boy who had never witnessed a production. What induced him to require three-dimensional pieces for a model stage and to ask a pertinent question about platforms on a real stage? Pictures in those drama editions in his father's library might well have stirred him to envision three-dimensional settings, virtually nonexisting in the theatre of the day. And perhaps with his interest in art he had become acquainted with good paintings and with the stage architecture of Greek and Renaissance theatres. But what could have caused Appia at such an early age to decide that in the theatre the actor is the first and foremost element to be considered? Maybe in reading books related to some course he learned about the predominance of the star actor or about the principles of the Classic period including a delineation of the importance given the human body by ancient philosophers. Of one thing we are sure—whatever the influence, it was a spark that lit a fire. His inquisitive mind was already examining everything that aroused his interest.

In his *Expériences de théâtre et recherches personnelles (Theatrical Experiences and Personal Investigations)* Appia writes that he "felt a passionate curiosity for anything connected with the theatre, with the presentation of every kind of drama," before he began to study music in earnest. His timid attempts at home to indicate his deep concern for dramatic art naturally found no echo, but there was little objection to his interest in music. Dr. Louis Appia may have preferred to see his younger son choose a career of a pastor, lawyer, physician, or businessman, but he probably realized that Adolphe would not succeed in any of these fields. Thus there was no serious argument. Adolphe knowing only too well that one did not raise an issue with his father who would simply ignore any suggestion he disliked, compromised with music. A musical career was tolerable, if not very welcome. Teaching music was at least an acceptable profession. Adolphe's first known instructor was Hugo von Senger, a native of Germany, who gained a good name as conductor and composer and who for several years directed the orchestra in Geneva.

With the choice of a musical career the problem of attending an opera became acute. Music played in concerts was an enjoyment approved by his father; yet opera was *theatre*. Nevertheless, finally with his parents' consent, he saw *Faust* in the new opera house which had been opened two years before. As we already know, it was his first opportunity to see a real production, rather than dream about one. To have that dream ruthlessly destroyed by a spiritless, conventional performance was a great shock. In one brief lesson he realized the emptiness of the contemporary theatre. In the following years whenever he attended operatic presentations he often listened to the music alone ignoring the stage as much as possible. Not until he witnessed some productions which somehow approached his own conception, did he change this attitude.

The Formative Years

UNLIKE other professionals Appia did not pass years in systematic training or apprenticeship. His manner of learning and acquiring know-how in the theatre was sporadic, atypical. His formative years may best be termed the period away from Geneva between 1881 and 1890. Officially he had left his native city to continue his studies in music, but he did not make much progress. A dreamer more than a doer, he never concentrated for long on technical tasks or regular work; he neither practiced the piano, or studied theory and harmony, his main subjects, with the necessary perseverance. His heart was in the theatre and only on something he liked to do would he work hard and long. From Geneva he went to Paris for the winter season. A year later he settled in Leipzig where he was registered for almost two years as a student at the famous Konservatorium. Virtually the only detail Appia tells about these years is that in Leipzig he was on good terms with his compatriot Willy Rehberg and with Felix von Weingartner, who also took

Figure 6. Adolphe Appia, ca. 1882. *Donald Oenslager.*

music lessons there and, in addition, was enrolled at the university until he moved to Weimar in 1883 to study with the old master Franz Liszt.

The lack of information about Appia's musical studies is quite characteristic of his attitude. We know far more about his theatrical experiences in those years as he elaborated on them in his writings and also talked about them to friends. The series of important impressions began at a production in the Festival House of Bayreuth where he had the good fortune to see Richard Wagner, the admired master. He repeatedly related with awe how he happened to see the great genius walking with hat and cane through the street just like an average human being. The tremendous devotion he had for Wagner's music dramas did not extend to the performance of *Parsifal*. Though the music moved him profoundly, he was dreadfully disappointed in the staging of this music drama. The pictorial impression he obtained in the festival house was hardly less of a shock than the one he had received in *Faust* two years earlier. All he could detect was the "unusual luxury" of the Bayreuth settings whose scenic style he basically detested. The singers' thorough training in acting under Wagner's guidance aroused his interest, yet he found cause for sharp criticism because of a "lack of harmony between scenery and acting except in the Temple of the Grail." Appia never changed his negative opinion about the festival productions although he returned almost every summer to see, first of all, *The Ring of the Nibelung* and *Tristan and Isolde*. The more he recognized what a production must project and the more he clarified for himself his vision of a scenic reform, the greater was his confidence in his first judgment. For all its marvels of technical perfection, Bayreuth represented for him an example of theatrical superficiality.

It is somehow strange that Appia never referred to the productions of the Meininger Court Theatre; he certainly must have had the opportunity to attend one of the performances as the principality of Meiningen was near Leipzig and quite easy to reach. Moreover, at that time the company of the Duke was touring several German cities every year. Since Appia was often driven by curiosity to see and hear something of interest to him, one can hardly believe that he passed up one of these productions. Or did he dislike the Duke's historical style and exaggeration of details so much that he never mentioned them? Yet the new conception of the Meininger regarding the arrangement of groups in depth often by means of platforms, or the use of levels in general, should have caught his attention, as such arrangements came close to his own *Raumgefuehl*. It is unfortunate indeed that we have no comment by Appia on that style.

He did approve of other productions which followed the predominant realistic style, yet made good use of platforms—that is to say, space. Of the many performances he witnessed during those years, the few whose principles of staging he accepted were those of *A Midsummer Night's Dream*, *Carmen*, and chiefly Goethe's *Faust*, all of which are discussed in the lengthy treatise, *Expériences de théâtre et recherches personelles.* In spring, 1882, he spent some days in Brunswick attending a few performances. The stage director of the Shakespearean masque, Anton Hiltl, "a fine cultured artist," as Appia reports, had been an excellent leading man (*bonvivant*) before he turned to directing; he was clever, imaginative and, in contrast to most of his colleagues, he cultivated the ensemble spirit as the Meiningen company showed it, and he worked hard to mold his actors into a good group.[2] The programs of the Court Theatre still to be read in the Brunswick Library give a clue to Appia's favorable reaction, for Hiltl based his new staging of *A Midsummer Night's Dream* on the scenic arrangement devised by Ludwig Tieck, as delineated in the Prologue. In this presentation Appia found some of his own ideas materialized: a variety of levels and platforms, a spatial setting with unconventional use of lighting effects, and a minimum of painted flats. Here everything was planned to support the actors instead of obstructing them. As Appia describes it, "the director obtained a vision of superior reality, a dream for the eye to behold." In Brunswick he also saw *Carmen,* but he gave no particulars about it except commending the setting of Act II in which several levels were employed to serve groupings effectively.

His most instructive analysis is that of the *Faust* performance. One learns more from his description in minutiae than from any contemporary reviews and pictures of the production, which was staged by Otto Devrient, son of the renowned actor, director, and author, Eduard Devrient. Appia attended *Faust, Part One* in Leipzig in May, 1883, in the version first tried out by Devrient in Weimar seven years previously. The analysis of the production, which Appia saw at least twice, was written forty years later, between 1922 and 1924. Seven typewritten pages were filled with the most detailed delineation of the setting, the part it played in each scene, of particularly impressive groupings, of lighting effects, and of the treatment of incidental music. To recall so much so clearly after such a long time bespeaks indeed a superior memory even if the author relied upon an old diary.

In addition to directing, Otto Devrient prepared the dramaturgical adaption and played the part of Mephistopheles. Influenced by his father, he experimented with a revival of the medieval Passion stage, as he defined it; thus he devised a simultaneous setting in which most of the scenes could be performed without lowering the curtain between scenes. It is difficult to believe that Appia accepted the over-all romantic flavor of the scenery; he certainly could not have been pleased with the prodigious use of set pieces and the nearly realistic painting of the entire setting. In his memoirs he concentrated on the aspects which were of prime interest to him: the actor, spatial setting, lighting, and music. His description of the scenic arrangement provides an eloquent picture of the performance.

The cathedral, built on top of a wide, high platform, dominated the entire stage; stairs, interrupted by a small landing, led to the stage floor proper where, left and right, the houses of Gretchen and Marthe and other essential acting areas

Figure 7. The death of Valentin in Devrient's staging of *Faust*. An artist made this drawing for a periodical. *Institut fuer Theaterwissenschaft, Berlin.*

were located. For Appia this kind of *Faust* arrangement must have been a thrilling experience, proving as it did that it is not necessary to devise an elaborate setting for every scene. The continuous flow of action permitted the characters to walk easily from one area to another thus taking the spectator along as though he were accompanying them. The future stage reformer was particularly delighted with the movements and groups across the platforms and stairs, such as in the scenes in front of the cathedral and that of Valentin's death, when townspeople filled most of the stage. This splendid impression must have made up for the nightmare of Gounod's *Faust* in Geneva.

There were still some solutions which Appia considered ill conceived, and he did not suppress his misgivings. Thus he strongly objected to the shifting of the scene in the cathedral to the area in front of it. For the sake of a good picture, he concluded, Goethe's drama was violated; it weakened the impact of Gretchen's situation, for the church is essential to create the suitable atmosphere. Appia furthermore pointed to the incongruity which arose in the relationship between the leading lady and the incidental music resounding from the church. But he liked the lighting effect in this scene when darkness covered the stage while the cathedral windows were dimly illuminated from within. His criticism was directed also against the meeting of Marthe and Mephistopheles in her garden; here Devrient gained a good blocking for Mephistopheles' entrance at the expense of the over-all mood since this scene should not be played close to the street where people pass by. Appia questioned, moreover, the arrangement of Gretchen's room because its window opening was so small that many patrons were unable to witness the action inside unless the actress stood close to the window; but again he was pleased with the light effect created by a candle in the room. With his deep musical understanding he analyzed Devrient's insertion of incidental music for Gretchen's entrance into her room. The very moment when the music stopped, he emphasized, Gretchen must not only be clearly seen but also distinctly understood. He was fully aware of the modification in timing and thus in space brought about by music, and was convinced that Devrient too recognized the problem involved; in the second performance he attended, the window was left wide open and, consequently, everything became clear but, as Appia added, this "nullified the scenic effect without adequate compensation." Lack of a satisfactory transition tremendously curtailed "the power of suggestive expression."

The elaborate account of this *Faust* production attests not only to Appia's astounding memory, but also bears witness to his deep understanding of the staging problem. It demonstrates, furthermore, that he was not merely interested in the art and technique of designing but equally, or even more so, in the art of staging. Obviously he considered himself the director in charge of the entire production. From both the strengths and the weaknesses of the *Faust* performance the young artist drew many conclusions which, before long, were to help him formulate his own vision of a *mise en scène*. His years in Leipzig were truly the first of his formative years.

The Friendship with Chamberlain

WITH his move from Leipzig to Dresden Appia entered the second phase of this period. In Leipzig he obviously did not concentrate wholeheartedly on his music studies; instead he spent much of his time observing productions, although theatre was still but a hobby. In Dresden his aim and outlook were unchanged; he went on studying music, specifically theory, and even won a first prize with a fugue he wrote for his course at the conservatory.[3] At that time his great urge to learn more about theatre and culture in general received a strong impetus which affected his development for years to come. Houston Stewart Chamberlain (1855–1927), who became his mentor, gave his life the new direction. It is not definitely known when and where the two men met for the first time, but statements made by Appia to others allows us to place this meeting in the year 1884. Chamberlain was then studying at the University of Geneva when Appia was home vacationing for a few weeks.

When Appia and Chamberlain are mentioned together, the spirit of Richard Wagner must be conjured at once, for only with the master of Bayreuth as a link is it possible to explain and to understand the long-lasting friendship of these two men. Yet it ought to be added that the genius had a different meaning for each of his two disciples. While Chamberlain was through-and-through Wagnerian and Bayreuthian, Appia sharply criticized the festival productions despite his infinite love for the master's music dramas themselves, or perhaps because of it. His chief concern was to present these great works in a form worthy of their true value. Chamberlain, on the other hand, considered Wagner not only the greatest of all composers and authors but also infallible as a producer.

Aside from Wagner, not many interests could possibly have united in close friendship, for about thirty years, two men fundamentally so dissimilar in their outlook on most human and cultural affairs. Chamberlain's extreme position on racism and politics struck no responsive chord in his friend. Appia's great admiration for German culture did not induce him to negate his Swiss Romande heritage; as a follower of Chamberlain he looked down on Latin culture, but no trace of any nationalistic inclination can be detected in the mature artist—he was in truth a citizen of the world.

Their temperaments were more alike. Both were nervous—Chamberlain more than Appia—sensitive and quick to react strongly to ideas and principles opposed to their own. This could have spelled conflict rather than harmony but it was coupled with gentlemanly deportment that prevented them from being tactless,

Figure 8. Adolphe Appia, ca. 1886. *Donald Oenslager.*

let alone aggressive. Throughout a period of over twenty years they moved in the same circle of friends, musicians, and music lovers, all disciples of Wagner. Yet they also cultivated groups diametrically opposed. Chamberlain, a brilliant though somewhat vain conversationalist, liked to be with famed personages and members of high society; Appia had an inveterate dislike for high living and sought instead the company of simple folk. He was almost invariably dressed in a very individual but unfashionable style whereas Chamberlain attached great importance to being well dressed. Early in the 1900's when Chamberlain communicated almost exclusively with the great and near great his friend increasingly withdrew from social activities and, primarily because of his grave stutter, lived more and more in seclusion.

It was indeed a strange and extraordinary friendship. Chamberlain, seven years Appia's senior, was the son of a British admiral; he received his schooling in three countries. The decisive influence on his development was exercised by Otto Kunze, a Prussian disciplinarian, who became his tutor when he was fifteen and continued in that capacity for four years. He imbued his young pupil with a love for German classicism and Prussian militarism. As a student Chamberlain majored in biology and botany and in due time obtained his doctorate degree. In addition he acquired a comprehensive knowledge of literature, music, philosophy, history, religion, and politics. Even when young he could converse fluently in French and German besides his native English, and he learned to write well in these languages. In comparison Appia would seem to be uneducated, but his inexhaustible thirst for knowledge made up for his lack of formal learning. He knew some German, learned more during his years of study, but never obtained a perfect command of this language. Later on he picked up some Italian. However, in addition to his trying speech defect, Appia sometimes had great trouble expressing his ideas even in his native French. An artist preoccupied with a vision and groping for a way to realize it, he found it difficult to state in clear sentences what absorbed his mind. Chamberlain on the other hand could discuss with great ease and in beautiful phraseology many complex questions and personalities. His universal knowledge and readable style of writing were the main reasons for his success in popularizing not only Wagner but also Goethe and Kant. Analyzing himself very cleverly he termed himself "not a scientist or philosopher but an onlooker of the world."[4] This incisively different background and development made Appia dependent on Chamberlain for a good number of years. Their relationship can be called that of teacher and pupil, or, as one of Appia's relatives put it, Chamberlain was Appia's substitute for Wagner.

The two men were rather quickly attracted to one another. Yet even after they became close friends they did not use the intimate *tu* in French or *du* in German as they did with some other friends. In the presence of French-speaking persons they too used that language, but they were said to have spoken German when by themselves. Their formality in addressing each other did not interfere with their otherwise informal manner of writing. From the mid-nineties, Appia signed his letters to Chamberlain with "Romeo"; Hermann Keyserling, a mutual friend, was the first to publicize this intimacy.[5] Mrs. Chamberlain is believed to have given Appia this nickname in keeping with his classic features and Latin temperament. Chamberlain was addressed as "Wotan," which may be explained by Appia's high regard for his omniscient friend on one hand and to the role assigned to the Teutonic god in *The Ring* on the other. Their mutual admiration for Wagner might have also led Appia to call Mrs. Chamberlain "Wala"; this could be an abbreviation of Urwala (roughly, "Mother Earth"), a term used by Wagner. Anna Chamberlain was about ten years older than her husband. When Appia met her, Chamberlain was kind and devoted to her, but she did not play an important part in his life. Giving her a nickname proves that Appia was on very good terms with her; indeed he respected and liked her very much.

The Chamberlains lived in Dresden for about four years; Appia arrived there probably in 1886 and remained for three years. Though he had not yet given up his music studies, he was now devoting more time to analyzing productions and familiarizing himself with the technical aspects of the theatre. At one time he also took lessons in sketching or painting, but not for long. Altogether he was a self-made man as a designer. Through Chamberlain, who had good connections everywhere, he was able to attend rehearsals at the Royal Opera House and to observe its technical installations. In Vienna too, where Chamberlain resided after 1889, he helped his young friend in a similar manner when Appia came to visit him for weeks or months. And again in Bayreuth. Thus Appia became well acquainted with the technical apparatus of the Festival House.[6] Returning from Dresden to Switzerland Appia did not take a permanent domicile for a long time; later when living in Bière, Canton de Vaud, he made prolonged visits to Munich, Paris, and with the Chamberlains. When separated, the friends kept close through a frequent exchange of letters. Occasionally they met not only in Vienna but also in Munich and Switzerland where the Chamberlains spent some summer vacations. Both men were nature lovers and took hikes where and whenever they were together. Enjoying the beauty of mountains and woods, they did not overlook the many interesting houses and churches of artistic value they passed on their countless walks.

Very few of Chamberlain's letters to Appia are known. Fortunately hundreds of Appia's letters to his friend are available and they are indeed instructive and informative. In these letters Appia gives free rein to his feelings and thoughts; every idea, observation, or experience seems to be mirrored in them. His full trust in Chamberlain let him write frankly and with an immediacy that gives those letters the appearance of talks with a friend. Sometimes notes were sent every day. Before an answer could arrive, which at that time took about four days, another letter from Appia would be in the mail with new observations and new questions.

Depending on what and how much Appia had on his mind, a letter turned out brief or long, occasionally extremely long, up to twenty handwritten pages. As in a conversation, Appia shifted from one theme to another, returning to the first later on. In the same nonchalant manner he added a postscript or started anew in case a letter remained on his desk over night. He wrote in French but every so often inserted German words and entire German sentences.

So extended and intensive a correspondence necessarily had some effect on the two parties—less on Chamberlain, the accomplished author with definite opinions, than on Appia, the young artist still in his formative years, who knew his goal but not the road to reach it. To a slight degree, Appia persuaded his friend to believe in his revolutionary ideas, at least in their possibilities. It may be doubtful though that Chamberlain really understood and approved of Appia's scenic reform. Some statements in his *Richard Wagner*[7] were obviously influenced by his friend; for instance, a reference about the role of the performer related to music, which can be found in Appia's first publication. In the same chapter Chamberlain emphasized in a footnote that the next great progress in operatic productions would not be musical but scenic. Later he referred to Appia's intention to reduce the scenic picture in *Tristan* to a minimum. Granted that Chamberlain was primarily anxious to do his friend a favor, the references make it clear, nevertheless, that those strange ideas actually impressed him. Many years later when their friendship had cooled he acknowledged his indebtedness to Appia for explaining to him "the diverse technical secrets" of the Bayreuth Festival House.[8]

Appia owed much to his older, more experienced friend—a good part of his higher education, his deep understanding of Wagner's principles, of esthetics, literature, and culture in general. The "higher education" consisted of advice about what to read, and of many conversations on manifold topics. As a consequence one could expect Appia to have fallen under his friend's influence so deeply that in his writings Chamberlainian thoughts and quotations might frequently appear literally or indirectly. However, this is by no means the case. The only sentence ever quoted was "Apollo was not only the god of songs but also of light"[9]—not very original and not too typical of Chamberlain. Appia was fond of quoting it since it expressed so tellingly his own conception. In his first booklet Appia inserted the strange term "Word-Tone Drama," coined by Chamberlain, and also "Word-Tone Poet," which the latter applied, for instance, to E. Th. A. Hoffmann, the German romanticist. Here again Chamberlain was not entirely original for, as he himself admitted, he found similar expressions in Goethe, Novalis, and the French encyclopedists like J. J. Rousseau.[10] In a letter to Cosima Wagner, Chamberlain writes, "He [Appia] has the term '*drame Wagnérien*' from me and employs it in my own manner, defining it as the Word-Tone Drama. . . . He takes up (without realizing it) an idea which already occupied Goethe . . . how music, through its cooperation with drama, determines not merely time but implicitly space as well."[11]

Indeed the relationship of time and space intrigued Appia throughout his life, and it is very likely that Goethe spelled out this vexing problem for him. The term "Word-Tone Drama" evidently pleased the artist so much that he simply inserted "WTD" in his French manuscript, just as he used Word-Tone Poet several times in his first publications. One sometimes gains the impression that Appia, in reading philosophers or other authors for that matter, hit upon passages which suddenly made his own hitherto vague conceptions clear to him. He would store such statements in his mind to quote them again and again whenever he felt he needed support in expounding his own principles. Therefore, one should not jump to the conclusion that, because Appia adopted some of his friend's terminology, he was decisively affected by him as far as Wagner's music dramas were concerned. It is true that Chamberlain contributed much to Appia's love for, and understanding of, Wagner's work, by conveying to his friend what he in turn had culled from Wagner, Goethe, and other intellectual leaders; in addition he called Appia's attention to the works of these authors, but there the influence ends. Although they relied on the same sources, the two men differed fundamentally in the interpretation of the great composer and in their approach, which revealed, as did all their principal opinions, the basic dissimilarity of their natures.

Their mutual high regard did not include mutual flattery. On the contrary there was no lack of critical remarks back and forth, for evidently it was not only Chamberlain who criticized Appia's writings, but strange as it may seem, vice versa—Appia examined Chamberlain's. Questions of content were seldom touched upon. Appia, for example, was mainly blamed for not expressing an idea clearly; his defense then was that he was fully aware of being a designer and director by talent, but a writer only by necessity. Nevertheless, he listened to his friend, and although he tried to find better wording for many passages, his style remained involved in most of his writings. Realizing that his conception of scenic art was entirely new at the time and hence difficult to grasp, he elucidated it from all angles and in so doing frequently overextended sentences and paragraphs; this, in addition to his bent for metaphors, left certain passages obscure. On the other hand, Appia did not hesitate to give his frank opinion about Chamberlain's manuscripts. When he recommended changes his suggestions were quite specific. To get his point across he even used German words and sentences he considered more suitable. Most amazing in this mutual exchange of corrections and suggestions is that Chamberlain—otherwise touchy and excitable—took his friend's advice seriously and without any sign of irritation.

Appia admired Chamberlain's book *Richard Wagner* which he thought excellent except for the passages dealing with production problems. In spite of his high praise he was rather unhappy about the pictorial material. If one is tempted to inquire why the author did not honor his friend with some of his fascinating designs for the music dramas instead of including the conventional ones by Brueckner, Joukowsky, *et al.*, the explanation may be that in his aim to publish a popular book he could not afford to display controversial settings; moreover he was quite conscious of Cosima Wagner's antipathy to any change in the Bayreuth tradition.

His volume of three dramas—it is hardly known that Chamberlain wrote plays and was anxious to be taken seriously as a dramatist—do contain two sketches by Appia; they are for *Der Weinbauer* (*The Winegrower*) and were executed according to the author's final wishes after a discussion of the scenic problems involved. The slightly sketched pictures do not allow any judgment about Appia's revolutionary art. Obviously he did not put his heart into working on this rather superficial play and doubtless had some secret misgivings about it. He could not have cherished this task for the play was written in a realistic style not at all in keeping with his art, and possibly he himself requested the omission of his name in the book form of the plays. In the preface Chamberlain expressed his thanks in general terms without giving the designer's name.[12]

In April, 1896, *Der Weinbauer* appeared on the stage of the Municipal Theatre in Zurich, and Appia went there to attend the so-called dress rehearsal and première. Cautiously he informed his friend who was unable to come to Zurich that the drama contained fine ideas but was ruined by the actors. For all the restraint he exercized in his criticism, the over-all tone of his message was still crushing. The upshot was that the play would have to be rewritten to create any impressive mood. A local critic was less polite in about the briefest review given any première. In some fifty words inserted under local news he expressed the hope that this "nonentity" had seen its first and last performance.[13] Chamberlain evidently hinted at this production when he spoke of "the execution" of his play for which he held the dramaturgist and the stage director responsible.

Appia also made sketches for *Der Tod der Antigone*, another drama included in this volume, but Chamberlain declined them with the explanation that the empty setting of the design failed to give an adequate impression of the essential role assigned to the grouping and the lighting in this drama.[14] A strange excuse indeed, since Appia demonstrated in several designs he made in those years, particularly those for the second act of *Tristan* and the third act of *The Valkyrie*, how the full force of lighting could be indicated.

The incidental music for *Der Weinbauer* was composed by Friedrich Klose who in 1902 obtained an artistic success with his "dramatic symphony" *Ilsebill*. He was one of the many young composers, conductors, and writers whom Appia met in Chamberlain's circle in Vienna and above all, in Bayreuth. Several were introduced by him to Chamberlain; for example, the gifted Robert Godet, who in collaboration with Ernest Guy Claparède translated Chamberlain's *Grundlagen des XIX. Jahrhunderts* (*Foundations of the 19th Century*), and Agénor Boissier, son of a noble Genevese family, who in those years counseled Appia. There were also Felix von Weingartner, the internationally renowned musician, and Hugo Reichen-

Figure 9. Sketch for Acts I and III of Chamberlain's *The Winegrower*. *F. Bruckmann, Munich.*

Figure 10. Sketch for Act II of Chamberlain's *The Winegrower*. *F. Bruckmann, Munich.*

berger, later a highly esteemed conductor at the Court Theatre in Munich. Hans von Wolzogen must be mentioned too. One of the most faithful disciples of Bayreuth, he wrote, regardless of Cosima's opposition to Appia's reform, a lengthy piece generally praising the artist's *La Mise en scène du drame wagnérien*. Wolzogen delineated clearly the main points; then he added hesitantly that the author was not quite right in his too symbolic interpretation of the master's precise scenic-dramatic requirements. Oddly enough this review appeared in the *Bayreuther Blaetter* (1895, n. IV/V).

One of the most brilliant personalities in this group was Hermann Count Keyserling who in 1901 as a student in Vienna had met Chamberlain. In no way did he share the political fanaticism of Chamberlain, he admitted however in his memoirs that he learned immensely from him, his "best possible guide and beacon."[15] The two men had some irritating traits in common: both became easily exuberant, took extreme positions, and liked to hear themselves talk. Thus it is amazing to observe how long they remained on good terms. In 1903 Appia met the young Count again in Paris and introduced him to his large group of friends. He must have shown great patience in tolerating Keyserling's arrogance in not merely directing every conversation but informing others, "I do not judge values, I create them." Later Appia somewhat ironically confessed to a cousin, "One must listen and be silent as though one would listen to the good Lord."

The queen among all the luminaries whom Chamberlain managed to assemble around himself was of course Madame Cosima Wagner; in fact, it is more accurate to say *he* belonged to *her* court to which he, the loyal Bayreuthian, had already been admitted in the late eighties.

Although Appia knew the other members of the House Wahnfried, it is doubtful that he ever met Cosima. His failure to do so depressed him greatly but did not disturb his relations to Chamberlain. When in 1904 tensions arose in his friend's marriage, Appia tried everything to be of help in this precarious situation. After Chamberlain's decision to dissolve the bond, Appia succeeded to remain a friend to both. Naturally Chamberlain meant more to him, yet he kept in touch with Anna, exchanging letters with her for several years. In 1908 Chamberlain married Eva Wagner, the master's daughter, and moved to Bayreuth. During the festivals, and Appia attended them almost every summer until 1914, he usually stayed at his friend's home; but somehow the relationship was no longer the same. In Vienna Chamberlain had still appeared to be an independent personality—to some degree, but after he became an official member of the House Wahnfried he necessarily succumbed to that atmosphere. This may have contributed to a slacking of the avid exchange of views with his old friend although Appia was hardly conscious of less cordial feelings; yet a slight shift in the latter's inner attitude must have begun by 1906 when he met Emile Jaques-Dalcroze whose rhythmic exercises opened a new vista for him. His collaboration with Dalcroze in the development of eurythmics made him intellectually independent of Chamberlain, and this too caused their strong ties to weaken.

In two important statements Appia expressed his deep admiration for Chamberlain. In spite of their waning friendship he continued to acknowledge his debt to his former close friend for everything he had learned from him. A clear reference to such appreciation may be found in *Expériences de théâtre et recherches personnelles* in which he describes how Chamberlain gave him "a pregnant and documented image of Wagner's personality, transfigured through the enthusiasm and adoration of a thoroughly informed artistic disciple." He emphasizes moreover that he could not have acquired this profound knowledge through any other method. A hidden but rather easily deciphered reference to Appia's relation to Chamberlain occurs in another essay in which Appia analyzes the role of a teacher as basically that of an "intermediary," the title of this essay. He tells of a friend who "was a very learned man. A humanist and scientist . . ." He then assures us that like a true intermediary, this teacher merely deepened his intellectual faculties, and with great understanding left alone "the core of my personality." "The ideal intermediary, he gave to me with one hand while he was willing to receive with the other. . . . Lucky the young man who finds such a friend on his way!" One can only add: lucky the friend who is paid such great reverence—equally moving confessions are not discovered in Chamberlain's writings; Appia's name and work were mentioned and praised now and then, and more important, attempts were made to win Cosima Wagner over to his friend's revolutionary staging ideas, but that is all. One senses, and not surprisingly in this case of mentor and disciple, that the friendship of the two men made a deeper impact on Appia than on Chamberlain.

Whether the latter was a great blessing for Appia is a moot question. There is no doubt that Chamberlain introduced the young artist to many facets of our culture; but his ultraconservative position in art and politics and his willful ignoring of any opinion other than his own contained pitfalls which Appia could not entirely avoid at first. If he had not come under the new influence of Dalcroze he might have drifted ever farther in a direction potentially dangerous to the full development of his genius, his sound instinct notwithstanding. In the final analysis Appia's close and long relationship with Chamberlain was fruitful while it lasted, but, on the whole, of limited and passing influence.

II

First Works

For Appia, the years in Dresden meant more than attending performances and studying music. Under Chamberlain's influence he began to take an analytical attitude toward himself and his reform ideas. He became conscious of his inner strength, of wider responsibilities. He was not yet sure how to attack the scenic reform he envisioned; all he knew was that there was a gap between his dreams and their potential fulfillment, between theory and its application. He realized that the next step must be to put on paper, both in words and sketches, what he had in mind. When he returned to Switzerland in 1890 he was determined to execute what he called his "imperative task"—to change from critic and analyst of theatre arts into a creative artist. His formative years had thus ended and he was entering the fruitful period of initiating his revolution of the stage. He had no illusion about the obstacles to be overcome; as he confessed later on, "I began to practice a completely unknown art for which all the elements had yet to be discovered and organized. Still I was convinced that following my own vision I would find the truth."

After his arrival in Geneva his first concern was to find a quiet place where he could live and work, undisturbed by any emotional strain. Hence the city itself was out of the question because of his family ties there and because he disliked city life in general. He visited several small towns near Lake Geneva spending a few days here, a few weeks there, with an occasional longer stay at one or another place. In between he also traveled to the Italian Riviera hoping to find a spot in which to settle for a while. Once or twice he tried, unsuccessfully, to share an apartment with Hélène.

For more than three years Appia's life was peripatetic. At last he chose Bière, a village in the Canton de Vaud, where he rented a room in a farmhouse. This became his permanent home from the summer of 1893 until the end of 1904. The term "permanent" however needs modification, for it does not mean that he stayed in Bière most of the time. He frequently showed up in Geneva to see friends and a few relatives, to attend a performance or a concert; moreover he made trips to Zurich, Berne, Lausanne, and other Swiss places. At the turn of the century he went to Paris quite frequently. Many weeks were also spent in Munich during the period preceding the publication of his *La Musique et la mise en scène*. And once in a while he visited the Chamberlains in Vienna and Bayreuth.

Relation to Richard Wagner

THE nineties were extremely productive for the young artist. During these years he created many of the designs which later brought him fame; in addition he wrote essays, a booklet, and a book, which contained his revolutionary ideas. His dreams and thoughts at that time concentrated on a single purpose: to find the perfect solution for the staging of Wagner's great music dramas and so to achieve the master's ideal of the synthesis of all the arts. He wrangled with the problems he had discovered when he attended the performances of those works. For years he had pointed out what, in his opinion, was wrong with the contemporary mode of staging. The exaggerated realism he saw in Dresden, in Vienna, and even in Bayreuth was proof enough to convince him that Wagner himself had failed to conceive the specific style of staging which his music dramas demanded. He found the performances in Bayreuth, preserved intact since the master's death in 1883, technically superior to those in other opera houses but otherwise they were basically like all operatic productions in the tradition of the day; that is, settings were painted in a mixture of romantic and realistic fashion in which every detail was neatly executed on wings and backdrops. Neither lighting nor acting had any inner rapport with the music and so Wagner's specific style which was audible in the musical presentation was not visible on stage.

Appia's disappointment in Bayreuth concerned solely the master's style (or lack of style) of staging. Indeed it was precisely his great admiration and love for the music dramas that made him so critical of their productions. He was in complete accord with many of Wagner's ideals—especially his dramatic principles, he shared his ideas about festivals in general, and he admired the Festival House in Bayreuth in particular, though not without reservation. Through Chamberlain Appia had become thoroughly acquainted with the classic theatre of Greece and so he understood Wagner's admiration for classicism. All three men agreed upon the importance of Apollo whom Wagner called "the main and national god of the Hellenic tribes."[1] Wagner's discussion of dance as an art in his *Das Kunstwerk der Zukunft* (*The Art Work of the Future*) and his combination of the "three sister arts"—dance, music, and poetry—in the same essay made a strong impact upon Appia. It is moot whether the young artist was more influenced by Greek ideas about the human body or by statements of the same kind in Wagner's writings.

Although Appia blamed Wagner for the conventional staging in Bayreuth, he conceded that the master had been extremely anxious to find a new scenic approach for the production of his works. According to some sources Wagner was so interested in directing his music dramas that in Bayreuth he had delegated much authority in the musical end of the production to the young conductor Hermann Levi while he himself concentrated on preparing the settings and costumes and conducting the acting rehearsals. But, except for occasional good acting and a generally well-disciplined performance by the singers, the Bayreuth productions adhered to the convention of operatic presentations. Therefore, Appia concluded, Wagner the musical genius, the creator of an entirely new dramatic form—the music drama, had not been truly a man of the theatre.

Somehow Wagner had realized that he was in dire need of a congenial scenic artist. He had thought of Arnold Boecklin, the famous painter, but he had to be satisified with collaborators who, while brilliant technicians, were unimaginative designers. Considering the taste of the 1870's, Joseph Hoffmann from Vienna and Paul von Joukowsky, a Russian artist, were excellent and indeed highly welcome. Yet it may be doubted that they really understood his new style, notwithstanding their admiration for Wagner, the man and composer. Even if they *had* understood him—Joukowsky never read Wagner's essays—their specific talent and training would hardly have enabled them to grasp the master's ideas, which did not rest in the past but pointed to the future.

Appia's criticism gives rise to the fundamental question whether Wagner himself recognized the incongruity between his music and the designs he accepted for the Bayreuth productions. In his insistence on a high degree of historical accuracy in settings and costumes Wagner the stage director was definitely a follower of the *Zeitgeist,* not a leader with a vision equal to his musical and dramatic genius. His innovations were of a purely technical nature; they did not bring forth a new scenic concept akin to his music. In Bayreuth the cyclorama, the swimming device, the *Wandeldekoration* were marvels of ingenuity. The master spared no effort or money to conjure up fascinating effects; but then again a forest, a wooded mountain, an interior were as conventional as in any other opera house, only more elaborate in their outfit. The boat in *Tristan* was extremely impressive if one believed in realism, and the street in *The Mastersingers* gave a true picture of a medieval German city. On the other hand the depth of the Rhine and the landscapes merely showed traditional settings devised without the least imagination for Wagner's unusual art. Technically there were some outstanding achievements such as the ship in *The Flying Dutchman* or the bear, the dragon, and the forging of the sword in *Siegfried,* the thunderstorm and the great fires in *The Ring.* All these effects could be observed in many theatres; however in Bayreuth they were executed with a precision and perfection unmatched anywhere else. Yet, one is tempted to ask about the real purpose of these technical extravagancies. Did they not aim more for the created illusion instead of arousing the spectators' imagination in accord with the symbolic character of the music?

Obviously Wagner the stage director did not always listen to Wagner the revolutionary creator who lashed out against the spectacles he had witnessed in other opera houses. He severely attacked effects for effect's sake and he objected to crude exaggerations of scenic events, such as the magic fire in *The Valkyrie* which should be subtly indicated. In reviewing the festivals of 1876 he confessed that some of the scenic solutions showed "weaknesses," but he was convinced that his collaborators were aware of the flaws and knew how to correct them. Evidently Wagner had technical, not artistic, problems in mind. At any rate, the basic style of his productions remained the same.

In regard to acting, the master of Bayreuth and the impatient young artist had much in common. Both considered the performer the heart and soul of the production; both were highly interested in rhythm and dance. Wagner's essays abound in valuable suggestions of how singers can make their gestures and movements meaningful, and their vocal interpretations intelligible. In his treatise *Über Schauspieler und Sänger (Actor and Singer)* he described his basic aim which was to eliminate overdone pathos and to teach expressive gestures. Thanks to his excellent collaborator Julius Hey, his singers made great progress in their diction. Wagner was less successful in realizing his ideas about movements except in some isolated cases such as in the scene of the Flower Girls and the Knights of the Grail in *Parsifal*. Wagner himself was a gifted actor who could jump with ease into any character to demonstrate how to synchronize music and action, yet few of the singers were able or willing to follow him. Most of them lacked his natural talent and probably were not eager to work hard enough to improve their acting. Appia recognized from the outset that singers needed training not only in voice and diction but in bodily expressiveness as well, and he suggested that "choreography" be included in their basic studies.

In an essay on *Tannhäuser* Wagner advised a careful examination of the score before devising the settings. This became one of Appia's main principles. When he studied the music dramas, he was pleased to see how often stage directions coincided with orchestra passages, but he also detected many a measure in which the description of the stage business was not directly underlined in the music. It is not known when Appia read Wagner's delineation of staging problems in *The Flying Dutchman* and *Tannhäuser*; possibly as late as the 1920's since he did not particularly care for these operas. In any case it was quite natural for him, the trained musician, to base his conceptions of the setting and every move on the music as did Wagner. His scenarios for *The Ring* and later for other music dramas are such splendid examples of his thorough knowledge of all problems involved and of his artistic conception for their execution, that Wagner himself could not have devised them more painstakingly.

Theoretically the composer and the designer shared a dislike for mechanization. In his *Das Kunstwerk der Zukunft* Wagner railed against the machine, "this heartless benefactor of human beings in need of luxury," yet he made wide use of mechanical devices on stage, and in life enjoyed the luxury provided by modern technology. Appia, by contrast, did not readily compromise with his aversion to machines and lived accordingly.

In literary matters Wagner and Appia would have found themselves on common ground. Had the two met, they certainly could have enjoyed discussing Wolfgang von Goethe whom they both highly admired, and they had similar opinions on other German classicists, too. From the philosopher Arthur Schopenhauer, Appia adopted several ideas and used some quotations, but in general he learned more about him from Wagner's use of those ideas. Some trouble would have arisen if Appia and Wagner had discussed composers. For Wagner, Mozart was the greatest of all composers, a gift from heaven; but Appia completely ignored this genius. Wagner wrote many pages about Ludwig van Beethoven, whom he revered. As a boy Appia was profoundly moved by the *Missa Solemnis*, yet he never mentioned the giant in later years. Appia's and Wagner's opinion on contemporary French and Italian music was very much the same although Appia cared for both even less than Wagner did.

For about three decades, Appia's musical taste was completely dominated by Wagner's music dramas which he considered the climax of all operatic art. But, whereas the influence of the music dramas on the young artist came as a direct emotional response to performances, his indoctrination with the master's writings was the result of Chamberlain's interpretation. When Appia returned to his native country from Germany he was a complete convert; his thoughts centered on the music dramas and his conversations were eulogies of the master of Bayreuth. He talked so passionately that people who had known him since childhood were shocked. "Without any doubt," Madame Anna Penel, an aunt, wrote to a friend, "he is the maddest Wagnerian I know of. He used to appreciate and love everything worthy, but now he is incapable of feeling and admiring any other music. Wagner has taken the place for him of religion, of love, of *everything*." She even suspected that Appia's fanaticism for Wagner had killed his own musical talent.

This extreme mood must be recalled when one evaluates Appia's early writings. It alone explains his exclusive concentration on *The Ring* and *Tristan*. In this state of total absorption his reform ideas began to take shape. His dream was to complete Wagner's synthesis of the arts by giving his music dramas the perfect scenic frame. Straight ahead he pushed toward this goal unwilling to digress, and he poured his mind and soul into the project. In his scenarios and sketches of *The Ring and Tristan* one can sense his infatuation. For a decade he gave himself completely to this "holy task," rarely taking time out to work on some other plan.

The First Essay

Notes de mise en scène pour L'Anneau de Nibelung (Comments on the Staging of The Ring of the Nibelung) written in 1891–1892—but not published until 1954—was Appia's first essay, as far as can be ascertained. It is important not merely because it represents his first attempt to write down his ideas concerning the production of *The Ring,* but above all because it offers the core of the reform the young artist was to expound in his following works. With one stroke he set forth his revolutionary conception. In a concise form his new principles are stated. Some of his explanations, it is true, were too brief to be clearly understood even by the expert, yet this essay is a most essential link between Appia the analyst and critic, and Appia the scenic reformer.

When he first began to put his thoughts on paper he was not thoroughly acquainted with Wagner's theories. He had seen his works in Dresden, Vienna, and Bayreuth but he relied almost entirely on the vocal scores in working out his conception, ignoring all the performances he had attended, even those in Bayreuth. *Parsifal,* incidentally, was the only one he saw under Wagner's own direction; he did not attend the other productions until after Wagner's death. The premises for his reforms had their wellspring solely in his imagination. Neither what he had seen in several opera houses nor what he had learned from Chamberlain gave him any clue to his visions. His concept differed fundamentally from all conventional presentations, those in Bayreuth included. After studying the score of *The Ring* he was firmly convinced he could devise the type of settings, costumes, and properties needed for a true realization of Wagner's intentions. Though he concentrated all his aspirations on the *mise en scène,* he never overlooked the performer. In Appia's opinion the main difficulty in a decisive change was related to the acting singer, and he therefore demanded that a method must be introduced to train the performer in gestures and movements. The method he had in mind was based on means similar to the musical signs which control the vocal interpretation to the most minute detail. For his new approach he borrowed the term "choreography." Generally he had no strong objection to the conventional style of acting—at least not in 1891—but he expected through his recommendations to raise the general standard of acting. Although at that time he did not offer a clear and definite solution for the performing singer, his preoccupation with the problem is evident. Aiming at a unity of purpose and execution Appia intended to develop "an organic whole in all its parts" which ought to include gestures, poise, stage settings, and the other scenic elements. His concern for the singer's performance grew with the years, but it is interesting to note that his concept was intact from the very beginning.

He requested radical changes in the use of space; in contrast to the prevailing way of staging, he defined his new principle as "movement in depth and height." In addition to his plan for three-dimensional settings he demanded that they should be simple and unobstrusive. He preferred a spatial arrangement that enhanced the three-dimensional performer and his movements in space. In his very first essay Appia stressed the part to be assigned to light in a production when he described how to "create an atmosphere through lighting," and in this connection he applied the term "living" which assumed great significance in his later thinking and writings. He realized thas the proper use of lighting is indispensable for a three- dimensional setting and the dramatic expression of the actors. He dismissed the prevalent notion by theatre people and spectators that everything and everyone on stage had to be seen. His reform was based on the contrasting effect of light and shadow, not on plain visibility. For its proper function he recommended the use of three types of equipment; namely, devices for diffused lighting, movable devices such as spotlights, and slide projectors.

A true artist, Appia always conceived his *mise en scène* as a whole. Thus in planning a setting he took into account all the other settings of the work; he did not think of lighting, properties, or costumes as separate units. His systematic analysis taught him to discern the style of an entire music drama and then to coordinate all scenic elements. Artistically speaking, the idea was not new; what was original was his intention to apply it to a strictly stylized production. For *The Ring* he concentrated on the fact that Wagner used the Rock of the Valkyries four times, each time to serve a different mood and a different action. The Rock therefore became the hub of Appia's considerations. The young designer was intrigued also by Wagner's preference for the outdoor, rocky landscape settings. Reading all of Wagner's scenic requirements he counted the frequent use of cave—Erda as well as Fafner (the dragon) appear at the opening of a cave, and Act I of *Siegfried* takes place inside a cave. Appia kept such details in mind when drawing his sketches unlike many designers of the day who were technicians rather than artists. He also observed as significant that in *The Rhinegold, The Valkyrie,* and *Siegfried* the action is carried by the gods and by the human beings related to them, while human beings as such were introduced only in *The Twilight of the Gods,* the last part of the *Cycle.* Finally, he was fascinated by the momentous role assigned to nature and natural phenomena; without clearly knowing how to achieve the necessary effects he began to think of a solution by means of lighting and even of projection.

He was altogether opposed to footlights, although he would condone sparing application for technical purposes. As he recognized, elimination of footlights would automatically force the singers to "avoid the tall wings" and move farther upstage to be seen; he was convinced that this strategem would also increase the effectiveness of the settings. He wanted the entire downstage area rather dim; this meant tackling a disturbing factor in all opera houses—the glow from the orchestra lamps and the reflection of light from white dress-shirt fronts and shining instruments. The less the proscenium frame and the downstage area are lit the softer will be the transition from the darkened auditorium to the bright stage. This is the first

Figure 11. *The Valkyrie*, opening scene of Act III. *Donald Oenslager.*

Figure 12. *The Valkyrie*, Act III. *Theater Museum, Munich.*

hint of his vision of an auditorium and stage all in one. Behind the suggestion of semidarkness downstage and brighter light upstage, lurk two basic elements of Appia's reform idea: the union of stage and auditorium, and the contrast of light and shadow.

His insistence on utter simplification in settings, costumes, and properties extended to wigs and footwear. He objected to their traditional picturesque style, despite Wagner's approval of it, and tried to design simpler forms for them.

The Scenarios of *The Ring*

Appia was not content to write a brief essay and draw a few sketches for *The Ring;* during the years 1891 and 1892 he created absorbing extended scenarios for the *Cycle,* in which he elucidated his new ideas. To our regret, that for *The Rhinegold* has been lost, but the three others are preserved. In Act I of *The Valkyrie* his request to have the hall built in three dimensions throughout was unheard of in opera. Walls and doors assumed plasticity without necessarily attaining full realism. Most interesting is his recommendation to show the roots of the large tree center stage by placing three-dimensional pieces around the part of the trunk which touches the stage floor. One of his main complaints about standard productions was that there was no real contact between the hanging pieces and the floor. For Act II and III of *The Valkyrie* Appia delineated the spatial arrangement as it became known through his marvelous designs. In the light plot, he called for a slide projector to create special effects. In discussing the magic fire in the last act he emphasized that no steam be visible. The only time he inserted the term "realism" was in connection with the cave in Act I of *Siegfried,* which he wished to see treated as if in a play setting, in contrast to the second act which was to be completely simplified; and he described in detail how the forest murmurs should be executed. Leaves and tree trunks were merely to be indicated and the over-all atmosphere was to be created through light. On a fly gallery in front of spotlights stagehands should weave branches creating the impression of leaves quivering in a breeze. Since this effect had never been mentioned before, Appia was possibly the first designer to think of it. In Act III the shift from Scene 1, at the foot of the mountain, to Scene 2, the Rock of the Valkyries, is worth noting. He emphasized that the spreading of the fire from the mountain down the slope—an effect obtained by means of a transparent drop and projection—must be synchronized with the music, that this is more important than the color of the fire. Here we sense again the signaling of an attitude which became pronounced when Appia relegated color to last place in his hierarchy.

Although in the scenarios much space was devoted to settings and scenic effects, Appia never forgot the performer. In prescribing positions and movements he frequently had one or another character placed in profile and thus, in relation to his particular light plot, in silhouette. Such a position was rarely seen, if at all, in operatic productions of his time. For the appearance of the dragon in *Siegfried* he recommended that the singer of this role be placed inside the frame of the beast instead of singing backstage while a stagehand somehow manipulates the feet, jaw, and tail. Evidently he expected to achieve more accurate acting from his new arrangement and better acoustics. He also ignored Wagner's direction in Act II of *The Valkyrie* for Fricka's entrance on a cart drawn by two rams. He simply let her enter on foot. The swimming of the Rhine Maidens was also revised. Instead of Bayreuth's elaborate and ostentatious machinery that let the Rhine Maidens appear as though they were swimming high above the stage floor, Appia suggested that they simulate swimming by motions of their arms while they climbed up and down several platforms. He thought of a different method for the Rhine Maidens in *Twilight of the Gods*. Lying on a kind of dolly behind a low platform they could move about by pushing the floor with their feet.

Every phase of the production was scrutinized in his scenarios. Every so often he returned to the performer and his problems, advising him to acquaint himself with the acting area assigned to his character. One of the principles on which Appia based his designs was to assume that all the characters except Wotan use a given area most of the time. Hence it was essential for the singers to have a relationship to their surroundings. Wotan, the god who directed his creatures, could therefore, as an exception, move across several areas. Furthermore, the scenarios contain suggestions for a type of gesture or a certain poise he wished to see executed; his aim was to give each character a symbolic meaning through poise and gestures peculiar to him.

These comprehensive scenarios give ample evidence that Appia saw himself in the dual role of designer and stage director. His extended description—each scenario consists of approximately sixty typewritten pages—demonstrate moreover that he was not only a brilliant designer with an entirely new conception of the *mise en scène* but also an extremely sensitive artist with a profound understanding of the performer's place and task in his scenic reform. Unfortunately the scenarios have never been published and hence are known only to a very few. They ought to be made widely accessible, for Appia's detailed presentation of his ideas should arouse great interest among students of theatre history and among directors, designers, and even singers. There are meaningful suggestions and valuable hints for all.

La Mise en scène du drame wagnérien

In his first book—briefer than any scenario, it might better be called a brochure —Appia elaborated the ideas and principles he had described in *Notes de mise en*

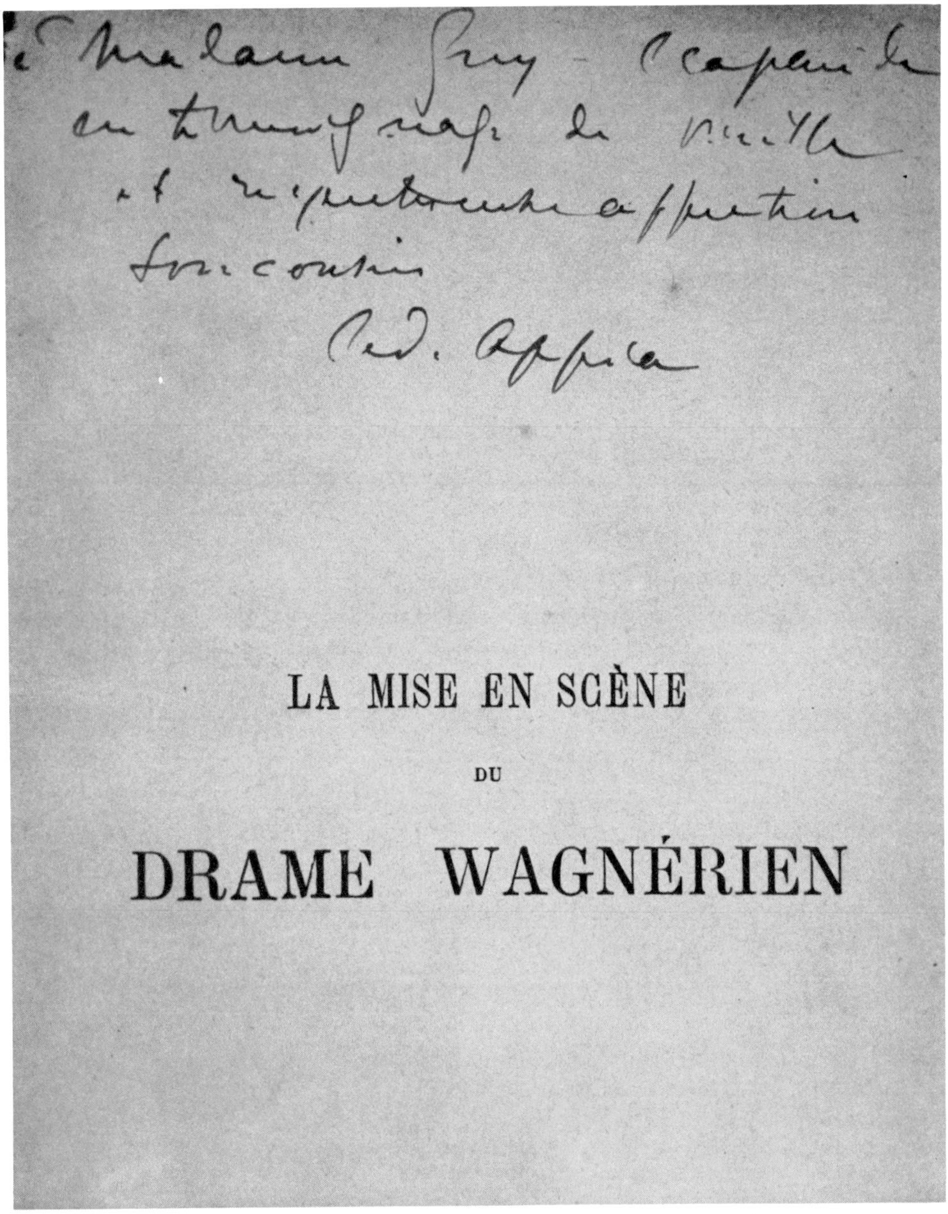

Figure 13. Title page of Appia's first book with a dedication to a cousin. *W. R. Volbach.*

scène pour L'Anneau de Nibelung. In the foreword he expressed his regret that its conciseness did not permit him fully to explain every problem and that consequently some of the points might not be as clear as he wished to make them. A student of Appia's work is advised to read his writings in chronological order to follow his development step by step. Just as *La Mise en scène du drame wagnérien*—not yet available in English translation—is the logical offshoot of its preceding essay, it antecedes in turn *La Musique et la mise en scène,* his largest work, which combined his dreams and thoughts of the entire decade.

Hitherto Appia had primarily dealt with practical matters touching only slightly on esthetic problems. In *La Mise en scène du drame wagnérien* he probed deeper into these problems, and one can note how his artistic concept matured between 1892 and 1895 when this booklet appeared. The change is immediately apparent in the first chapter where he explained his reason for taking the spoken drama as point of departure and for concentrating on Wagner's music dramas. It is here too that the unusual term "Word-Tone Drama" is used for the first time. His esthetics was based on the premise that music determines the time duration for gestures and movements and represents the expressive element in the music dramas. Settings and action must be subservient to the music which alone expresses the inner life of the characters. From this he concluded that a drama set to music can, under no circumstance, have the same scenic style as a spoken play. This guiding thought returned in variations in Appia's later writings. It led him to other important questions, above all to that of the relationship of time and space.

Appia did not delude himself about the possible reaction of the theatregoers to his scenic reform. He anticipated their passive attitude for three reasons; their inertia resulting in indiscriminate acceptance of conventional staging; their incapacity to immerse themselves in passionate music; their inability to consider a masterwork in terms of the whole. Yet he did not accuse the audience alone for its indifference; he included the author (composer) who failed to bring his powerful position to bear in resolving the urgent production problems.

In the second chapter of his brochure he conveyed some of his principles far more than previously. He pointed out the position of the performer who, during the past centuries, became slowly separated from the setting that surrounded him. Without going into details Appia indicated his opposition to the development of stage and scenery since the late Renaissance, particularly to the scenery which had lost every contact with the performer and had turned the stage into "a lifeless picture," a condition further aggravated by the negligible treatment of lighting. As antidote he suggested his spatial arrangement which must be subordinated to and dominated by the performer and his actions. A setting must serve the performer who is the intermediary between the drama and its scenic form.

Only in the last chapter did the author comment specifically on the problems involved in a production of *The Ring.* Unlike some Wagnerian experts, he did not look for mythological significance everywhere in this monumental work. To him the mythology from which this music drama originated was of minor importance; he preferred to think of its foundation as being "typical, not symbolic." Consequently he interpreted the gods merely as "members of a higher society." On the last pages he then described again his solution for a scenic reform, a reform in which lighting played a strong, active role.

His friend Chamberlain was instrumental in finding a publisher for *La Mise en scène du drame wagnérien*. It is not known, though, whether he helped directly or through the Wagnerian circle in Paris. One of those who served as mediator was Edouard Schuré, an admirer of Wagner and a disciple of symbolism.[2] The treatise was published by Léon Chailley in 1895. It was mainly intended for German readers, and of course Appia hoped it would attract the attention of Cosima Wagner. Publicity was sent out; friends led by Jean Thorel[3] made propaganda; but this revolutionary treatise did not create a sensation. Those few who knew and believed in the genius of Appia were delighted, some followers of Wagner in France listened, but otherwise it was virtually ignored. Except for the review by Ernst von Wolzogen in the *Bayreuther Blaetter*, this important publication hardly made a ripple in Germany, the country for which it was written. The small edition—300 copies were said to have been printed, paid for by Appia himself—did not even find enough buyers among the professionals in the theatre or among opera lovers. Twenty years later, when Appia's fame had grown, it was impossible to hunt up a copy anywhere, and now it is termed a rare book—very rare indeed, worth a high price. Perhaps it was a mistake to push a French publication instead of trying harder to have a German firm accept it. A year after it appeared in Paris Appia missed an opportunity to have it issued in a German translation. Toward the end of 1896, Otto Lessmann, publisher and editor of the renowned *Allgemeine Musikzeitung*, approached the author through Moritz Wirtz about the possibility of publishing it in his periodical. One or another condition made Appia hesitate; the reason may have been that Lessmann intended to print merely a condensed version. The negotiations quickly broke off.

Plan for an Opera

WITH the manuscript of his first publication out of the way Appia set himself a different task, that of creating an opera. He had entertained the idea for a long time; he began before 1895 and did not abandon the project for ten years. The subject he fell in love with was *Ondine*. Where and when he became acquainted with this romantic story cannot be traced. Perhaps Chamberlain mentioned it to him; perhaps Appia discovered it while playing the scores of German operatic versions by E. Th. A. Hoffmann or Albert Lortzing. It may be that he did not conceive the idea until he read Jean Thorel's French translation of *Undine* by Friedrich Karl Heinrich Fouqué (Baron de la Motte). This had appeared in 1894 and was praised as the first acceptable French version. Appia carried with him a copy of Fouqué's novel in a Reklam paperback edition for several years.

The basic plan was that Thorel would write the libretto (in French, of course) while Appia would devise the scenic form and, having conceived the whole enterprise, would in addition serve as a kind of supervisor. Since the manuscript of the libretto is unavailable and the sketches are lost, it is difficult to draw final conclusions about this opera, although letters to Chamberlain contain several pages with details of the plot and scenery. Appia's collaboration with the librettist must have been profitable for he was well pleased with the libretto as Thorel developed it. The important question of who was to be the composer remains. Appia vaguely talked about *Ondine* with close friends but he never stated definitely who would compose the music. Late in the winter of 1895 he paid Claude Debussy a visit in Paris; but was this merely a friendly visit to obtain his advice or an attempt to persuade this great musician to take on the composition? We do not know. Some time later Appia went again to the French capital; this time to submit his plan to Gabriel Fauré who indicated an interest in the libretto and pondered its composition. However, he apparently dropped the idea after a while, and later on Appia consulted with Wolzogen and other friends to obtain their recommendation. Nothing came of it, still Appia did not give up his plan and searched for a new collaborator. Could it be that, however secretly, he felt tempted to compose the opera himself? He was proficient in theory and composition, composing short pieces as a student and later for his own enjoyment. A few of his pieces of the nineties have been preserved by a favorite cousin of his. Strangely they show a style derived from the French school of that period rather than from German romanticism. There is, then, an ever-so-slight possibility that Appia actually made musical sketches for one or more scenes. At any rate *Ondine* was not dropped abruptly when he failed to find a trustworthy composer. He continued to think about and work on it while his main effort was devoted to the preparations for his next book.

La Musique et la mise en scène

SINCE 1892 Appia had the intention to write a full-length book describing his scenic reform and related problems as perfectly and as completely as he was able. He did not wish merely to repeat and expand what he had written and published but to elucidate his ideas from every angle lest anything be misunderstood. Everything he had on his mind was to be said honestly. From the very beginning he selected *La Musique et la mise en scène* as the title of his new book, and it was the title of the final manuscript. The organization of the material too is as he originally devised it. Only the last chapter underwent a thorough change; very early he conceived the idea to include an appendix in which he intended to delineate the precise procedure for the staging of *The Ring* and *Tristan,* his favorite music dramas, and a series of designs for the production of these works.

When drafting the outline of the new book he was convinced the manuscript could be finished within a comparatively brief period, but this proved to be too optimistic an appraisal of the complex task. He knew exactly what he wished to discuss, and in his mind he had, to a high degree, clarified most of the problems; yet the actual writing turned out to be far more difficult than he had anticipated. The year or so he had scheduled for it was not nearly enough; the manuscript on which he began hard to work in the fall of 1895 was not ready for a publisher until two years later.

In the dedication of this volume Appia expressed the friendship he felt for Chamberlain. "To Houston Stewart Chamberlain who alone knows the life which I enclose within these pages," so read the first and the final version. His faithful mentor again took great pains in finding a publisher for Appia's second book, this time trying to interest a reputable firm in Germany rather than in France. In a short while he was able to tell Appia that his friend Hugo Bruckmann, head of a well-known publishing company in Munich, was willing to take a look at some chapters and designs. Direct negotiations between Bruckmann and the author began, but for several months Appia hesitated; he was not sure whether it was better to have his new book appear in a German translation than in French. Agénor Boissier urged to have it published in the original and advised to seek a firm in Paris while Chamberlain favored a German edition. Appia weighed the pros and cons; naturally he preferred his French language, but the book was meant for the German reader. Finally he agreed to the German translation but not until he was assured of Chamberlain's willingness to supervise both the French and the German versions and to give suggestions.

Progress in writing the chapters was neither fast nor smooth. The subjects Appia knew best caused only minor difficulties in the enlarged form. The main obstacle arose when theories had to be expounded. A few times Chamberlain recommended clarification of basic principles, above all greater variety in the wording and a precise formulation of theories. Often Appia himself was dissatisfied with his writing; he had a notion that divers passages sounded too abstract and enigmatic. Part Two especially caused endless worries, because it was a delicate task for him to state clearly and precisely the principles upon which he based his staging of the Wagnerian music dramas. Part Three of the book did not take long to put into final shape; he actually enjoyed writing down his critical thoughts about Bayreuth, but what gave him the greatest satisfaction was the series of new designs which were simpler and showed more than his previous ones his reliance on three-dimensional pieces.

In spring 1897 Bruckmann offered an acceptable contract containing among other things the condition that the printing of the first 500 copies were to be subsidized. This request was taken care of very likely without the direct knowledge of Appia who understood little about financial matters and usually did not concern himself with them. His friend Boissier offered to serve as guarantor and Hélène, his sister, carried a smaller portion of the expenses. More troublesome was the question of translating, no mean task as everyone acquainted with Appia's treatise in the original French realizes. Bruckmann suggested as translator the princess Elsa Catacuzène. The prospect of collaborating with a woman was not to Appia's liking at all but in the end he decided to travel to Munich and meet the lady. After an exchange of views with her he forgot some of his misgivings. It required almost two years to see this project through, and during this period Appia referred frequently to the pain and agony suffered by an author; nevertheless the demanding task made progress thanks to Bruckmann, the princess—who became his wife, and the cooperation of the Chamberlains. (Mrs. Chamberlain occasionally helped with the German version.) With patience and understanding all dangerous problems were smoothed over.

During the winter of 1897–1898 Appia spent many weeks in Munich. This made it possible for him to work directly with the publisher and the translator. He had no major complaint except about the reproduction of the designs; the first prints he examined were such a poor sight that they depressed him considerably.

Like all sensitive artists Appia had his good and bad moods and even a slight remark could easily upset him. Thus he was annoyed when some people—not the Bruckmanns—called him a modern artist; he despised this term in general and he hated in particular to be identified with any movement. To his deep satisfaction his publisher understood his conception and tried to be of help. This encouraged him, for the Bruckmanns were staunch followers of Wagner and Bayreuth; hence he was all the more grateful that they accepted his manuscript in spite of its considerable critical passages about Wagner and a consummate rejection of the Bayreuth productions. During the year 1898 Chamberlain had gone over the entire German draft giving his friend many valuable suggestions which were greatly appreciated, for by that time Appia was so steeped in his work that he was unable to examine it objectively.

The appearance of *Die Musik und die Inscenierung,* as it was titled in German, in the middle of 1899 left a deeper mark than his preceding booklet. It received sundry reviews though not immediately, for in those days the custom of reviewing books regularly was not yet established. A comprehensive appraisal by Alfred Dutour for the *Journal de Genève*[4] acknowledged that the main principles were well delineated and, as a pertinent factor, that the author had a profound musical feeling for Wagner's music dramas and their production problems. Of particular interest is that Appia's concern for the relationship of time and space was duly mentioned. His reform idea was in general accepted by other writers too, though, in one case, with the ironical connotation that Appia, a Frenchman [*sic*], had digested German culture "with a thoroughness rare for his race."[5] The impact of this book has increased with the years. Thus Lee Simonson could write: "The first one hundred and twenty pages are nothing less than a textbook of modern stage craft."[6]

Appia wrote two prefaces for this book. One was included in the German edition; the other, in French, was intended for an English translation, but did not become known to a larger circle until *Music and the Art of the Theatre* was published in the United States in 1962. Both prefaces are highly instructive with reference to Appia's attitude as well as to his conception and execution of this volume. They must be read for an understanding of some of the author's intentions. Appia's ideas are difficult to grasp in their original language; the translation into German by no means alleviated this difficulty. Several passages are awkward and troublesome. Probably the princess was not always sure of the artist's aim; Chamberlain's florid style did not render some passages more intelligible, and Appia's command of the German language was not complete enough to recognize some misinterpretations.

Indicative of Appia's esthetics are the two mottoes he included in the publication; namely, Schopenhauer's "Music never expresses the phenomenon but only the inner essence of the phenomenon" and Schiller's "When music reaches its noblest power, it becomes form." Both tell about Appia's concept of the part played by music in the staging of a work. Since he used these quotations or at least referred to them in later writings, they almost stand as leitmotifs and should be remembered by every student of Appia's art.

In the preface to the German edition the first statement to hold the reader's attention is that Appia was fully aware of his limitations. "I am, by nature, not a writer," he confessed. He considered himself a musician who, fascinated by the theatre, became a designer, and as designer he relied on his feeling for rhythm which he translated into space. In the second preface he added that his task was the more complex because he dealt with the art of staging and also with dramatic art in general at a time when no one else seemed to be concerned about these topics. In the same preface he pointed out his interest in rhythmic movement, which had occupied him more than a decade before he met Jaques-Dalcroze. Lastly he presented the "three different aspects which correspond to the principal parts of my study." Included in the 1899 issue were:

1. Can the existing elements furnish, independently of any particular dramatic work, a principle applicable to the *mise en scène*, and if so, what will be the effect of that principle on existing theatre technique?
2. What obstacles prevented Richard Wagner from exercizing his creativity on the visual elements of the drama?

3. What effect will the theory of production, developed in the first part of this book, have on the artist of the theatre and on today's audience?

In Part One Appia touched upon the theme—the signal role of the performer—for which he did not discover a perfect solution until his collaboration with Dalcroze. Early he had shown a profound interest in dance and pantomime, and observations induced him to designate the performer, rather than the setting, the core of his reform. Appia considered the singing actor, later the performer in general, the intermediary between the ever-flowing mobility of music and the permanent immobility of the scenery. All of a performer's actions, gestures, and movements are determined by time durations and by rhythm. Consequently, before he can execute a step or a gesture, he must be familiar with the musical time pattern to which he must relate his actions. On this premise Appia based his conclusion that music must determine all phases of staging. In his opinion "music is transported into space and there achieves material form." And in accordance with Schopenhauer's dictum he opposed the realistic approach to scene design and wished to replace it with three elements in this order: spatial arrangement, lighting, and lastly painting since the task of coloring would mostly be assigned to light. At the summit of this hierarchy, of course, is the performer.

Appia divided a setting and its three-dimensional arrangement into three parts: the lower section, that is, the stage floor and the platforms placed on it; the middle one, the section most noticeable to the spectator; and the upper section, consisting of the borders and backdrops. Since his boyhood he had thought about the floor on which the singers stand and walk. In this book he again emphasized the importance of that portion of the setting; he regarded it as the "most critical" and further voiced his objection that trees, pillars, columns, rocks, and legs were never truly connected and integrated with the ground. He likewise attacked the exaggerated use of detailed painting and instead pleaded for utter simplicity; in quite strong words he called for sacrifice as "the most important principle in a work of art," a principle totally ignored by the contemporary leading designers and producers. His spatial arrangement needed only platforms of different levels, stairs, ramps, pillars, and plain walls and drapes. His description of a previous attempt at a similar reform clearly refers to the Shakespeare Stage used in the National Theatre in Munich which he had seen a few times. The flaw in this experiment was its inconsistency; while some settings were well devised in their plastic form, others retained the conventional style.

Appia's emphasis on the performer as the central element of the production and his insistence to provide for him a three-dimensional setting represents a complete break with tradition. Added to his new lighting method that played down, even eliminated, borders and footlights, accentuating instead the importance of spotlights to obtain complete plasticity, the thoroughness of his reform is truly striking, and distinguishes it from all former attempts.

Costumes before 1900 came under sharp scrutiny. In opera, Appia found them elaborate and ornamental but wanting in significance; in plays, completely subordinated to the historical style of the particular plays; making it even more difficult for the actor to become one with the purely decorative setting. His approach to costuming was based on two points:

1. The harmonious relationship between the actor's form and the poetic musical proportions.
2. The harmonious balance between the actor's form and the rest of the stage picture.

Relieved thus from the fetters of realism and sumptuousness the costumes can assume their proper function—to serve the performer.

Problems related to the Festival House in Bayreuth are discussed at the end of Part One. Even before he had seen it, Appia favored the construction of the building over the prevalent Baroque type of opera house. His own concept is a blend of three sources: the classic amphitheatre, Wagner's Festival House, and the auditoriums used for divers pageants in Switzerland. His rejection of the conventional structure with its boxes and galleries stemmed primarily from his aim to bring spectators and performers in close contact. Furthermore he wanted the audience to have a direct, unobstructed, and undistorted view of the entire acting area. Lastly he preferred the amphitheatrelike auditorium that does not separate the privileged classes from the other theatregoers. The Festival House fulfilled many of Appia's dreams and impressed him deeply when he first saw it. He loved the "fortunate optical effect" as well as "the wonderful acoustics" and praised the arrangement of all spectators directly in front of the stage, overlooking the fact though that a selected few still had their boxes in the rear. His reservations indicate his artistic approach. One concerned the proscenium frame which was too narrow for his taste. He would have liked to see it as wide as feasible, virtually flush with the side walls. This would provide a smoother transition from the house to the stage, eradicate the traditional peephole and offer an even better view for the patrons on the extreme left and right. He admired the so-called Wagner curtain as a great improvement over both the drop and the draw curtains which, whenever they close or open slowly, interrupt the mood of the spectators. The Wagner curtain, opening sideways and upwards at the same time, eliminates this trouble.

Appia also approved wholeheartedly of Wagner's innovation of the orchestra pit. In the contemporary opera house the pit was open, just a few feet below the level of the auditorium. Schinkel had been the first architect to conceive of lowering the pit, an idea later developed by Wagner to the "mystic gulf" in his Festival House. Appia, like every true musician, rightly decided that the orchestra could not be located backstage or below the stage as some extremists had suggested, but that it had to be in front of the stage and thus remain part of the auditorium. In Bayreuth he discovered to his pleasure that the partly covered sunken pit removed most of the disturbing spill of light thus giving the scenery an almost dreamy quality.

For Part Two of *La Musique et la mise en scène* Appia chose as motto Wagner's slogan "The German builds from within." Quotations from the master's essays, *Das Kunstwerk der Zukunft* and *Oper und Drama* form the nucleus, for Appia used them extensively to express his admiration as well as his criticism. Fully aware of Wagner's view of the relationship between libretto and music and the problems involved in handling scenery and singers, Appia had strong words of disapproval for the staging in Bayreuth. Some sharp reservations were unavoidable when he re-examined the style of the productions. Reluctantly he had to confirm his previous conclusion that, for all the technical improvements in Bayreuth, in essence the master was satisfied with the contemporary staging. In vain did Appia search for a new concept Wagner might have set forth in devising his own scenic style. "Obviously his sense of visual form was not appreciably developed beyond this convention, which did not offend his own vision," Appia wrote. Hesitantly he called this attitude "a defect which explained why he failed to recognize the limitations of the decorative methods of our stage."

Appia's devotion for Wagner concerned exclusively the tone poet, the composer of the great music dramas, *The Ring of the Nibelung*, *Tristan and Isolde*, *Parsifal*, and *The Mastersingers*. He paid little attention to his earlier works; which, like *Rienzi*, either belonged to the French form of grand opera, or were strongly under Italian influence. Since he disliked the romantic style of that era, he more or less ignored *The Flying Dutchman*, *Tannhäuser*, and *Lohengrin*. Appia was nearly sixty years old before he began to occupy himself with *Lohengrin*. His concept of a complete unity in art drew him naturally and logically to Wagner's *Gesamtkunstwerk* of his later period.

Appia had dealt thoroughly with *The Ring* in his previous writings; thus new material is primarily offered with reference to the other music dramas. Here he stated for the first time that only a modicum of visual effect should be given to a production of *Tristan*. *Parsifal*, as he interpreted it, is a miracle play "which is taking place within the soul of the pure and innocent hero." Based on this definition he drew his sketches in which the Spanish historical element gave way to simple symbolic settings. Only for *The Mastersingers* was he willing to concede some scenic realism; yet the connotation of this term was not so strict for him as for his colleagues; he was convinced of being able to find a solution different from the conventional productions of this comic opera. In the nineties he did not consider *The Mastersingers* important enough for a thorough study. His vague indications make it impossible to visualize distinctly how he would have devised its four settings. He did not take up this task for nearly twenty-five years.

"The Word-Tone Drama without Richard Wagner" is the heading of Part Three, which combines a series of loosely related topics. Here Appia left his own ground, theatre and esthetics, venturing further afield into general cultural questions which, at that time, he had not yet quite mastered. He was then still groping for a solid foundation to his own philosophy. As a result, this last part does not equal the magnificent ideas presented in the preceding chapters. There is no difficulty in following the author through the beginning passages in which he defined music as "essentially a living art." In applying this epithet to music as well as to light Appia let us anticipate the importance he attached to the word "living"; as a matter of fact it became the lodestar in his philosophy. Further contemplations on Wagnerian music contain no new views; Wagner stood in the center of Appia's analysis until he discovered Gluck's works later on. Of great importance in this chapter is one of his rare statements about Beethoven, when he wrote that Beethoven's music "in drawing near to drama" made us aware that we were "no longer concerned only with the expression, but with its objects as well."

In the last part the author referred once again to Bayreuth, extolling Wagner's genius which had created the festival idea and the Festival House. The remaining pages were devoted to a comparison of German and Latin—read "French"—culture. In all sincerity Appia stressed that not "the slightest political notion" was attached to his use of the terms "race" and "nationality." Undoubtedly he concurred with Wagner in that matter, who was not as extreme as Chamberlain in his views. He was even well disposed to commend certain conditions in Paris, such as the close contact between artists and patrons. But when his comparison extended to creative works, Appia found little cause to praise French art and had no word at all for Italian art. Although he conceded that French composers had a strong sense of form he added with regret that this quality was abused and ultimately led to an "exploitation of form for its sake or a more or less skillful imitation of German forms." He criticized moreover the position of the poet who merely served as an assistant to the composer, and referring to Debussy's style, he pointed out that as a result of the poet's subordination, "at times the music goes so far that it virtually assumes the role of the reader of the poem—the hearer is positively involved in the work of art."

Among the sundry topics Appia assembled in this part are two complaints still valid today. Many concert goers can still sympathize with him for assailing "the sickly orgies of the concert halls" where singers and conductors cut up his beloved music dramas, presenting portions of those masterpieces out of context, as separate arias, overtures, and symphonic interludes, although one has to confess that they are extremely effective as individual music pieces independent of their theatrical value. Appia's disgust with "the monstrous translations" that could be heard in French opera houses is also à propos in our time. Fortunately, during the past generation, improvement has been achieved in spite of the fact that occasionally an important opera is still being translated in a hurry, often by people who are, to boot, insensitive to the style of a given work. At any rate Appia's condemnation of the first French translations of the music dramas was absolutely justified. It seems strange that he did not raise the same issue with *Carmen* in an equally poor German translation which he must have heard at least once. Later in his life he adopted a somewhat milder position; then he was willing to assent to translations of the Wagnerian music dramas into other Teutonic languages, such as Swedish and Flemish.[7] He still excluded French, but in Milan he accepted Italian in his *Tristan* production and even liked the translation.

In a review of a *Lohengrin* performance in Geneva early in 1899 a critic suggested that a production of *Tristan* for the next season be scheduled, using the designs of "our fellow countryman Adolphe Appia."[8] Since the writer mentioned Appia's forthcoming book and in general disclosed a good knowledge of his works, he must have been one of Appia's friends or at least closely related to his circle. Appia, who suspected Agénor Boissier to be the instigator, was quite upset about this proposition, for the performance was supposed to be sung in French and he had no wish whatever to be associated with such a venture. His excitement evaporated as soon as he learned the plan would not materialize.

The appendix to *La Musique et la mise en scène*, planned as an expansion and explanation of staging ideas for *The Ring* and *Tristan*, turned out to be two almost independent scenarios written in essay form. As to *The Ring*, Appia did not include information beyond that contained in his previous writings, mainly because he still hoped to have his comprehensive scenarios of the *Cycle* published, an expectation never to be fulfilled. Nevertheless this part of the appendix is quite important, since copies of his preceding brochure *La Mise en scène du drame wagnérien* are so scarce. Of the highest value is Appia's delineation of staging ideas for *Tristan*. Unfortunately many professionals in the theatre have so eagerly concentrated on the practical outline of the spatial arrangement of the three settings and of their light plots that they have sometimes overlooked his other statements. His basic conception of *Tristan* was inserted earlier in the book; in the appendix he then described the mood of this music drama in poetic and moving phrases. The description of his scenic vision is equally fascinating. His outline of the floor plans enables every designer to draw them to scale and thus to obtain a clear picture of the execution of the stunning designs which are part of that edition. The light plot, stated almost cue by cue, makes it possible to visualize the intentions of the artist. The passages about the lighting in *Tristan* had a tremendous influence on the development of lighting, one is inclined to say, as a specific art. Here designers and directors can learn what he meant by employing light as a living element synchronized with the score; that is, with the mood expressed through the music. Appia clarified the use of a *crescendo* or *decrescendo*, how to emphasize or de-emphasize the presence of a character, and he showed how to achieve the original effect of a light beam falling from upstage toward downstage. All these new ideas had little relation to the external plot but they tellingly expressed the reality of the inner action.

The First Designs

NINETEEN sketches were included in this volume; they are admirable though Appia himself made "no claim to artistic perfection." Apologetic as he frequently was about his drawing and writing, he volunteered another reservation based on his observations backstage during the mounting and shifting of Wagerian operas. He was afraid that the backstage area of many theatres was too small for the handling and storing of the multitude of three-dimensional pieces required for his settings. This fear was unnecessary for the opera houses in Dresden, Vienna, and Munich had ample backstage area. Of the large opera houses known to Appia before 1900 only the Bayreuth House can be said to have had limited space. Many middling theatres might have faced difficulties in executing some of his wishes, but this should not have perturbed him since technical requirements can, in most cases, be solved by an ingenious technical director, as Appia himself was to experience in Basel in the twenties.

Appia's modesty concerning his designs was in line with his constant striving for perfection. The restless artist was seldom satisfied with his work; he even confessed that the more he designed the less he knew about the craft. This is typical of the true artist who is never content with what he has already accomplished, but an objective viewer has to disagree. It seems unimaginable that anybody interested in designing and in the theatre would not be impressed, even fascinated, by most of these sketches. Immediately striking are the simplicity, purity, and clarity of Appia's conception; then the extraordinary effect of space, the monumentality of these settings; the impressive atmosphere which all the settings breathe because of the treatment of light, the use of dark and lighted areas; and lastly the harmony of a world in which musico-poetic sensitiveness and logical thought are fused. If Appia had left no more than these designs he would still count among the greatest scene designers of all time.

A brief glance at the five sketches for Act III of *The Valkyrie* will remind the viewer that Appia had the definite intention of obtaining cloud effects through projection. Each of the sketches shows a different scene and a different mood which would have been created by clouds projected on the cyclorama (backdrop), clouds and more clouds at the beginning of the act, and then quiet serenity before the magic fire. Appia never stated where and how he conceived the idea to use slides for such scenic effects. As a child he almost certainly played with a *laterna magica*, but its adaptation for the stage can not be so readily explained. Later he may have read about an elaborate device invented by one Athanasius Kircher before 1700, or about the ocular harpsichord of Robert Smith about 1750. In Appia's day there

Figure 14. The Rhinegold, Scene 2. *Donald Oenslager.*

Figure 15. Siegfried, Mimes' cave in Act I. *Institut fuer Theaterwissenschaft, Cologne.*

were the Chase Electric Cyclorama about 1890 and other experiments with slide projectors in France and Germany. Perhaps he had heard of a new scenic projector which La Loie Fuller introduced at the Paris World's Fair in 1900. Whatever inspired his approach, he was convinced that a slide projector represented a great asset in his aim to eliminate realism. He predicted a wonderful development for this device as soon as adquate electric equipment would be manufactured; then, he thought, it could become "all powerful." Since Wagner in *The Ring* had nature and its phenomena play so essential a part, it is not surprising at all to find Appia dreaming of, and working on, the use of projection for a whole series of effects.

Only by drawing several sketches of a scene was Appia in a position to present his staging ideas. He did not find it easy to clarify the role he assigned to light and shadows. His several sketches for Act II of *Tristan* prove this point best, for he demonstrated the eye-catching effect of the dominating oversized torch and the interplay of lighted and dark areas, ideas brillantly realized in the designs. For Act III Appia included only two examples, showing the atmosphere at the beginning of the act and toward the end. Our only regret is that he did not draw sketches for the other scenes he had outlined in his light plot.

The sketches he initially drew for *The Ring* were replaced by a new series when the publication of the book became a distinct possibility. Fortunately there is an opportunity to compare the designs of the first group with those of the second. We see, for instance, that the setting of Scene 2 of *The Rhinegold* is basically the same in both cases. The background is treated alike, but the acting areas with their numerous levels show slight changes. Thus the high platform on the right was originally more abrupt, there were no ramps downstage right and left. A more obvious modification con be detected in the plan for Act III of *The Valkyrie*. Again the basic concept remained unaltered; there is hardly any change in the size and height of the platforms; the difference stems from a new version in the treatment of trees. In 1892 just a few crowns of firs were seen in the background, but years later a large fir was added downstage left; its branches dominate the particular area close to the tree which also provides a fine balance to the summit of the rock on the opposite side. Even an intensive study of Appia's scenarios does not give any satisfactory clue to why he decided on these modifications; slight as they were they demonstrate how he continuously pondered improvements.

Appia's style does not fit any known term. He himself resented attempts to associate him with a movement, or even to call him modern; he merely wished to be himself. While fully recognizing that realism on stage had brought about some improvements, such as the introduction of three-dimensional pieces, he abhorred verisimilitude. Extreme symbolism was not to his liking, though he applied symbolic elements, such as the torch in *Tristan*. This was when he was closest to romanticism, yet he lashed out against its misguided use as he observed it in so many productions. There are traces of impressionism, the movement which definitely affected his concept of contrasting light effects. Finally the strong influence of classic principles is noticeable in the simplicity and clarity of his designs. He digested all these elements and united them in his own style; he truly was and remained himself. That the disciples of Wagner under the leadership of Cosima objected to Appia needs no emphasis. Madame Cosima, as Appia learned, compared his designs with the empty ice fields at the North Pole. Less-prejudiced observers were inclined to accept part of Appia's interpretation, but somehow wondered how to combine the rich romantic music of the Bayreuth master with the almost ascetic pictures of the young Swiss artist. Is there a contradiction? A critic merely examining the sketches may conclude that Appia went too far in his simplification. But this opinion cannot be held by someone who is acquainted with Appia's light plot which is as richly varied as the music and in direct empathy to it; those who attended a performance of Appia's *Tristan* in Milan in 1923–1924 should certainly deny any discord existed between his *mise en scène* and the music of this work. Appia avoided everything that could distract from the music and thus succeeded in giving it the dominant role. Whenever he was not absolutely true to himself he was not really convincing. Examples of this are the first scene of Act III in *The Twilight of the Gods* which is not far removed from a conventional setting, and the Flower Garden scene in *Parsifal* which resembles an impressionistic sketch. The designs that made Appia famous have hardly any trace of realism, merely a hint of impressionism, but speak a romantic language, though unlike that of the usual artist of his time. There is no sentimentality in Appia's drawings, for in his strength he created an atmosphere through a minimum of means.

The sketches of that period are drawn with black crayon and black and white chalk, on either a light tan or bluish paper. Most of his effects were achieved by "smudging, rubbing and erasing with very little actual drawing," as Donald Oenslager described the artist's method. None of his designs was done in color. No one ever saw him working with brush and watercolors. In his scenarios several colors are mentioned; he was willing to apply grey and brown, neutral shades, but seldom green, red, or blue. Although he intended to add some hues he did not show them in his sketches. According to his principle, of course, light was to be the coloring element; "color that is light," he told his friend Jean Mercier. Jacques Copeau, who knew Appia intimately, was convinced that the lack of color in the artist's designs had nothing to do with his esthetics, it was part of his austere nature.[9] Appia saw his settings in black and white and simply did not think in terms of colors. Only much later did he wonder whether this omission could somehow weaken his conception.

How many sketches of *The Ring, Tristan* and *Parsifal* did Appia draw around the turn of the century? It is interesting to discover that, once in a while, the master made his sketches in different sizes; that, moreover, he copied those he considered particularly well executed. Some of his originals show needle holes along the outline of "tree trunks" and "hills"; this simple method evidently allowed him to redo a design using the same basic proportions of the original. He certainly finished more sketches than we know of since he made several of many settings. He kept a good number of them wherever he happned to live, storing others in his sister's apartment; later he gave some to friends and admirers. It is doubtful that a reliable listing could now be made, though after his death the Adolphe Appia Foundation in Geneva took great pains to do so. Numerous drawings have been lost, for Appia, the perfectionist, threw away whatever he did not quite approve of. Some are surely in private hands yet unknown to researchers; a family mishap accounted for innumerable losses; and, World War II contributed, when some designs in the possessions of friends were destroyed or perhaps stolen during the Nazi occupation of France.

Other Essays

WAGNER's *Parsifal* is not treated thoroughly in *La Musique et la mise en scène*, but remarks Appia made to friends and above all an essay about *Parsifal* allow the conclusion that he seriously considered to include extensive passages in his book or add, respectively, a scenario to its appendix. The essay, written about 1896, remained unpublished until 1912 when it appeared in an abbreviated German form in the periodical *Der Tuermer*. There was good reason for revising and shortening the essay, for Appia devoted more than a third of the first version to *Tristan* before touching on his ideas for a production of *Parsifal*.

Disregarding Wagner's directions for the settings he examined the score; that is, the music and the libretto. Again he tried to extract the inner action from the external events. To achieve this he suggested that all the scenes in and around the Temple of the Grail should be presented in a "profound and unforgettable solemnity" in contrast to the scenes in Klingsor's castle for which he devised an atmosphere of "artificial fragility and mobility." The designs for *Parsifal* demonstrate again how he succeeded in expressing magnificently each scenic idea with a minimum of means. Unfortunately we do not have his sketch, or sketches, for the Temple. But his description of the change from Scene 1 to Scene 2 in Act I gives a fairly clear picture of what he visualized for this setting. Appia was not completely opposed to Wagner's request for the use of a *Wandeldekoration* to execute this change, but he discarded all purely decorative items from the Bayreuth production. He relied basically on the tall tree trunks of the first scene which, during the interlude would gradually move across the stage. The tree trunks would slowly assume more and more the shape of pillars until the pillars would finally form the sacred interior. The most significant role, of course, was given to lighting, not only in the softly lit opening scene, but even more so during the shifting until it would progressively turn into "supernatural clarity" in the Temple. Appia made the original

Figure 16. Parsifal, the Sacred Forest. *W. R. Volbach.*

series of sketches for *Parsifal in 1896* but he kept working on them for almost a decade. Maybe he was undecided regarding a definite solution, and this could have been a reason for excluding a scenario and sketches from his second book.

The setting of the Sacred Forest seemed to fascinate him most, and he devised it in different sizes and with different lighting effects. This sketch remains one of the master's most striking creations: the foreground dominated by dark tall tree trunks, the brighter background with its indicated outline of wooded hills, the prominent effect of light falling from the rear toward downstage center. This monumental though simple spatial setting affected generations of designers.

A year after the appearance of *La Musique et la mise en scène*, Appia wrote again about his reform principles. The new essay published in 1904 has the title *Comment reformer notre mise en scène (Ideas on a Reform of our mise en scène)*. It supplements the preceding volume and was probably motivated by his reaction to remarks he heard from friends and foes alike, accusing him of being too abstract in his thoughts and too diffuse in the presentation of his scenic reform. So he decided to set down his principles clearly and precisely in a terse essay. The printed version is identical with the original manuscript of 1900, except for a footnote praising Mariano Fortuny's "excellent invention," the new system of indirect or diffused lighting.

Compared to his previous writings the essay is tame and mild; besides, following the advice to be more lucid and concrete, he illustrated his sometimes abstruse theories with concrete examples which could be grasped by the lay reader. Thus, when he conceded that Parisian theatres had a workable approach to staging realistic plays, he mentioned the company of André Antoine. Slyly he then inquired how directors and designers would proceed with works of a nonrealistic style such as *Troilus and Cressida, The Tempest*, and the Wagnerian music dramas. The question was, of course, rhetorical, and was left pending, but another example may be taken as his answer to it. Referring to *Siegfried* he raised the fundamental issue: is there mainly a forest with characters moving in it or is the audience interested in the characters who happen to be in a forest? In his answer he took the theatregoer as point of departure, the spectator who wishes to witness on stage a dramatic action, and logically he came to the conclusion that the living, moving performer alone was in a position to fulfill that wish. For the audience, he emphasized, "scenic illusion is the presence of the living actor." This issue and Appia's solution were and are frequently quoted by directors. In the same essay Appia also succeeded for the first time to express his hierarchy for the production in a concise form. Without any deviation he simply stated it in a few words: the actor, spatial arrangement, lighting, painted flats. Likewise he indicated a problem which occupied him deeply later on: the task to solve the integration and participation of the audience in the performance.

At this point it would be beneficial to review what Appia had achieved during the decade from 1890–1900. A summary yields the various ideas presented in his scenic reform. Some had been suggested or tried out before him, some are indeed the fruit of his particular conception, all represent a new, unique combination of esthetic principles. The ideas he blended are:

Wagner's synthesis of the arts can obtain its perfect form only after the prevailing contradiction between the master's musico-poetic conception and his production style in Bayreuth has been eradicated.

It is wrong to place the three-dimensional moving actor in front of two-dimensional painted flats and drops.

Only a setting conceived in a spatial arrangement is compatible with the living performer.

Lighting must play a much larger role than heretofore. Portable devices (spotlights, slide projectors) must be used more extensively while border and footlights should only serve as general illumination; footlights in particular are to be kept at a minimum volume.

A notation has to be initiated to enable the performer to execute his action as a singer by using the notation of the vocal score for his interpretation.

The performer should receive training in a physical discipline similar to that of ballet in order to improve his acting ability.

Stage and auditorium should not be strictly separated. On the contrary, everything must be done to provide a smooth transition from the darkened house to the well-lit stage.

The foundation of all his detailed ideas is the hierarchy in which the performer occupies the highest position to be followed by spatial arrangement, lighting, and color, in this order of importance.

Appia and Bayreuth

THE essays and books Appia wrote, the sketches he drew, all his thinking were directed toward one single aim: Bayreuth. In his desire to be heard, to be read by Cosima Wagner, he devoted all his time and effort to the development of a perfect production plan for the music dramas. The hope he expressed in his writings was to be granted a favorable reaction, perhaps to be accepted. No rebuke could stymie his optimism. And rebuked he was. Whatever he tried, or more correctly whatever Chamberlain tried, remained without positive result. Yet Appia kept urging and urging, hoping against all hope to surmount Cosima's prejudice.

In 1892 Appia sent Madame Cosima several designs with a few lines of consummate dedication. Chamberlain brought them to House Wahnfried. In spite of the strongest recommendation the guardian of Bayreuth did not even open the package and Chamberlain was obliged to return it to his friend.[10] Thirty years later

Appia stated that his purpose was to impress Cosima Wagner so that she might consider his designs for the festivals in 1896. In the middle nineties Appia inquired whether his friend could arrange for him to attend some of the festival rehearsals. Evidently Chamberlain succeeded in fulfilling this wish, but another more delicate request by Appia was beyond his influence. Appia asked that certain items be eliminated and others be changed in the production. Around 1895 Chamberlain brought Cosima a second portfolio with Appia's sketches for *The Ring;* stubbornly she declined to look at them. As Appia told his friend Jean Mercier about this disappointing experience, she stated, "Exactly as if Richard were still alive, nothing related to his esthetic principles will be changed."

From the published correspondence between Cosima Wagner and Chamberlain we know that he mentioned Appia to her several times. In one letter he offered as excuse for not being at home when she called that he was with his "dear friend Appia," who had been demonstrating how lighting for a production of *The Mastersingers* should be plotted "so that light and music would fuse."[11] At another opportunity he informed her that he was looking ahead to hearing *Tannhäuser* with Appia. Not only artistic, but personal events too—for instance, how they hiked and climbed in the Vienna woods—were inserted in these letters. However, all his allusions to his high regard for and intimate friendship with Appia fell on deaf ears. Cosima's answers leave no doubt that any attempt by Chamberlain, no matter how discreet, would be rebuffed. During the winter of 1895 she read Appia's first booklet, which Chamberlain had sent her. Her conclusion showed her prejudice when she informed Chamberlain that "the *mise en scène* has been precisely determined in the orchestra score and therefore this work is of no value ." A bit ironically she added that in France perhaps this treatise may serve some purpose. Shortly thereafter Chamberlain indicated in a letter that Appia would be participating in an operatic production in Paris. This news did not move Cosima to abandon her indifference either. In May of the following year she read Appia's first essay and of course her reaction was again absolutely negative. The only concession she permitted herself was to be interested in the way Appia described his lighting ideas, but even here she found fault with his choice of bright and dark areas. All other suggestions were bluntly rejected; she did not care at all for his spatial arrangements, his simplified costumes, the omission of properties, the blocking of the action; in short, the entire plan of his scenic reform. Cosima's letters lead one to believe that she rejected Appia's new concept primarily out of her blind reverence for the late master which would not allow her to question his infallibility. In addition, however, it is unlikely that as a conventional romanticist she could have grasped Appia's revolutionary ideas.

The Festivals nevertheless did not remain untouched. When influential followers of Bayreuth urged some changes Madame Cosima finally gave in. An important speaker for those who disagreed with the tradition in Bayreuth was Henry

Thode, the eminent art historian, who was Cosima's son-in-law; he was in favor of abandoning historical verisimilitude and relying on unfettered imagination.[12] Cosima made slight modifications in *The Ring* production of 1896, and in 1903 she agreed to an entirely new *mise en scène* for *Parsifal*, though not a modern one. In Bayreuth, as in many other theatres, vested interests posed an insurmountable obstacle to any necessary change. Whatever the cause of such a resistance—personal or artistic loyalty, antagonism against everything new, inertia, or financial consideration—it is agonizing for any young artist and can impede his development, perhaps beyond repair. Appia suffered such a fate.

The only time Cosima considered it opportune to answer one of Appia's letters occured in 1902. This single occasion, however, had nothing to do with his wish to be acknowledged as a designer. In that year an article of Appia's was published in which he made a penetrating comparison of the Bayreuth Festival House and the new Prinzregenten-Theater in Munich. With only a few, brief reservations, he praised Wagner's creation for its form, color, arrangement, its visual and optical advantages in contrast to the unsatisfactory solution of these points in Munich.[13] Cosima Wagner acknowledged receipt of this article but for obvious reasons refrained from offering her opinoin about the new opera house. Although the festivals in Munich were a competitive venture she was not anxious to be drawn into any public controversy. Appia was very disappointed when he realized that she would not support him with a frank statement. Unlike Madame Cosima, he was no diplomat.

III

Appia and Paris

At the age of nineteen, Appia visited Paris as a starting point of his musical studies. He was not to return until he had spent years in Leipzig and Dresden. How often he then went to the French capital and how long he remained each time is difficult to ascertain. He himself mentioned in a general way that he spent a total of two years in Paris before the end of the century. Although he was imbued with French culture, indeed grew up surrounded by volumes of the French classics, Wagner had so strong an impact upon him that, upon his return to Paris around 1890, he was quickly drawn to the Bayreuth circle which flourished in those days. His entry was provided by friends of several relatives and by Chamberlain. Many musicians, writers, and philosophers of the younger generation were disciples of Wagner, to the extent that author Romain Rolland wrote, in retrospect, "The entire universe was seen and judged by the thought of Bayreuth."[1] Even a special periodical, La Revue Wagnérienne, edited by Edouard Dujardin, was in circulation.

Outside of the Wagnerian circle, Appia found little he appreciated. Among all the French operas he liked only Carmen, a work that broke through the rigid tradition of French grand and comic opera. The story and music strongly appealed to the sensual side of Appia's nature. In spite of his complete surrender to the Wagnerian music drama which, theoretically at least, should have excluded the acceptance of Carmen, he was fascinated by this opera. He studied it so thoroughly that he was able to play the score and sing the diverse roles from memory; he enjoyed doing this for close friends. Later he would even have a chance to stage some of it.

When Appia referred to any other French opera, it was to criticize or ridicule it. This negative attitude extended even, in a way, to the work of Claude Debussy whom he greatly admired. As he explained to Mercier, he loved the composer not for his modern style but for the atmosphere of his music. Appia had met Debussy sometime before 1890; although the contact cannot have been very close, Appia called occasionally on the master for advice. For about a decade he praised Debussy's compositions; then he attended a performance of *Pelléas and Mélisande*. He was not even willing to acknowledge that this opera developed a style indicated by Wagner in *Tristan*. He condemned *Pelléas et Mélisande* as intolerably boring and Debussy's new operatic style a misconception; and his criticism included the play by Maurice Maeterlinck whose other writings he had quite enjoyed.

He shared a longer-lasting and more intimate relationship with Gabriel Urbain Fauré to whom Appia was introduced by Robert Godet. A few hints in Appia's essays and vague remarks to friends permit the assumption that Fauré was Appia's theory and counterpoint teacher, at least for several months. Since Fauré has been described as being "less a teacher than a guide,"[2] he was precisely the teacher for Appia who was more anxious to receive suggestions and advice than to be taught methodically. In his essay *L'Intermédiaire (The Intermediary)* Appia described how, after a lesson, his music professor would take him for long walks discussing "subjects and observations unrelated to music and yet connected with my studies." This, he confessed, induced him carefully to examine his own self and his art. These conversations and the friendship surrounding them taught him the meaning of Goethe's term "the spiritual bond" (*das geistige Band*).

Fauré was known mainly as composer of chamber, symphonic, and church music; but he created a few dramatic works too. With his interest in opera Appia found in Fauré an understanding adviser and, around 1900, he may have obtained from him the impetus for his later attempt to stage Aeschylus' *Prometheus* (see Chapter V); Fauré himself used this subject as libretto for one of his dramatic works. The acquaintance with the composer probably dated back to 1880 or even a year earlier when Appia, after his graduation, stayed in Paris for a longer period of time. He certainly met him again ten years later and kept contact with him until about 1905. Letters were exchanged and whenever Appia came to Paris he called on Fauré who remained his sounding board and, as previously mentioned, was also approached to compose the libretto of *Ondine*.

In Paris Appia saw many productions in legitimate theatres but in his letters and later in essays he hardly mentioned musical performances. Perhaps he could not accept their conventional style, although in the Opéra a few presentations ought to have at least partly attracted his attention because of their interesting use of three-dimensional set pieces. On the other hand, silence can be explained by his first and foremost concern with the over-all style rather than the execution of details. The only operetta he took note of was Offenbach's *Orpheus in the Underworld*, which he saw at the Variété. Although he thoroughly disliked the production as a whole, its sumptuous settings and costumes, and the display of scantily dressed women on stage, he applauded the lighting, especially various spotlight effects and the minimal use of footlights. Play productions seemed to have chiefly impressed him for their intense preparatory work and the discipline of all concerned during rehearsals. Yet disapproving the prevailing realistic style of playwriting, he could only deplore that so much effort was wasted on mediocrities. As an example he referred to the company of the Théâtre Libre of André Antoine whose penchant for imitating life Appia was unable to appreciate. Thus his theatrical observations confirm that, true to himself, he was exclusively on the lookout for a realization of his ideas and gave unstinted praise wherever he discovered a similar approach.

The First Production

THE first opportunity to execute a production such as he had dreamed of and written about came to Appia in Paris in the early 1900's. Probably by a letter Chamberlain introduced Appia to Countess Zichy, a Hungarian, in the spring of 1901. She was fascinated by the artist and his work and soon introduced him to a friend in Paris, Countess René de Béarn. This delicate, vivacious, and remarkable lady, then in her early forties, loved to sponsor exceptional artistic events in the private theatre attached to her magnificent mansion at 22, avenue Bosquet. The Countess, related to the Singer family of sewing machine fame, was wealthy. Her husband, himself quite rich, remained in the background and played no part in these evenings arranged by his wife. About the time the Countess was considering the project with Appia, the couple separated and after their divorce she was known again under her maiden name, Martine de Béhague. A third lady, frequently mentioned in connection with the project, was Countess de la Tour who was well known in artistic circles of Paris.

The intimate theatre of Madame de Béarn was designed by the Venetian architect Forini in a basically Byzantine style; its walls were covered with Persian silk rugs. Here nearly 400 guests enjoyed concerts, recitals, and a few theatrical performances until the thirties when the Countess retired from her soirées. Performers of international renown were engaged for these gatherings of a sophisticated society, as were promising young artists who gained thus the unique opportunity to show their talents or to experiment with new ideas. Evidently the Countess was convinced that Appia could offer a production unlike any other heretofore presented.

Appia's original suggestion was to stage parts of *Tristan and Isolde*. It seemed an intriguing idea and he was asked to start with the preparatory arrangements. For his efforts he was paid an honorarium of 300 francs a month which probably included his traveling expenses for the forthcoming production as well as his living costs for the many weeks he spent in Paris. The first plan, to present Act II and scenes from Act III of the music drama, was plagued with problems. *Tristan* calls for an orchestra of at least sixty or seventy musicians, while the pit of the private theatre could hold thirty-five or forty instrumentalists. Without alteration, the stage was not adequate for Appia's demands. Finding and affording good singers for the leading roles was a problem. Then there was the publisher's attitude. Leading firms generally do not like to grant the rights for a performance such as Madame de Béarn's. Most of the difficulties would have been resolved because the countess seemed willing to shoulder the ever-mounting expenses, and with that in mind, Appia was a happy and busy man. For weeks discussions centered around the re-modeling of the stage and the pit. One suggestion was to build an entirely new theatre; another to enlarge and modernize the stage; a third to rent a legitimate house for the performances. The Countess finally agreed to have the stage and pit enlarged. During these months of planning and organizing Appia was often in Paris for talks with madame and his collaborators. He traveled to Munich and other cities to meet with singers and conductors; in between he returned to his home in Bière. Nothing apparently disturbed him; no problems, no difficulty could dampen his elated spirit. He was even very pleased with his hostess, the "perfectly charming" Countess de Béarn, a compliment he seldom paid a woman.

Appia had several collaborators. Alfred Guy Claparède, a distant cousin and good friend, maintained contacts with the Countess and with some artists and technicians during Appia's absences from Paris. Alfred Guy's home was often Appia's mailing address while the latter was so much on the move. This cousin was close to Mariano Fortuny, son of the Spanish artist of the same name. Fortuny was important to the forthcoming production because his fascinating lighting experiments promised to fulfill Appia's dreams. His new system called for a group of strong floodlights to illuminate a cyclorama indirectly while at the same time spreading diffused light across the upper stage area. In addition to this general illumination, spotlights were planned for the acting area proper and for special effects. Like Appia he discounted the use of footlights. The two men spent many hours together, often joined by Alfred Guy, to talk about lighting problems and how to solve them on an ideal stage. Fortuny was also interested in building a semi-spheric cyclorama consisting of two canvas layers which could be inflated to form a dome around and above the acting area. The first experiments were evidently not too successful and the plan was discarded. To what extent the Fortuny system of lighting was ready when Appia finally presented his production is not quite certain. At any rate, there was no cyclorama and consequently few, if any, floodlights were employed. It is known though that the stage and the pit in the intimate theatre were remodeled, with the original plan providing for a new lighting equipment. Since reports and reviews emphasize the stunning light effects, it may be taken for granted that Appia's and Fortuny's revolutionary visions were at least partly realized. Shortly before opening night the two men told Raymond Penel, another cousin of Appia's: "If we do not succeed in pushing this thing through, we shall burst." The final success demonstrated Appia's brilliant idea as materialized by the more practical Fortuny, an engineer.

In December, 1902, Appia met Lucien Jusseaume, the great designer, whose settings for *Pelléas et Mélisande* had made him famous overnight. Appia admired his style and was very happy when he attained the cooperation of this congenial artist. Countess de Béarn too was highly pleased to see this rising star connected with the forthcoming event. Due to contradictory reports it is not quite clear what part Jusseaume played in the production since, after all, the settings were designed by Appia. However, the fact that Appia disliked technical work and particularly had no patience for details permits the inference that Jusseaume was kind enough to give his expert advice on these matters; he may even have served quasi as a technical director coordinating all phases of the production and he must have spent considerable time on it. Whatever he did was of great value to all participants, for Appia left no doubt about his gratitude for, and satisfaction with, the work of his new friend.

From the beginning an urgent problem was to find an outstanding conductor. Early in 1902 Appia had reached a vague understanding with Felix von Weingartner. With this eminent musician behind his production Appia could expect the engagement of first-class singers for the roles of Tristan and Isolde to be comparatively easy. Weingartner had seen Appia's designs and admired their artistic simplicity. Yet in spite of an agreement of sorts Appia somehow felt that Weingartner would not in the end join the team. This thought and technical difficulties so worried him that he nearly became ill. In order to get a clearer picture, Madame de Béarn invited Weingartner to call on her in Paris. At this meeting he suggested she look around for a gifted younger conductor and for less-known singers who would more readily adjust themselves to the new style. Thus the serious question of finding a suitable conductor was wide open again. During a visit to Munich late in the same year, Appia tried to talk to Siegmund von Hausegger in nearby Partenkirchen, and he was also in contact with Hugo Reichenberger, conductor at the Court Theatre in Stuttgart. Time was pressing and still no results. In December Weingartner definitely declined to interrupt his regular work in order to serve as musical director in Paris. Who in the end took the baton, Hausegger or Reichenberger, cannot be determined from the available material.

During these dramatic weeks the plan to stage scenes from *Tristan* was finally discarded and a new program was discussed and devised. It contained scenes from *Carmen* preceded by scenes from Byron's *Manfred* with music by Robert Schumann. In view of Appia's distaste for melodrama in general and his description of *Manfred* as a crude creation in his book *La Musique et la mise en scène*, his compromise cannot easily be explained except as an appeasement to his patroness.

The change in the program heaped more work upon the collaborators whose nerves were already strained. During the winter months the entire project was in jeopardy more than once. Appia was particularly upset about the remodeling of the theatre which was behind schedule, and it looked as if the original production date in early March, 1903, would have to be postponed. The Countess too became nervous, probably irritated and even annoyed because the preparation made so many demands for her time and patience over and above the demands for her money. Appia's ever-changing moods must have worn her out; she was not accustomed to dealing extensively and intensively with theatre people. Yet as a rule, she was able to control herself and to remain a kind hostess to a group of artists who invaded not only her theatre but also her mansion almost every day. The weeks when 1902 turned into 1903 were hectic indeed; plans had to be and were altered. For a while the presentation was postponed to a date in May when nothing seemed to develop as projected . Yet suddenly everything fell into place and opening night was again foreseeable in March. Appia was of course much relieved when all the troublesome problems evaporated: the rebuilding in the theatre came along rapidly, all parts were cast, the settings took shape, the rehearsals could commence. He confessed to all his friends that he was well pleased with his designs and his scenarios.

Three performances of the scenes from *Manfred* and *Carmen* introduced by some concert pieces were scheduled; the first, on March 25, 1903, was reserved for invited guests while the other two on March 27 and 28 were thrown open to the public for the benefit of a charity. On opening night members of the nobility, finance, and business mingled with prominent musicians, authors, theatre managers, and actors. Sarah Bernhardt was probably the guest best-known internationally; those present remember distinctly how she staged a splendid entrance, arriving late and walking slowly and majestically to her seat. Although the evening was an event of social and artistic signficance, editors in 1903 showed no particular interest in covering a private performance. Thus it is not surprising that no review appeared in the Parisian newspapers. Nevertheless three reviews are available; one published in Germany and two in Switzerland.[3] Hermann Keyserling, Appia's young friend, wrote an elaborate article, about 4,000 words, almost immediately after opening night. The two writers for the Swiss periodicals did not have their reports published until the second part of May which leaves the impression that they decided to write about the production in Paris after learning of Keyserling's article; this assumption is strengthened by the open references to and quotations from the German newspaper. Both writers became admirers of Appia and were to write other articles about him in later years.

In his review Keyserling ignored the introduction of the evening, the concert pieces, evidently to put greater emphasis on the importance of Appia's work. The Count had been in a position to observe the entire development of the venture from its inception to opening night; he had even lent an occasional helping hand in the preparatory work. His review commences with a delineation of Appia's ideas which he thoroughly understood and fully supported in the conviction that they would lead the way in the future. The second half of his report is devoted to the production proper. First he describes the charming little theatre and the suspense in the audience when the house lights were dimmed and Schumann's overture to *Manfred* sounded forth from the invisible pit. Since this drama was not well known, Keyserling briefly explains the situation of the scenes that were performed. The only actor he mentions is Edouard De Max, a highly esteemed artist and partner of Sarah Bernhardt at that time, who played Manfred. Much space is then given to the description of the setting whose salient features were typical of Appia: platforms of several levels and light effects created by spotlights. The Hall of Arimanes, the Kingdom of the Dead, was indicated by a series of platforms with the lowest level on stage left (from the spectator's view) and the highest on the opposite side with steps connecting the different levels. A few heavy pillars of a dark reddish color surrounded the acting area. Appia introduced a new method of masking the upper part of the stage. Instead of the conventional borders, he used drapes hanging not straight across the stage, but lower on the left and higher on the right, thus, in a general way, following the contour of the platforms. When the curtains opened, a red beam was falling from the left occasionally striking the moving Manfred. This gave the impression of a torchlight illuminating his face. At other times he was merely a silhouette in front of strong light. When later, Astarte appeared on the highest level she seemed to float in a silvery light that made her look almost unreal, a spirit. The area between the two performers remained dark throughout. The entire arrangement, the spatial setting, and the sharply contrasting light effects, had a stunning impact.

Manfred was very well received by the audience; even more enthusiastic was the reaction to the scenes from Act II of *Carmen*. Keyserling stresses that "no more perfect staging could be imagined." The tradition was completely ignored; a new conception initiated. Moonlight filtered through branches of a vine arbor forming a capricious pattern on the floor. Candlelight, barely noticeable, came from the ramshackle inn heightening the contrast between brighter and darker areas. The dancers, quickly moving from one area to another, were at one moment well illuminated while at the next almost invisible. For this scene Spanish dancers had been engaged who, like the singers, appeared to be totally "oblivious of the audience," thus creating an atmosphere of abandon as though they were all dancing and singing solely for their own enjoyment.

"A revelation of powerful and original art," the performance was called in *La Semaine Littéraire*. The execution of Appia's revolutionary principles was a complete success. His insistence that the whole production be focused on the performer, who would be supported, not dominated, by the scenery and light, was overwhelmingly vindicated; and his hierarchy was definitely established as the guidepost for a revitalized modern theatre. The spectators were deeply impressed. Even Sarah Bernhardt, more accustomed to be flattered than to praise others, told everyone who would listen that this was "an exquisite artistic sensation" (*une exquise sensation d'art*). In his review Keyersling reports that a renowned actor who himself had staged a production of *Manfred* and had played the leading character congratulated Appia telling him he would call himself fortunate if some day he could have his advice. This must refer to Aurélien-Marie Lugné-Poë who was highly acclaimed for his fascinating characterization of the Byron hero in his production at the Théâtre de l'Oeuvre in December, 1902.

The Aftermath

UNDER the impact of his great success Appia nourished high hopes for the future. The Countess de Béarn had let him believe from the beginning that, though this production was an experiment, it could be followed by others. Appia lived under this assumption. Members of society as well as professionals of refined taste and great influence expressed their profound satisfaction with the artistic endeavor; one guest, a professional theatre manager, even indicated his willingness to engage Appia. In those years the artist, always optimistic, trusted everyone without reservation; he accepted every word literally and did not doubt that promises would be followed by deeds. He was not the first idealist to experience the fickleness of people and fate. Feelings on the morning after seldom equal the excitement experienced immediately following the moving event. In that first flush promises may have been made in all honesty, but they are soon forgotten in the routine of daily life, or they are dismissed in the face of practical considerations. Appia had good reason to expect that his consummate victory would at last bring forth the opportunity he had so longingly awaited to work in a professional theatre with better technical equipment and with greater authority so that he might be able to accomplish his reform.

Soon after the three performances, he returned to Bière, for he could not afford to keep a permanent studio in Paris. A few times he made the journey waiting anxiously for a word from Madame to start another production, or better still, for a word from the manager to open the doors of his theatre to him. He tried every way to keep in touch with any development in Paris, for conditions, as he interpreted them, promised a positive outcome in the near future. During his absence cousin Alfred Guy kept him informed. When in early summer, 1903, no clear word came from the avenue Bosquet, Appia's suspicion arose. The Countess did not answer his inquiries and recommendations or circumvented them with polite vague statements. In the fall he finally succeeded in seeing her again and learned that for several reasons no other event was scheduled for the current year. Appia, returning to Switzerland, was troubled but nevertheless did not grasp the negative gist of that conversation. His usual good spirits flagged but at the same time so did some of his tensions, for Madame had been very kind. But when, during the succeeding months, he received not a single encouraging word from Paris for a production in 1904 he suffered such anxieties that he ran a fever. No longer able to stand the strain of uncertainty he planned a trip to Italy where he hoped to get his mind off the depressing situation. He loved the Italian people and the art of the Early Renaissance, and besides, he knew that Countess Zichy was in Venice. Apparently he sought refuge in her presence. This lady proved to be his only reliable supporter in Parisian society but was unable to influence Madame de Béarn, who had a mind of her own. Late in the fall, Appia left for Italy, staying first in Florence and before Christmas moving to Venice to see Countess Zichy. Except for the satisfaction of talking to an understanding soul, the unfriendly December days brought him no consolation.

Appia no longer held hopes for a professional engagement. All his aspirations still rested in the theatre on the avenue Bosquet. Because Alfred Guy and Mariano Fortuny were continuing work on the cyclorama and the lighting system, Appia felt they could and should persuade Countess de Béarn to agree to another performance. However, his faith in Fortuny came to an abrupt end. When Appia's essay, *Comment reformer notre mise en scène,* was published in 1904, he sent him a copy. Fortuny's reaction was a series of ironical remarks about Appia's emphasis on the performer; he now favored the conventional concept of the contemporary stage. Claparède tried to mediate, but his attempts did not bring about a reconciliation. The subsequent total break was a terrible shock to Appia who was unaware of, or unwilling to recognize, the superficial character of the well-to-do, yet brilliant, young man. Leaving Appia's letters unanswered, Fortuny thwarted all efforts by his former friend to approach him. This disappointment came on the heels of another personal blow. At that time Appia was collaborating on *Ondine* with his friend Jean Thorel, a good journalist but not so great a writer as Appia believed. Thorel suddenly cut off his relations with Appia without any plausible explanation. Thorel's sister and cousin Raymond's mother probed for Appia's sake but in vain for a reliable clue to the unhappy circumstance. Appia himself mentioned, without naming Thorel, only that the break with a friend for whom he had the highest regard was "a debacle."

He finally had to face the fact that Countess de Béarn did not wish to be bothered further; she too had left his inquiries unanswered. Indirectly he learned then that Eleonora Duse was soon to perform in the Countess's theatre. His dream to stage at least part of a Wagnerian music drama in Paris had come to naught and the artist had to admit to himself that he could expect no further support in the French metropolis.

So the opportunity which, at first, had seemed to imply magnificent possibilities turned out to be a mere episode. On this pessimistic note ended an important chapter in Appia's life. Just as his passion for Wagner's music drama found no response in Bayreuth, his desire to find acceptance for his new style in Paris remained unfulfilled. The consequences were immeasurable. One can hardly imagine to what heights Appia's genius might have carried him if his successful staging in Paris had launched a career in the French theatre to which he was tied by language and heritage. And there is no telling how differently his personality might have developed. Perhaps he would have thrown off the overpowering influence of Wagner's music which had made him a captive of German culture for too long a time to the detriment of any positive interest in the cultural life of France. The saddest result of the bitter experience was enforced inactivity which caused an irretrievable setback in his development. For several years Appia continued to grope for a clearcut direction. Instead of being allowed to mature through work in a legitimate theatre, or at least in Madame de Béarn's intimate theatre, he could not get hold of himself. At times the personal and artistic tribulations were too much for him to bear, and his nervous system was definitely affected. Much of what went wrong in his life can indeed be traced to the shocks he suffered in Paris.

But his was not the only loss. Paris' failure to give that great artist a more substantial recognition by availing itself of his genius was its own loss. How much he would have enriched its theatrical life. At that time Jusseaume alone reached beyond the conventional staging; still, though an enormously gifted designer, he was not a revolutionary of Appia's scope. Fortuny did not grow to become a great artist at all; he remained a lighting expert. Lugné-Poë envisioned a new theatre; however, he was more concerned with new authors than with new staging conceptions. Firmin Gémier and Jacques Rouché were then mere hopefuls; their great achievements were yet to come. Rouché and others incidentally tried their best later to provide another opportunity for Appia to demonstrate his revolutionary ideas, but they had no luck. In Paris the first breakthrough did not occur until Diaghilev presented his stunning ballets in 1909 and the succeeding seasons. With them a new breeze blew through the Parisian theatre. Appia however was not part of the change.

Meeting Jaques-Dalcroze

During the following years Appia found no peace. Restlessly he moved from place to place, unable to remain long anywhere and incapable of concentrating on any work. A few times he returned to Paris, merely to see friends and to attend performances. Most of his time was spent in small towns of the Canton de Vaud; whenever loneliness overcame him, which was frequently, he looked for companionship. He would visit Raymond Penel, who was a general practitioner at Viry and later at Samôëns in the Haute Savoye, or meet Chamberlain; and above all he made his annual pilgrimage to Bayreuth. He seldom went to Geneva and then only for a few days to see his sister Hélène and aunt Emilie. Yet most of the time he was alone.

One evening in the spring of 1906 Appia, in his usual curiosity, went to an auditorium in Geneva to attend a lecture-demonstration arranged by Emile Jaques-Dalcroze (1865–1950). It was a revelation! Suddenly he saw the road toward a realization of his own ideas. Eleven years earlier he had somehow sensed that rhythmic movement might serve as the connecting link to create a close contact between music and performer. In the new discipline of Dalcroze, who succeeded to put an end to the existing separation of music and body, "I found the answer to my passionate desire for synthesis," he wrote in his second preface to his *La Musique et la mise en scène*.

Though Appia and Dalcroze lived near one another for many years, fate kept them apart until the time was ripe for both to meet and to collaborate. Prior to that moment they had followed their own specific vision and made basic attempts at reform in their respective fields of theatre and music education. When they finally exchanged ideas and combined their efforts these two artists achieved a sublime means of presenting the human body in dramatic action on a stage and in a building most suitable to such a performance.

Appia and Dalcroze had much in common. Their long-lasting friendship was founded on a strong bond—the aim to liberate the human body from the fetters of meaningless conventions and give it the opportunity of becoming alive and expressive of the soul. This bond was strengthened by the lack of success experienced by both men. Dalcroze and, in a greater measure, Appia had met with ridicule, ignorance, and indifference from a majority of their colleagues, the music educators and theatre experts who should have been concerned with the new conception. Indeed the two artists needed indomitable confidence to pursue acceptance for their ideas.

Dalcroze was born in Vienna of Swiss Romande stock and spent most of his life in Geneva. Like Appia he decided to study music; among his teachers were Anton Bruckner and Leo Delibes. In 1892 he joined the staff of the Conservatoire in Geneva to teach classes in theory and harmony. As a composer he was quite successful in his own country as well as abroad; his five operas were widely performed. He became best known however for his *Chansons romandes et enfantines*. As a teacher he was highly regarded; yet he himself was not fully gratified with the results of his educational efforts, for he was puzzled by the difficulties many of his pupils encountered in keeping rhythm. Since his training and experience did not provide a satisfactory answer, he tried to find another means. Around 1900 musical discipline was firmly established in a misinterpreted "classic" method and those in power were not inclined to change it. But Dalcroze was, very much so. He looked for an approach that would lead to a harmony of soul and body, the Greek ideal which he shared with Appia. But in that period of "intellectualism" little attention was paid to the body.

One of Dalcroze's first discoveries was that rhythm varies with the individual. He set out to train the hearing perception of each pupil, then found out that some youngsters whose hearing developed at a normal rate were unable to measure various time and rhythmic values precisely. Trying to have the pupils react to music with their body he invented exercises in walking and stopping; these were in his words "the origin of my Eurythmics.[4] Opposed to the traditional ballet schooling which he considered mechanical and hence unnatural, he took great care that in his exercises the body moved naturally. This system was expanded so that every rhythmical detail of a composition would be expressed through a move of the pupil's body. Later, influenced by Appia, Dalcroze also devised exercises for the body to transfer an emotional value of the music into a particular posture on stage. In a general way he aimed at a "lyrico-plastic unity," fully aware of the time and effort required to explore his theories and make them work. Early in this experimentation he also introduced the exercises which enabled the pupil to move each arm at a different rhythm or tempo.[5]

As his superiors disapproved of "dancing" in music lessons, Dalcroze rented a small hall where every free hour he practiced with volunteers. Confronted with a host of worrisome problems he sought the counsel of experts and thus he obtained great help from Prof. Matthis Lussy, a physiologist, who, upon Dalcroze's request, probed into the question of musical movement in time as related to the corresponding body movement in space. Prof. Edouard Claparède, a psychologist, distantly related to Alfred Guy, then formulated the scientific basis for the new conception which Dalcroze described thus: "Fundamental to all individual training is the discipline of emotion and the practice in reaction. This I try to achieve through my eurythmics."[6] In other words Dalcroze thought of himself as the intermediary to the students and the music they were expected to express. The lectures and demonstrations he regularly gave in Geneva attracted much attention. By 1903 he was invited to present a series of his extremely charming *Kinderreigenspiele* at the annual meeting of the *Allgemeine Deutsche Musikverein* in Basel. After this event several German cities invited him to come as lecturer and guest teacher, while in his home town the conservative circles prevailed in opposing his innovations. Many of his colleagues, particularly the dean of the music school, rejected any dealings with a musician who was foolish, perhaps immoral, enough to let children jump around barefoot, in leotards and tunics.[7]

At last, in 1906, the musician-turned-educator met the musician who became a reformer of the theatre. Although Appia's ideas had crystallized, they still lacked definition. The Dalcroze demonstrations in the auditorium Odier du Casino de Saint-Pierre impressed him so deeply that he sent a letter to Dalcroze, and soon the two met, discussed their mutual aims at length. In his enthusiasm Appia wrote an article for the *Journal de Genève* about his impressions of and reactions to Dalcroze's ideas in order to introduce—or, better, to publicize—an advanced course for teachers planned by Dalcroze. Appia emphasized the importance of the new conception to "make music vibrate" in the body and to render it "an integral part of the organism."

Dalcroze took his new friend to his classes. Since the students knew of Appia's work, his visits were anticipated with great interest. A former student gives us an example of how Dalcroze proceeded; she relates that after a brief introduction he asked the pupils to execute a stylized movement to an improvised Greek mode. The young ladies pretended to fill a well with water, but the well would continue to empty itself. The short scene was beautifully devised and executed. Although only a few measures of music were used and were repeated over and over again, the effect was forceful and the inspiration perfect. Appia returned frequently to the school and became so closely associated with Dalcroze that by 1909 the names of the two men were always mentioned together.

A pair less similar could hardly be imagined. Appia, fairly tall, had bright shining eyes, a sharp Roman profile, and a beard that made him look like a prophet; his dress was unconventional, consisting of a sweater, knickerbockers, and sandals. Gentle and reticent he was particularly shy in the presence of strangers. Dalcroze, by contrast, was below average height. His friendly round face had a goatee; his small nearsighted eyes twinkled behind glasses. He was jovial, outgoing, but shrewd. While Appia shrunk from addressing a group of people because of his stutter, Dalcroze was completely at ease as a speaker even at the largest meeting; as a matter of fact, lecturing was one of his salient talents.

Until 1909 the collaboration did not bring about any noticeable change in the ideas of either artist. In that year Appia, after attending another demonstration, returned home dissatisfied with the scenic arrangement and immediately began to devise an entirely new plan which would provide an ideal setup for the rhythmic exercises. Within a few days he had finished about twenty sketches, "Espaces rythmiques" (*Rhythmic Spaces*), as they were called in his next book. These settings were based on platforms of various levels, ramps, stairs, simple walls, and pillars. The monotonus flat stage floor disappeared giving way to a spatial arrangement through abundant use of those manifold levels. Appia sent Dalcroze the new sketches accompanied by a letter in which he told his friend that heretofore "the pupils moving invariably on a flat surface gave the impression of alpinists ascending a mountain on a bas relief spread on the floor." Dalcroze accepted the new ideas with great enthusiasm. The Rhythmic Spaces were never transferred onto a stage—it would have been impossible to execute them under the limited conditions of the Dalcroze Institute—but the resulting experiments helped Dalcroze in his teaching and Appia in finding a different style for his designs. The "corporeal space" as he termed his previous designs became now the "living space" for the moving actor. Thus he gradually freed himself from the last traces of tradition.

Musical rhythm and body rhythm remained the core of Dalcroze's teaching;

Figure 17. One of the Rhythmic Spaces. *Theater Museum, Munich.*

Figure 18. Shadow of the cypress, another example from the Rhythmic Spaces. *Theater Museum, Munich.*

incidentally, neither man liked to speak of a "method." Dalcroze never overlooked the purely technical ear training, but emphasis was put on making the student feel the music through listening. Under the influence of Appia, Dalcroze next extended his experiments to working with entire groups rather than individuals. Harmony of body and spirit was to be achieved through a coordination of "physical movement and sound movement, musical and spatial elements."[8] First the nerves and muscles were taught to react to music; the final goal, harmony of body and spirit, was to be reached by concentrating on ear training and listening, eurythmics, improvisation, and musical plasticity.[9]

The basic ideas of Dalcroze and Appia derived from classic and neo-classic esthetics. The relationship of rhythm and body movement had been investigated by the Greeks, and Dalcroze followed their principles. Goethe and Schiller gave music an important place in life and their writings were as familar to both men as was Richard Wagner's synthesis of all the arts, the union of speech, gesture, and music. Traces of François Delsarte's method, too, can be discovered in some of Dalcroze's movements and postures. But the application of all the ideas originated with Appia and Dalcroze and was a tremendous step toward creating a new style in the performing arts. When their conception was applied to an entire production, every rhythmic detail of a composition found its equivalent in a body movement of the performer, every emotion was expressed through a characteristic posture or move on stage. In the end the Dalcroze students were capable of transferring every musical nuance into dramatic action. A perfect synchronization of musical and acting elements had thus been accomplished.[10]

In his ceaseless campaigning to promote eurythmics Dalcroze relied more and more on Appia. He needed his advice and support against outsiders who urged him to try different techniques and external effects—promptings that Dalcroze feared might pull him in a wrong direction. Again and again he insisted that he was not after a new art, but merely "a road to art." All his exercises were therefore planned with one goal in mind, to help his pupils transform music into simple gestures and movements without artificial effects. In his struggle against critics who were incapable of envisioning that goal, Appia's unshakable confidence in the eventual triumph of his work gave Dalcroze strong support.

Hellerau

DALCROZE, in deciding what step to take next in establishing his ideas increasingly depended upon the congenial Appia, whom nobody could dissuade from pursuing an ideal. In the spring of 1910, Dalcroze had received an enticing offer from the brothers Wolf and Harald Dohrn, manufacturers of modern furniture and real estate developers, to come to Hellerau, their newly created suburb of Dresden, as director of an institute to be built specifically for him and his work. The negotiations were successfully concluded and in the fall of that year Dalcroze and his family departed from Geneva followed by about two scores of his students. Appia's name was on the list of the faculty and also on that of the committee which held the annual examination at the *Bildungsanstalt Jaques-Dalcroze*. Appia however remained at the old château de Glérolles (see chapter IV) near Vevey and went to Hellerau only to participate in the initial plans, the annual demonstrations and examinations, and in the two festivals. The exchange of views ensued mostly by means of letters. Generally speaking, Appia served as a consultant rather than as a regular faculty member.

Hellerau offered the two Swiss artists splendid opportunities. Dalcroze obtained an almost free hand in devising the large auditorium with the adjacent classroom building and the dormitory. Evidently all important questions were first discussed with Appia who saw some of his own dreams come true on a grand scale. There is no doubt that the basic plan of the auditorium was his. He had once described how during a staged demonstration in Geneva he had suddenly decided the conventional theatre curtain was a "ridiculous and barbarous" phenomenon. Consequently he had dreamed up a hall in which the acting area and the audience were no longer separated. And there was no separation of stage and house in the Hellerau Festival Auditorium. The entire hall, measuring 49 meters in length, 16 in width and 12 in height, embraced both spectators and performers; only a sunken orchestra pit recalled the standard opera house. The rows of approximately 600 seats, steeply raked, rose from the floor level amphitheatrically. Only one of Appia's suggestions remained unfulfilled in this building; namely, to make the rear wall of the stage removable, thus granting the audience the view of the landscape behind the auditorium. For financial reasons this detail had to be dropped.[11] Nevertheless Appia was highly pleased with the modern building whose architect, Heinrich Tessenow, executed all plans as originally recommended and accepted, notwithstanding many objections by artists and other influential persons.[12]

In Alexander von Salzmann, a Russian artist, Appia found a kindred spirit to collaborate in planning the stage and its lighting equipment. Together they adapted the system on which Appia had worked with Fortuny in Paris. The combination of soft general illumination and special spotlight effects was modified by Salzmann for Hellerau. Walls and ceiling of the large hall were covered with a transparent fabric (light canvas); behind it about 3,000 lamps were installed, and their indirect light was enormously impressive. This luminous space left no sharp break between the semidark house and the brighter light effects on the stage. Salzmann believed such an arrangement "indispensable whenever the relative value of color, form, motion—all inspired by music—are at stake. . . . Light is dominated by music which gives movement a soul. Light explains movement."[13] These sentences, of course, could have been written by Appia. Here at last he had met another artist who shared his conception of a predominant role for light.

In summer, 1912, everything was ready for the first festival. On July 4, 5, and 6, performances were given of *Echo and Narcissus,* based on a poetic story by Jacques Chenevière with music by Dalcroze; this dance drama, which was well received, was followed by the scene in Hades from Gluck's *Orpheus and Euridice.* Guests from many countries witnessed the production and regarded it as a revolutionary step in the development of theatre arts. An even more international crowd assembled during the last week of June the following summer when 200 participants performed the entire Gluck opera three times. The garden city of Hellerau turned into a famous cultural center with an atmosphere all its own.

Appia designed the settings and, with Salzmann, was in charge of the staging. Salzmann devised the light plot, and Harald Dohrn, an engineer, handled the light console with its forty-six curcuits. Two opposing groups had argued about the general production style. Appia and Salzmann rejected any adherence to tradition, demanding instead complete stylization of settings, lighting, and costumes. They were opposed by those who favored illusion on the stage or, at least, more illusion than the two were willing to grant. The opposition included Wolf Dohrn, and probably even Dalcroze himself, who was trying to find a compromise; in the end pure imagination remained victorious.[14]

For *Echo und Narcissus* a shadow effect was used as dancers appeared in silhouette behind a scrim. Otherwise, with its platforms and stairs, the decor was extremely simple. Two of the *Orpheus* settings were similarly stylized whereas the arrangement for the scene in Hades was more elaborate, more monumental. A tremendous staircase in the rear dominated the entire acting area. No photograph, sketch, or description can regain the visual effect of the total arrangement in which lighting powerfully created every mood. Obviously everything was done to focus attention on the soloists and on the dancing and singing choruses. As early as the end of the 1912 festival Appia had every reason to state proudly: "for the first time since the Greek era, a perfect fusion of all media of expression, in close mutual subordination, has been realized. . . ."

The musical conception and execution for which Dalcroze was responsible were somewhat less applauded than the staging in spite of Emmi Leisner, the magnificent leading alto of the Berlin Court Opera, who created the role of Orpheus. She immersed herself in the delicate task of adjusting to the new style by taking a course in eurythmics for several months prior to the rehearsals. Her performance was "in perfect harmony" with the ideas of Appia and Dalcroze.[15] G. B. Shaw, a critic always hard to please, called the production "one of the best" of *Orpheus* and praised Emmi Leisner very highly with the one qualification that the aria *Che faro* was taken too slowly. In his opinion the performance needed a few more rehearsals with Harley Granville-Baker and himself "to be perfect."[16] Other experts found several details open to criticism but they generously overlooked the fact that the

Figure 19. *Orpheus and Euridice,* the Hades setting of the Hellerau production. *Editions de la Baconnière, Neuchâtel.*

choristers, who, after all, were not professionals, did not keep in strict accord with the conductor as they moved about. The elimination of the overture, however, was openly disapproved and so was the changed ending of the opera. In the last act the two leading singers moved toward the audience while a traveler masked the up-stage area, an idea certainly initiated by Appia who later used a similar solution in his *Ring* production for Basel in 1924. When Euridice died she sank into the folds of the drapes which then hid her. After Orpheus' famous aria Dalcroze repeated the lamentation from Act I with the chorus placed in the orchestra pit; thus the revival of Euridice was deleted and the basic tragic mood of the opera was maintained.

The treatment of Amor was considered good. His piece in the last act was cut because of the new ending. In Act I the god of love did not appear on stage; his presence was indicated by a light beam while his voice came from backstage.[17] The settings, even the one in Hades, were extremely simple consisting of platforms, stairs, and curtains. The latter were predominantly blue while the set pieces were kept neutral. In the first act drapes formed a kind of corridor which Orpheus used for his exit at the end. A high platform and stairs placed against a greenish white background made up the third setting—an arrangement which was not thoroughly acceptable as it was too functional, not monumental enough. The staging of the scene in the Underworld became the climax of the performance and invoked jubilant enthusiasm. Early in the century the opening music of this scene was usually played with the main curtain closed. Now Appia and Dalcroze made full use of its dramatic impact through the dance of the Furies. The towering staircase upstage was, figuratively speaking, leading from Earth to Hades. The spatial setting gave Dalcroze and his dancers marvelous opportunities for groupings and evolutions, choreographed by Annie Beck. Particularly fascinating were the dancers pushing up against Orpheus when he descended the steps and then upon his soothing song, recoiling to the lower level. And the sharp contrast of the bright light beam striking the hero against the chiaroscuro and the darkness in other areas was duly recognized as an important innovation.[18]

A few persons caviled; mockingly, the small square platform pieces were called "building blocks for children"; more serious was the criticism of Appia's stage, divided in dark and bright areas, as "too monotonous" or as unfaithful to the score's deep tragedy. Dalcroze's conducting met some reservations because of slow tempo and off-key singing.[19] However the wide majority of critics regarded *Orpheus* as the most striking experience in the modern theatre. A Frenchman pertinently remarked that what he had witnessed in Hellerau was as different from the conventional theatre "as truth from falsehood."[20] In general the highlights seemed to have been the funeral procession in Act I; the demonic movement of the damned souls, and the ethereal gliding and floating of the blessed spirits in Act II; one reviewer was immensely impressed by the utter harmony between the music and the magic lighting. The writer for the important *Berliner Zeitung am Mittag* called the production "a renaissance" of Gluck.[21] Not all the participants were considered capable of adopting, or, rather, ready to execute the revolutionary conception though the underlying theories were fully approved.[22] Appia and Dalcroze virtually attained their aim of making everyone a participant. Karl Storck, an admirer of Dalcroze's achievements for years, expressed this sense of sharing when he confessed how much he was captivated by "the compelling power of space, the soulful power of light, and the beauty of the human body." He foresaw in this "space-creating" production a possible "salvation for Bayreuth."[23]

The listing of those who attended these festivals reads almost like a Who's Who af the arts. There were Paul Claudel, Georges Pitoëff, and Jacques Rouché from France; Alfred Roller from Austria; G. B. Shaw and Harley Granville-Barker from Great Britain; Upton Sinclair from the United States; Serge Diaghilev and Serge Wolkonsky, the General Director of the Imperial Theatres in St. Petersburg, from Russia; and, of course, most of the well-known critics. German opera houses were well represented by, among others, Ernst von Schuch (Dresden) and Max von Schillings (Stuttgart). Max Reinhardt, the great stage director, came from Berlin to see one of the performances. One name, strangely, can not be discovered—that of Houston Stewart Chamberlain. Fully informed about Appia's collaboration with Dalcroze, with whom he had corresponded in the nineties, he evidently preferred for reasons of his own not to go to Hellerau.

Dalcroze was a perfect host; he had a remarkable talent for keeping all of these celebrities interested in his projects and his work. But where was Appia whose ideas were the artistic backbone of the *Orpheus* production? No eyewitness recorded that Appia actually conversed with any of the famous guests and patrons, although photographs show him with some of them. Presumably he was too withdrawn to join in the conversation with strangers, for it should be taken for granted that Dalcroze made every effort to introduce his collaborators, especially his close friend Appia, to some of the influential personages. In any event there is no way of knowing whether Schuch or Schillings, who exercised decisive power in their opera houses, were so deeply moved by what they saw in Hellerau that they considered an invitation for Appia, Dalcroze, or perhaps both artists. Nor is there any proof that Reinhardt was interested in having Appia design the settings for one of his productions. However, since Reinhardt had had contact with Gordon Craig a few years earlier and was always keen to experiment with new designers, we may assume that he seriously weighed such a possibility. There is more than a general hint that in Zurich serious consideration was given to invite Appia to take charge of a new *mise en scène* of *Tristan and Isolde*. Also Jacques Rouché evidently hoped to succeed in bringing Appia to Paris to supervise the staging of one of Gluck's operas. Perhaps other opera houses too would have engaged Appia and Dalcroze if it had not been the year 1913. A year later the outbreak of the first World War destroyed many a dream.

Some months after the festival performances another event attracted visitors to Hellerau: the German première of Paul Claudel's *L'Annonce faite à Marie* (*Tidings Brought to Mary*). This play was planned to be presented a few days after *Orpheus*, but the opening night had to be postponed "because of a new staging idea," according to a newspaper report.[24] This venture was the idea of Wolf Dohrn and Alexander von Salzmann who managed the production without Appia and Dalcroze, both of whom were in Switzerland at the time of the three performances on October 6, 11, and 19. The author himself supervised the last rehearsals. The settings were designed by Salzmann whose scenic solution evoked a medieval mystery stage with its different levels serving as acting areas. In spite of an outstanding cast—Alexander Moissi from the Deutsche Theater in Berlin playing Jakobaeus—the reception by the press was not unanimously favorable. The critic of the *Dresdener Anzeiger*, for instance, had no praise for the play and condemned "the unbearable theatricality" of the production.[25] Salzmann received full credit for having "achieved great things with plasticity that made the scenes in form, movement, and color often reminiscent of old paintings of the saints."[26] The description of the setting indicates a reliance on Appia, who had been impressed by similar staging in Devrient's *Faust*, and the general plan of the spatial arrangement suggests that the designer participated at least in the preparation.

La Fête de Juin

THAT same fall and the following winter Jaques-Dalcroze spent several weeks in Geneva in answer to an invitation to prepare a pageant for the city. A multitude of volunteers, about fifteen hundred of them, underwent thorough training in eurythmics to enable them to execute the countless movements in the forthcoming demanding production. Appia was not officially connected with the festival but again served his friend as adviser on many details. Hence it is of some interest to cull from the finished production and from eyewitness reports the items which were based on Appia's ideas or, in general, were the result of his long discussions with Dalcroze.

The pageant, *La Fête de Juin*, was conceived to celebrate the centenary of the Republic of Geneva's joining the Swiss Confederation, and the performances were scheduled for July, 1914. It was not a new kind of festival for Switzerland, a country with a long tradition of events which combined purposes of health and acrobatic discipline with the often beautiful synchronization of music and movements for "an emotional as well as an esthetic effect."[27] Dalcroze had written music for several pageants. They were often performed by large groups of amateur singers, dancers, and acrobats on simple stages which formed a unit with the audi-

Figure 20. *La Fête de Juin*, a dramatic arrangement. *Blanche Bingham.*

torium and were sometimes so built into the natural surroundings that the latter took part in the action. His collaborator was Firmin Gémier, the famed Parisian stage director, who supervised the entire production. He too was thoroughly acquainted with this work as he had cooperated with Dalcroze in the staging of a large festival in Lausanne in 1903 and of the *Fête de Vignerons* in Vevey the following year.[28] Since Gémier had a high regard for Appia's art, the rehearsals in Geneva must have proceeded harmoniously in Appia's spirit. Appia had attended the Vevey festivals and had written in his essay *Style et solidarité* that they "have taught us that art must spring forth from the heart of all of us and must be represented by all of us."

La Fête de Juin, a patriotic spectacle in four acts, was written by Daniel Baud-Bovy and Albert Malche with music by Dalcroze, who was also in charge of all dances and rhythmic movements. An ideal location was selected on the north shore of the lake. A city official submitted the plan to erect a special hall and this time Appia's dream was fully realized: the rear wall of the stage could be opened giving the thousands of spectators a breathtaking view across the lake toward distant snow-capped mountains, topped by Mont Blanc. The 50-meter-wide stage was subdivided into several acting areas on different levels. From the curtainless platform which served as the main acting area, stairs led down to the orchestra and the audience. The only discrepancy in the otherwise splendidly devised setting was a row of Greek columns encircling the stage; they had little relation to the over-all atmosphere of the pageant.[29] The entire event, the auditorium, the drama, and its presentation, aroused immense enthusiasm not only in the local population but among foreign visitors as well. Only a few scenes were criticized because their operatic character spoiled the guilelessness of a folk play. One of the most impressive moments was the opening of the rear wall when barges could be seen moving across the lake toward the hall; from these boats soldiers landed below the higher platform to join the action. Another thrilling moment occurred during one of the large-scale rhythmic evolutions when men raced across the platforms, down the steps, and through the audience, waving flags of all the Swiss cantons.[30] A folk festival of this kind in which the audience and the performance become one was the realization of Appia's ideals. In describing this "great national and patriotic" event in his book *L'Oeuvre d'art vivant* (*The Work of Living Art*) he concludes that it "presented an imposing and unprecedented example of this esthetic phenomenon. It realized the simultaneity of the two principles. The spectator had simultaneously before his eyes first animated historic themes . . . and second, their purely human Expression. . . . " The execution of this two-pronged affair was for him "a revelation . . . masterfully handled by the author [Dalcroze] and his collaborators."

A few weeks after the last performance of *La Fête de Juin* war broke out. Dalcroze canceled all work in Hellerau and settled in Geneva for the duration, unaware that this was an end, not an interlude. Events had developed so rapidly

Figure 21. *La Fête de Juin,* one of the high points of the pageant. *Blanche Bingham.*

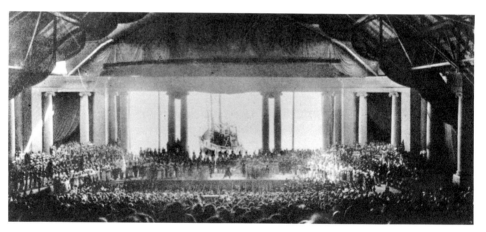

Figure 22. *La Fête de Juin,* general view of the setting. *La Patrie Suisse.*

that he left his Hellerau Institute without even taking his last salary. When in fall of 1914 German armies bombarded the Cathedral of Reims and burned the Library of Louvain, he signed an international protest by artists and scholars against these military misdeeds, a step which did not endear him to the nationalist circles in Germany. The relationship of Dalcroze and Hellerau changed and it looked as though Hellerau might proceed without its founder. At that time Percy Ingham offered to transplant the school and its director to England; the proposition was considered by all concerned but did not materialize.

Friends, particularly Professor Claparède and the poet Jacques Chenevière, succeeded in organizing a new school of eurythmics in Geneva, and so Dalcroze was in a position to go on with his work, if at first on a much smaller scale. Appia, who was still at Glérolles, remained in touch with his friend. Though there was no intention to prepare a major production, demonstrations by the students were presented every year. Perhaps plans existed for a full production in the postwar period, but we know merely of a revival of *Echo and Narcissus* in 1920 and similar brief dance dramas on the small stage of the new Jaques-Dalcroze Institute. In spring, 1923, Dalcroze was very active in the June production of *Fête de la Jeunesse et de la Joi*, yet less is known about Appia's part in it than about his work for *Fête de Juin* nine years earlier. Future grand projects evaporated when Dalcroze left Geneva in 1924 to look for better opportunities in the cosmopolitan atmosphere of Paris, where he had spent much time since 1917. He remained in the French capital for two years and when he returned to Switzerland in 1926, Appia was living in a sanatorium, a retreat he rarely left.

Deeds, observations by common friends, and letters from Dalcroze to Appia (unfortunately almost all written by Appia were destroyed) attest to their mutual admiration. Having had Appia put on his staff in Hellerau, Dalcroze had provided some financial aid for him, and to be sure, the unique opportunity of making the work of his friend known. But in his writings Dalcroze hardly referred directly to his collaboration with Appia; once, acknowledging many sources and influences, he stated that "the ideas of Adolphe Appia about the *mise en scène* have been of great help to me in my rhythmic and plastic experiences."[31] He also remembered his friend in the dedication of his *Le Rythme, la musique et l'education* and in a chapter in his *Exercises de plastique animée*. Still, we miss a frank recognition of his debt to the genius who self-effacingly served as the artistic spirit behind eurythmics.

As may be expected, there were disagreements and conflicts between the two friends, all the more so as Dalcroze was not always acceptable to criticism. Yet such conflicts could have been settled probably without further ado if Dalcroze's sister, Madame Brunet-Lecomte, and possibly his wife had not aggravated them through their interference. In their zeal to enhance the fame of their brother and husband the two ladies, above all, Madame Brunet-Lecomte, kept a jealous watch over his reputation.

Appia, by contrast, was more magnanimous, using every opportunity to delineate and propagate Dalcroze's ideas and art. During the Hellerau era he wrote four essays in which he explained in detail these ideas and their potentialities for the theatre arts. While Dalcroze described his findings as teacher and musician, Appia approached his theme from the importance of those ideas for dramatic art in general and their application to its divers phases in particular. His article on *L'Origine et les débuts de la gymnastique rythmique (The Origin and Beginnings of Eurythmics)* is the most reliable and perceptive discussion of this topic. In addition to biographical and historical data this essay is interesting because of Appia's selfless appreciation of and devotion to his friend whom he called a "pedagogical genius" and a "genius for synthesis," which he defined as "the compelling urge to combine all the means of expression of an integral artistic life." Appia also extols Dalcroze's extraordinary "gift of life" and his role as "an unequaled inspirer" who was always willing to listen to suggestions from a student. His description, though a bit exaggerated in its eulogy, provides a lucid image of Dalcroze the teacher.

The articles on eurythmics are as indicative of Dalcroze as they are of Appia himself; he always looked at his friend's work from his own point of view. This is especially true in *La gymnastique rythmique et le théâtre (Eurythmics and the Theatre)* and in *La gymnastique rythmique et la lumière (Eurythmics and Light)*, to a lesser degree in *Du costume pour la gymnastique rythmique (Eurythmics and Costumes)*. In the first of this series he repeated his criticism of the conventional theatre which failed to fuse house and stage into one unit to integrate spectator and performer. He hoped that Dalcroze's use of space would result in a better understanding of the basic requirements for a reform but at the same time, he warned against applying eurythmics directly to the conventional staging. He foresaw the time when spectators would actively participate in a performance instead of merely watching it, and he was convinced that the Dalcroze method was the most decisive step in this direction. Implementing his own ideas he included both the singer and the actor as being able to benefit from learning how to relate their bodies to the space surrounding them. In discussing the relationship of eurythmics and light Appia referred of course to the relation of light to music, and in addition he suggested the development of hearing as well as sight, "the two noblest senses." Light was for him "the esthetic ruler of clarity" and he predicted that as soon as lighting can really be mastered on the stage it will become "luminous sound." The last article is noteworthy for giving us interesting data concerning the uniform of the students. Appia explained how and why Dalcroze proceeded in six steps from street dresses to the final one-piece tights with a light tunic. Each change is described: how items such as shoes were discarded and sandals substituted; how a short skirt was introduced and a blouse leaving neck and arms uncovered; then the skirt and blouse were replaced by a kind of knickerbockers and pullover; later the stockings were removed; before the last step (the one-piece tights) was taken, the sandals were eliminated and the exercises done with bare feet. Here Appia may have served as adviser for he had seen Isadora Duncan dancing barefooted years before he met Dalcroze. In explaining how Dalcroze arrived at his final choice Appia emphasized the importance for the human body to feel free in exploring space, and for the costumes to be simple in order to allow the study of light effects.

Besides these articles Appia wrote notes for some programs of the Dalcroze school in Geneva and for a book on the Hellerau Institute. He devoted, moreover, much space to his friend in his treatise entitled *Expériences de théâtre et recherches personnelles*. Praise for Dalcroze is abundant also in the early essay, *Style et solidarité* and in another written in the twenties *Le Geste de l'art (The Gesture of Art)*, in which he called eurythmics "an art of devotion." The finest document honoring his collaborator is the dedication of *L'Oeuvre d'art vivant* to Dalcroze, "the faithful friend to whom I owe my esthetic homeland." Many passages in this volume, in which he directly and indirectly referred to Dalcroze's ideas, bear witness to his unqualified gratitude.

In their collaboration the two artists supplemented each other ideally. Appia, the great visionary and theorist, provided most of the decisive ideas and, above all, prompted his friend to think in terms of the production as a whole, a union of performer, spatial arrangement, light, and music, rather than of the training of each individual pupil. Since Appia's predilection for the grand design was coupled with a dislike for details, whether technical or organizational, he left the execution of his ideas to Dalcroze who, in turn, benefited from Appia's genius and steadfast drive toward an ideal. Dalcroze, the practical man, clever in persuading people to accept and support the new conception, was in turn of great help to Appia; not the least of it was that through eurythmics, Appia discovered the means he had sought for so long to make his vision of living art come true. The unique collaboration culminated in the revolutionary production of *Orpheus* in which many of their dreams were realized. Appia rightly predicted that Dalcroze's new approach would prevail in the future. It took firm root during the musician's life and he could thus enjoy the fruits of his splendid work. In the twenties when modern dance ascended to its definite victory, Dalcroze, together with Isadora Duncan, was frequently mentioned as one of the initiators of modern dance. As had so often happened to Appia, his great contributions to the success of this new art form remained unknown to his contemporaries apart from a comparatively small circle of experts.

Figure 23. Château de Glérolles, seen from a hill with a view across Lake Geneva and the Alps in the background. *Editions du Griffin, Neuchâtel.*

IV

Appia and Copeau

On October 22, 1913, Le Théâtre du Vieux Colombier in Paris was inaugurated in a special event with speeches, and on the following day opened with *Une Femme tuée par la douceur* (*A Woman Killed by Kindness*) by Thomas Heywood, and *L'Amour médecin* by Molière, two plays which the new management and stage director presented in an utterly unconventional form. There was no setting in the accepted sense; on an almost empty stage the audience saw merely a few platforms, stairs, and screens. Lighting too was against all tradition since no footlights were used. Attention was entirely focused on the splendidly costumed actors and their interpretation of the two comedies. Jacques Copeau (1879–1949), highly regarded as an interesting author and a brilliant critic, was the director of this venture which he had initiated with his friends and colleagues of the periodical *Nouvelle Revue Française*, among them, Gaston Gallimard, André Gide, and Jean Schlumberger.

Their aim was to fight the commercialism of the Parisian Boulevard theatres which had strangled every modern artistic development. Outlining their program in the *Nouvelle Revue Française,* Copeau emphasized that he hoped to regain "the soul of the theatre."[1] He prepared the opening production with a clear view of that goal. Before he made a final decision concerning his reform he probed into the work and esthetics of Harley Granville-Barker, Gordon Craig, Adolphe Appia, Constantin Stanislavsky, and others. His observations in Paris had made him reject the star system and superrealistic staging. He wished to center interest on the performer and hence to use a minimum of scenic effects. A rundown theatre, which had been used as a kind of music hall or for vaudeville, was acquired and François Jourdain was put in charge of remodeling the auditorium and the stage, while Copeau and his actors retired to Limon, about an hour's train ride from Paris, where he conducted the rehearsals.

The first season of the Vieux Colombier ended in a draw. Attendance was not good enough to create a solid financial foundation. Artistically Copeau was fully accepted by a rather small group of intellectuals, but most of the critics, considering his style "puritanism," remained cool. His adaptation of *The Brothers Karamazov* secured a kind of artistic success, and his production of *Twelfth Night* was widely acclaimed. Moreover, a brief appearance of the company in London caused much favorable comment. With this meager background he planned the second season which, because of the outbreak of World War I, never materialized.

Copeau used the following months to examine and re-examine his artistic aims and he decided to discuss them with Craig and Appia in order to clarify everything for his own sake and simultaneously to see for himself what these two great artists, to whom he somehow felt akin, could teach him. At that time, he considered Craig the "only theoretician of value," but after his visit with him in Florence in September, 1915, he came to the conclusion that Craig's principles remained "incomplete" because they had no "solid foundation." Yet less the artist than the man must have disappointed Copeau, who missed a sense of magnanimity in him.[2] Consequently, although he continued to admire the great British designer, the stage was set for Copeau's decisive meeting with Appia.

After about three weeks of discussing all pertinent theatre problems with Craig, Copeau moved directly to Geneva in the middle of October for he was extremely anxious to meet Appia and Dalcroze. A talk with the latter was essential, as Copeau wanted to learn everything about the thorough training of the actor's body. Dalcroze explained his approach and took his guest to some classes to demonstrate his eurythmics. On October 28, Copeau and Dalcroze went by train to Rivaz and then walked to the château de Glérolles to have a long visit with Appia. The first meeting must have been very stimulating indeed, for Copeau returned the following June to discuss problems of mutual interest with Appia.[3]

At the first meeting Copeau, of course, had the opportunity to delineate his plans. His basic conception approached Appia's in its striving for utter simplification. He had no definite style in mind; however, he was resolved that no realistic element must intrude into his productions and that the setting must be architectural. The "hermit of Glérolles," as he called Appia, deeply impressed him—the magnificent features—the large, sparkling eyes; the sensual lips from which words and sentences came sometimes hesitatingly, sometimes growlingly, sometimes explosively. He was immediately aware of Appia's extreme sensitiveness. In contrast to many others who met Appia, Copeau never considered him a dreamer or mystic, but rather an exceptional artist who saw the theatre's problem far more clearly than anybody he had met. What intrigued the Frenchman most was Appia's firm stand against any compromise with the "banality" of the current conditions.[4]

Appia and Copeau were drawn to one another from the moment they exchanged their first sentences, which is not surprising. Appia found in Copeau a stage director who had the same concept of the theatre as an art form, and Copeau met in Appia the artist who could explain to him what he had been groping for. They were on common ground in their love for Molière and Shakespeare. Copeau did not share Appia's predilection for opera, in particular for Wagner's music dramas, but he understood his principles regarding musical values in their relationship to dramatic action and dialogue. Copeau needed no persuasion to accept Appia's hierarchy. He had, of course, already given predominance to the performer on his stage, using a spatial setting, assigning a major role to lighting and a minor one to painting. The two men found a binding force born out of profound understanding in their idealism, their enthusiasm, and the earnestness with which they went to work. Though Appia would be vehement in defending his ideas, he was not stubborn when it came to executing them. His main concern was to reach agreement on fundamentals; he did not insist on having his designs merely copied or his statements taken literally. The principle most important to him was that the artist who intended to accept his style must have "an inner attitude toward the work he is creating or performing."[5]

On this basis it was not difficult to discuss, in a friendly manner, all questions related to the Vieux Colombier. Copeau continued to materialize Appia's main theories, including the actor's training in eurythmics, which he later introduced in his drama school. He became a great admirer and strong follower of Appia to whom he remained devoted throughout his life. Early in their relationship, in gratitude, he called himself a "disciple" of Appia, whom he respectfully addressed as *"maître"* or *"cher seigneur."*

The new friends were not to meet a third time for several years, but letters were often exchanged. Appia never again traveled to Paris and missed the opportunity to attend a postwar performance at the Vieux Colombier. But in the mid-1920's, Copeau began a tour of Switzerland with his new company and was thus able to see Appia. Copeau seized every occasion to talk about Appia and his art, and it is likely that, due to the prestige he subsequently gained on the international scene, Copeau contributed more than anyone else to the growing fame of his friend. Admittedly he had little, if any, success in this respect with his colleagues in Paris, but in New York a young generation was to listen to him.

When Copeau made his decision to put all emphasis on the actor, he naturally considered rehearsals, as heretofore conducted, inadequate; above all he needed his actors better prepared for the important new role assigned to them, and he opened a school to train them. The body of the actor had to be made supple, his nerves sensitive to any and every task. He charged Suzanne Bing, an outstanding member of his company, with the preparatory work for this project which in 1915 had been inaugurated in a separate building.[6] The body exercises were largely based on Dalcroze's eurythmics, yet Stanislavsky's influence was also noticeable in the training of dramatic expression. In his school as well as in the rehearsals

Copeau practiced his principles, handling his actors and actresses with immense patience and discretion.

Upon the request of the French Government, Copeau spent part of the winter and spring of 1917 in New York lecturing on problems of the modern stage in general and the scenic reform in particular.[7] Copeau left an unusually strong impression on all who met him. As an immediate consequence, Otto Kahn, the noted Maecenas, invited him to bring his company to New York. While Copeau rehearsed in Paris for the guest appearance, Louis Jouvet supervised the remodeling of the Garrick Theatre near Herald Square, to be known as the Vieux Colombier of New York during the company's occupancy. Even the auditorium was reshaped to fit the forthcoming productions. The boxes, left and right close to the stage, were eliminated and new ones were built in the rear of the auditorium. The scenic frame was extremely simple; with a wide apron jutting out from the stage and doors on both sides, it was reminiscent of a Renaissance stage. The acting area, of course, showed no realistic settings. For the opening production, which included Molière's *Les Fourberies de Scapin* and Copeau's *L'Impromptu du Vieux Colombier* as curtain raiser, a large platform, with stairs leading from every direction to the highest level, dominated the stage proper. A bench needed for the action consisted simply of three cubes. Screens and drapes confined the acting area. Upstage, a balcony occasionally became part of the settings; when not in use it was masked by a curtain. There was no distinct color except in the orange curtain in the rear; everything else was neutral.[8]

Among those who eagerly expected the guests in November, 1917, were the young leaders and members of divers artistic enterprises in New York, Boston, and Chicago. Lawrence Langner, Robert E. Jones, and Lee Simonson were in the forefront of those who welcomed the scenic reform. Some writers joined them in praising the new spirit of the French company, but the typical Broadway critics, accustomed to the Belasco program, were by no means enthusiastic. In fact they attacked the unconventional settings and evidently did not care for the plays, which were mostly French classics, by Molière in particular. Since the financial returns of the first season were disappointing mainly because of language difficulties—perhaps also because of too highly priced tickets—Copeau changed his repertoire for the second season; he included some of the well-written French plays which were better known in New York, such as Henry Bernstein's *Le Secret*, but he declined to compromise with the style of his staging. A sound decision, for the more popular program had the desired effect of attracting more patrons.

Belasco's and his followers' hold on the New York theatre was too firm to be broken at once; however, the impact of Copeau's appearance should not be underrated. The directors of the Theatre Guild, which was initiated in 1919, were so impressed that in 1927 they invited him to stage for them his version of *The Brothers Karamazov*. The production found much praise and many of the actors who had worked with the great French director loved him. It is regrettable that in his memoirs Lawrence Langner, the clever manager of the Guild, did not choose to write more than an insignificant anecdote about this event. After Copeau's visits, arguments went on about how much he had affected the development of the American theatre. He himself concluded in later years that it was influenced by two foreign companies, that of Stanislavsky and his own.[9] He could also have given credit to Appia's indirect but decisive contribution to his own reform.

Upon his return to Paris in 1919 Copeau had the Vieux Colombier remodeled. He added a large apron, one step lower than the stage floor, to be used particularly in Shakespearean productions. Upstage a high balcony supported by four columns was erected. Steps led to the platform which had three exits toward backstage. As in the Garrick Theatre, the balcony could be masked by a simple draw curtain.[10]

His new scenic arrangement, devised in accord with Appia's ideas to bring actors and spectators in close contact, did not enlist new friends. Those who believed in his approach remained faithful, but wide influential circles fervently opposed him, and he heard himself called a "Calvinist," as did Appia a few years later. Financially the theatre did not stand on solid ground; even good attendance did not suffice to cover all expenses, especially with the large apron cutting out several rows of seats in the auditorium, which was only of medium size at that. Copeau's greatest success in the postwar period was with Shakespeare's *A Winter's Tale*.

In the early twenties, making no headway artistically or financially with his theatre, Copeau gained great satisfaction from the work in his school which had been closed by the war but reopened in 1920. Shortly thereafter he transferred his teaching to Pernand-Vergelesses in Burgundy where he could rehearse to his heart's desire and perfect his productions. Several times Appia went to Pernand, a town with a population of 200, to see his friend and to attend rehearsals.[11] Jean Mercier, a pupil of Appia's, remembers, moreover, that plans were discussed in the middle twenties to invite Appia to spend a longer period at Pernand as teacher and adviser. But in 1926 and thereafter the aging master felt no longer strong enough to travel so far. Had such a visit and extended exchange of views taken place, a more definite blueprint for a new type of theatre might have resulted. Copeau thought of building one that would afford the actors close communication with the audience mainly through the complete removal of the proscenium frame.[12] As we already know, Appia had entertained this idea for many years and once, in the Festival House at Hellerau-Dresden, he had seen it realized.

Copeau's new ensemble, trained in Pernand, obtained its baptism in the cities of Burgundy. Later on, he also toured other parts of France, Belgium, Germany, Italy, the Netherlands, and Switzerland. In September, 1924, he gave up the Vieux Colombier and left Paris for good after making an agreement with Jouvet, who promised to execute his original program at the Comédie des Champs-Elysées.[13]

This left Copeau free to devote all his time to the training of his enthusiastic young actors in Pernand.

When in 1926 the company appeared in Geneva and Lausanne, two cities not far from Nyon, where Appia had been living since 1923, the master was the honored guest at all performances. A close tie with the actors blossomed, in which Appia's role was that of "fatherly comrade." The actors adored Appia for his nobility, kindness, unassuming charm, and deep understanding of the art of the theatre. Appia in turn had a high regard for *les petits*, as he called them and, moved by their artistic spirit, had great hopes for their future. Copeau considered Appia the "ideal spectator" who noticed even the most minute detail of stage business and line interpretation. After attending a performance, Appia regularly appeared backstage to discuss his impressions with the entire cast. Such sessions turned into a second performance when Appia interspersed his review with demonstrations. Every cast member received a friendly remark. Keyed up though he often was, in his enthusiasm he never forgot anyone; even for the actor with the smallest part, he had a word of praise.[14] Appia rarely had any reservations regarding the productions of his friend. Once he criticized the staging of Copeau's *Illusion* but added kindly that he was delighted "to bow before a performance of such sincerity and admirable purity."[15] When the two men parted after four happy days in Geneva, during which they had much time to talk about their favorite subject, they embraced in a mood which Appia described as "beyond time and space, or rather in Time and Space."[16]

Meeting Craig

THAT Appia gained Copeau's admiration and friendship was of great importance for the development of theatre arts. Earlier, before World War I, Appia had had another unforgettable experience in his meeting with Edward Gordon Craig (1872–1966). This happy event occurred on the occasion of an international theatre exhibition in Zurich where, upon Craig's suggestion, the designs of the two giants of scene reform were placed in the same room of the Kunstgewerbemuseum. The two artists were well acquainted with each other's work. Appia never mentioned when he first saw Craig's designs but it is assumed that friends interested in scenic art—perhaps Keyserling—gave him a hint fairly early. Reliable information states that Craig had known about Appia since 1904 through Henry Thode. Four years later Craig saw reproductions of Appia's early designs, which he admired, for they seemed to be conceived in a style related to his own. Upon inquiring where he could meet the designer he was told that he was dead, but in 1911 he learned in Moscow from Prince Wolkonsky that Appia was very much alive. Craig decided to use the first opportunity to meet "the foremost stage designer of Europe."[17] If nothing else, these facts alone refute the assumption, still occasionally advanced, that Craig simply adopted Appia's ideas.

In February, 1914, Craig arrived in Zurich ahead of Appia and went to the station to welcome his colleague. Unknown though they were to one another, they recognized each other from a distance. Craig, dressed in his customary cape, held his arms wide open to embrace his new friend and the cape "enfolded" both. Neither of them ever forgot the few days they spent together. Unfortunately, Appia left no notes about their discourses, but in conversation he repeatedly referred to this meeting with admiration and affection for Craig. For three days the two met mainly in cafés and restaurants for hours and hours to discuss what was closest to their hearts, the scenic revolution. These talks must have amused eavesdroppers since Appia could speak no English and Craig hardly any French; the latter could use some German which indeed Appia knew, and both shared some Italian. Somehow they managed to project their ideas, mainly by drawing sketches on the tablecloth in front of them. Appia related how Craig wrote his own name on the tablecloth and next to it that of Appia; then he drew a circle around both names adding the word "music" to Appia's, thus outlining the relation and difference of the two great artists.[18] Craig was more elaborate in his remarks about the Zurich meeting. He described how he was at once impressed by Appia's imposing head; the man looked to him "very much like Jupiter."[19] He found the first talk "excellent, very pleasant" and the following ones "exciting." In his diary he delineated the course of the conversation: how Appia's concern for the actor made "less and less sense" to him; how his own blunt statement that "Wagner detested the theatre and used it as a prostitute" made Appia "furious," although it did not impair their further discussion, which was devoted to the importance of light and movement, "the only true material for the art of the theatre." As an afterthought Craig concluded that Appia's emphasis on the human body and music interfered with his clear understanding of the scenic problems. He wondered furthermore whether his reliance, first on Wagner and later on Dalcroze, revealed "a weakness" or "perhaps his strength."[20]

After this first and only meeting both men came to an interesting if strange conclusion: they believed it possible to collaborate on a production. Craig wrote a remark in this sense in 1932.[21] Appia had uttered a similar opinion in 1915 when he expressed the wish to form a partnership with Craig. Six years later he was more specific in a letter to his friend talking about their "parenthood" of the scenic reform. He was inclined to discount their dissimilarities which, he thought, existed more in the eyes of the public, and he considered Craig and himself "brothers in suffering as well as in joy."[22] These statements invite intriguing speculation. What would have been the outcome of a collaboration? One cannot really visualize the two artists working together for any length of time in the tense atmosphere of a theatre. They had much in common and much that was not. Their basic conception was similar. Appia thought of himself not as a designer but definitely as designer-director as did Craig; both believed the true playwright should actually be his own director, and here Craig surpassed Appia in his desire to write, to direct, and to design.[23] There was further a strong resemblance in their views on space settings, the role of lighting, and the importance of movement in staging. However, their conflicting opinion about the actor's place let them go in opposite directions; while Appia had the actor dominate all the elements of staging, Craig considered him less essential. This is the decisive difference in their scenic concept. In Craig's often monumental settings, the performers appeared like insignificant personnel, while Appia drew his sketches with the function of the actor in mind; his spatial surroundings were devised in scale to the size of human beings. Moreover, it is almost inconceivable that the two men could have come to an understanding on the treatment of dialogue and action which, in Appia's concept, were subject to musical interpretation. Indeed they would have had to be angels, not human beings, to collaborate successfully; for how could Appia, the sensitive introvert, stand his ground against the irrepressible Craig who, often unable to control his sharp tongue, was easily provoked and controversial? It was therefore perhaps fortunate that these contemporaries met at ages in life which made any collaboration just wishful thinking.

On the other hand, it is a pity that they met but once. At least they exchanged many letters, some of which have been published. Several years after Appia's death Craig requested the return of his letters. The Fondation Adolphe Appia fulfilled his wish, and now only a few of these are in its possession. In 1960 Craig gave his entire correspondence to the Bibliothèque Nationale in Paris. Its hoped-for publication will be a most instructive volume; it will give a moving picture of the two lonely reformers, of their mutual high regard, deep understanding, and their frank, exceedingly interesting discussion of theatre arts.

The designs of both artists were again shown at the 1922 International Theatre Exhibition in Amsterdam. Appia was extremely pleased and satisfied that once more their works were linked together, and he advised his young friend Waelterlin not to miss the exceptional opportunity of seeing his fourteen sketches and "the superb room devoted to Craig." Apparently he was not acquainted with Craig's recent designs because he inquired of Waelterlin whether he had "developed a bit" since Zurich. With her notorious lack of modesty Sarah Bernhardt paid Appia an extraordinary compliment when after a long look at his designs she exclaimed at last: "The great well-known in front of the great unknown" (*La grande Connue devant le grand Inconnu*)![24] An attempt was made to bring the pieces from Amsterdam to London and afterwards to New York; however, the plan did not materialize. From some of Craig's letters it can be culled that he tried hard to have Appia join him in sending a series of sketches to the United States. Appia hesitated, then evidently declined. Finally Craig stated categorically he would not participate without him. This insistence on the part of Craig ought definitely to destroy the widely spread rumor that he was jealous of Appia, his older colleague, and that he made every effort to stand in the limelight everywhere. Craig, like Appia, was extremely kind to people he liked and admired. Meanness was not in his nature when he could write to his friend, "You are, my dear, the most noble expression of the modern theatre."[25]

Appia kept Craig informed about the opportunities which came to him late in life. By the twenties Craig stood aloof from all practical work in the theatre while Appia at last saw his ideas executed on the stage of La Scala. The animadversion and ridicule heaped upon his *Tristan* designs by critics and patrons alike did not surprise his friend. Craig was convinced that people never gave Appia appropriate support he so desperately needed for the realization of his vision. He even speculated that Appia's co-workers in the opera house may have "exclaimed 'Wonderful' and added aside 'Unpractical' without attempting to aid him." In this respect Craig was a bit mistaken as will be seen in the presentation of the Scala experiment, but in his general conclusion he was right; namely, that "a large theatre like La Scala, like the Opéra in Paris, is somewhat like an old fashioned court—intrigue is despicable in such places, and paramount." He made this statement after his friend's death, when he also concluded that Appia's collaboration with Dalcroze was "very successful" and his sketches for Wagnerian music dramas "perfect."[26]

The War 1914-18

THE period prior to the outbreak of the First World War was indeed one of Appia's happiest for, in addition to his stimulating experiences in Hellerau and Geneva, he won the friendship of Craig, later of Copeau. The air was full of hope, when in August, 1914, the war broke out, killing every opportunity for new theatrical experiments. Appia maintained his correspondence with old and new friends, his talks with Dalcroze but, living alone in Glérolles, he was essentially left to his own resources. Thus he had much time to meditate. This was a "creative pause" during which conditions permitted him to re-evaluate his relation to German culture and, at the same time, to determine and strengthen his position vis-à-vis the art of the theatre. The war turned out to be a hard but good teacher.

Naturally, as an artist he was nonpolitical; no one ever heard him discuss national or international politics. The few remarks he made were incidental rather than intentional. The one country he disliked, or rather feared, was Russia; he had almost a terror of the Czars and their despotic system of government. When asked whether he was capable of committing suicide he spontaneously answered, "In case the Russians should enter Switzerland." A brief reference in a letter written in the middle twenties could, at a first glance, be interpreted as favoring fascism, but it simply expressed his satisfaction with Mussolini's introduction of rhythmic gymnastics in the Italian prison system. He had once made a sharp comment against France, in Paris early in the century. In a circle of artists the conversation turned to the merits of France versus Germany. Suddenly Appia, intensely irritated, uttered the remark that the German victory in the War of 1870 was of great benefit to the future of civilization and added something about Latin corruption of the arts. Such an extreme position was not consistent with his basic belief in fairness and justice and his passionate concern about the welfare of the human being regardless of religion and nationality. His leanings toward Germany were purely intellectual and emotional, by no means political; they might be termed philo-Germanic, but indeed not pan-Germanic. His attitude toward France was evidently conditioned by the deep disappointment he had experienced in Paris but he never lost great interest in, and understanding of, certain French authors and composers. Essentially he was proud of his native Switzerland, though not in a narrow, chauvinistic sense. Rather he loved the beauty of his region, the hills and woods between Lake Geneva and the Jura mountains, and also the way of life in French Switzerland since he was, in a friend's words, "very sensitive to the Latin atmosphere of freedom and gracefulness."

Long before 1914 Appia was fully aware of the political tensions between France and Germany and he pondered all their implications impartially. Still, the outbreak of the war came as a terrible shock. For a while he hardly spoke to anyone; in taking no stand against Germany he alarmed his friends and relatives. In that French region his silence was easily misinterpreted and even caused the rumor he might be "in the service of Germany." From the very beginning his sister Hélène worked in the Red Cross Office for Prisoners of War; there is reason to assume that he too thought of joining this charitable work, perhaps he did so for a brief period. When in early fall, 1914, Dalcroze and Hodler, the renowned Swiss painter, signed their names on the international protest against some barbaric misdeeds of the German armies, Mrs. Anna Penel, his aunt, wanted to know whether Appia too gave his signature. He did not react to her inquiry until October when he sent a letter to the editor of the *Journal de Genève* for publication. The occasion was the cancellation of concerts in Geneva's famous cathedral; since this almost unknown statement is significant of Appia's views about the interrelationship of music and people and vaguely about the erupted hostilities, it is here reprinted in translation:[27]

WHILE LISTENING TO THE ORGAN AT SAINT-PIERRE

Saturday evening the listeners to the concerts at Saint-Pierre left our cathedral with deep sorrow.

Indeed that evening gave us not simply the last of a series of concerts. No, we all realized how much those hours of meditation answered an inner necessity.

In view of the present destructions of our culture, and those yet to come, we have some difficulty to maintain, before the work of art, the serenity it requires: the war which occupies us today does not seem to be an object for artistic expression.

Nevertheless, who among us did not carry away last Saturday—and the preceding weeks—a vision of architecture that appeared *new* to him, an echo of music that appeared equally *new,* a certain feeling of communion and harmony never before experienced? Whoever listened to the thunder of the organ and the human voices bursting forth in the vault and between the columns, then drifting down again and hovering above the crowd like a supreme prayer —whoever glanced over the devoted assembly where each individual concealed in his soul the same anguish, the same painful hope—whoever did so and felt not impelled to recognize that the serenity exacted from us by the work of art is the result of an inner conquest, and that this conquest must be achieved *together* to be truly alive? . . .

War is an incomparable school. We have heard this said but we have not yet been aware of it, and we are still less aware that war is—absolutely—a school in every field without a single exception: it is a harsh, pitiless revealer; coldly it exposes the woes we conceal under our clothes.

One of these woes is the worthlessness of our artistic life. True, we wanted to bring art into our life—but we intended to do this as *individuals.* And now war is going to demonstrate the absurdity of such efforts. Its loud voice shouts at us: You must suffer together; but then, like your sufferings, you also express your joys together. Otherwise everything is futile.

Climbing the stairs to Saint-Pierre as well as descending them, we have felt how powerful is the desire for an expression conveyed together and what an inner strength such an expression confers upon us.

Experiences like that one have an incalculable bearing. Therefore it is regrettable that they cannot be relived at least once a week and that these hours of meditation—I might almost say of revelation—are suspended.

Our eminent organist, in cooperation with his valiant Little Choir and also with several soloists, has put his whole heart and all his art into the execution of a great idea. He has done this through programs discerningly arranged, in which nothing was sacrificed to the too facile emotion that conditions might suggest. He did so as an artist. Our full gratitude goes to him and his zealous and unselfish collaborators.

May their efforts and their perfect good will not be halted by considerations important as they undoubtedly are at this time. The difficulties involved would be quickly overcome if we could convince ourselves of the importance of these collective manifestations for the participants as well as for the listeners.

A warm "thank you" to the participants! See you again! We are sure of this!

Our cathedral is there, silent, waiting to witness our return.

This article disappointed his aunt as it indicated his unwillingness to take sides in the war. Officially he did not turn against either country but remained neutral. In private conversations, however, he sharply condemned the country whose culture meant so much to him. In a conversation with Mercier after Germany's defeat he compared the catastrophe with Wagner's *Twilight of the Gods.*

Under the impact of the war his admiration for Wagner lost some of the spell it had on him. The transition had begun during his work on *Orpheus,* but now he really freed himself from Wagner's too powerful influence; more important yet, from that of Chamberlain. As previously indicated, the two friends began to drift apart from the moment Chamberlain married Wagner's daughter and Appia met Dalcroze. But the decisive blow came when the hostilities brought to the fore the profound difference between the two men. Chamberlain, who had become a German citizen, openly propagated the war aims of extreme pan-Germanism while Appia, a citizen of the world, abhorred force and brutality. This fundamental conflict could not be bridged and irrevocably cut the old bond. From his peaceful retreat at Glérolles Appia wrote Chamberlain once that the *Tauben* (doves) he could see flying by his window told him the truth in contrast to the German *Tauben* (name of a fighter plane). Chamberlain's reaction to this blunt allusion and similar insinuations is not known. He later allowed the publication of three letters he wrote Appia during the war. In these the amicable feeling for the longtime friend is still alive, yet a strange air may be discerned between the lines. In a resigned mood he confessed that "at the moment there does not exist a trace of sympathy that can serve as a bridge for an understanding between the two of us. Sometimes silence is the friendliest thing one can offer a friend. . . ."[28] This pessimistic utterance illustrates their changed relationship. As Appia, furthermore, made bitter remarks to a close friend about Chamberlain's lack of sincerity, it is surprising that the sharp differences did not result in an open break. In fact, the two men corresponded much in the postwar era. In those years Chamberlain was incapacitated by Parkinson's disease and dictated his letters to his wife Eva. Appia enjoyed reading them because Eva's handwriting reminded him of that of Richard Wagner.[29] There is no sign that Appia ever again met his former friend, who died in 1927.

Appia the Man

BESET by many problems which piled up or were aggravated during the war, Appia withdrew unto himself ever more. As a child he was, like most children, talkative, frank, and open until his father's inexorable strictness and the altogether chilly atmosphere in his home weighed too heavily on him and he began to keep his own counsel. In a stirring document entitled *Introduction à mes notes personelles* (1905), he analyzed himself and, detecting some unfortunate traits he had inherited from his father, complained bitterly at one instance that "solitude" was his father's "only intimate company . . . which did not bore or tire him, which forever held his interest . . ." and about himself he added that although he knew he was well able to communicate if he so wished, "contact with others disturbs my harmony of mind." As a music student he tried to overcome this tendency by indulging in whatever pleasures life offered him. He went through several superficial adventures, lived a bohemian existence unconcerned about a definite career. Seemingly without ambition, he read at random and saw and heard in the theatre whatever he liked, or he simply dreamed in the countryside. From his student years until his dismal experiences in Paris after 1903 he was carefree, perhaps happy.

In the end, distressing experiences taught him to rely more on himself than on others. The professional as well as personal disappointments in Paris made him sadly aware that, at the age of forty-three, he had not achieved anything positive in a field to which he had devoted his life. Without work and influence he was an outsider, unrecognized, a lonely man. Pondering his position as designer he realized that unlike the work of painters and sculptors, his creations depended on the collaboration of other forces. To be fully appreciated his designs had to be executed and shown in a theatre. Giving himself an account of what he had accomplished until 1905, he confessed that by that time he had expected to be the head of a large studio working on many orders to devise new settings and consequently to be in constant contact with artists and theatres. Instead, as he wrote at that time, he saw himself "more and more isolated, even alienated from the theatre and its artists" without "a knowledge of worldly matters" or "a sense of work." Underlying all his troubles was, of course, chiefly his very pronounced stutter. According to his friend's observation, the condition of this embarrassing impediment varied very much in later years; it seemed related to his anxieties and tiredness. In the company of close friends he felt at ease and his stuttering almost disappeared. But it definitely made him shun speaking before groups. Mercier concluded that the handicap gave his personality "a certain flavor of sorrow which made him more sympathetic." In general however the stutter was "a cross he carried through life."

His deep-seated frustration and serious speech defect notwithstanding, Appia left a lasting impression on everyone he met. (And one may add on anyone who sees a picture of him). Everything about him was unusual: his whole appearance, the way he dressed, his extraordinary kindness, his nonconforming attitude. The beautiful head—a clear-cut face framed by long dark auburn hair and the famed beard that gave him the look of a prophet—was set upon a strong, well-proportioned body. His hazel-colored eyes were soft, dreamy, unfathomable; only in moments of excitement, that is whenever he discussed dramatic art, they would "flash full of life and joy, otherwise they also showed signs of tiredness," as a friend described them. His hair turned gray in his late fifties, but it never became really white. Like most of the Appias he was of the dark Mediterranean type, except his height was above its average. Some even thought he had similarities to the Indian Hindu. As several pictures show, Appia was extremely photogenic, and it is not surprising that artists were eager to sculpt his head or make a sketch of him.

Figure 24. Appia playing with two dogs, ca. 1910. *Blanche Bingham.*

A fine bust, made in his Dresden period, alas, is lost; fortunately a few portraits are preserved, one by his cousin, Theodore Appia, and another, better known, by the excellent painter René Martin who was introduced to Appia by Ernest Biéler in 1920.

Appia was determined to remain completely independent and to live in utter simplicity. He seldom wore the normal city suit, and in fact he looked strange when he did, for his was usually quite out of fashion. He preferred the more comfortable sport clothes; in inclement weather a loden cape protected him. In 1920 he told his friend Mercier, "You will see how men's fashion will one day resemble my outfit; they will copy me without knowing it." Economy undoubtedly had something to do with his almost monastic mode of living. Brought up in Calvinistic austerity and, as a Swiss, frugal by nature, he seemed to need very little so that scarcity of money did not bother him. There was no symptom of any luxury whatever in his personal appearance or his room. Although he liked fine things and fully appreciated them, he could readily do without them. In his essay *Après une lecture de* Port-Royal *(Sainte-Beuve) (After Reading* Port-Royal *by Sainte-Beuve)* Appia injects the term *"Lebenskuenstler"* (an artist of life) defining it as a man who has made his choice and is satisfied with what he has. It is almost a description of himself toward the end of his life, a man essentially at peace with the world, except for his severe personal and artistic frustrations.

All who knew him intimately agree that he was never interested in money, did not even know its value. During his student years in Leipzig and Dresden and those following them, he was financially supported by his father. After the latter's death in 1898, he received a legacy which was put in trust of his brother Paul, who doled it out to him in monthly rates of about 180 Swiss francs. Here Paul obeyed an order, not an inclination. Cousin Raymond Penel remembered that "this arrangement did not please Adolphe, but he knew too well that if he had a free hand the capital would be spent quickly." At any rate Appia "never complained about his pecuniary situation; his freedom satisfied him." The small monthly grant increased a little after the death of a well-to-do uncle and that of his sister Marie; yet, according to reliable sources, there was altogether less than 300 francs available monthly; not much, but sufficient for a modest man like Appia. A few times he earned a small sum; he received a fee in Paris and a honorarium from Dalcroze for his work in Hellerau and Geneva, and finally an adequate remuneration from La Scala in Milan and the Municipal Theatre in Basle. But this amounted to very little, too little to sustain him, and after World War I his small income really spelled hardship. Occasionally friends succeeded in assisting him without hurting his pride by offering useful presents which he gratefully accepted. When expenses for a stay in a sanatorium exceeded his financial means, his sister and friends somehow managed to pay the difference without his knowledge.

The little money he had went for the bare necessities; in addition he needed material for writing and designing. Outside of room and board he had few expenses whether he lived in Bière or Glérolles, in Paris or Munich. And so it was when he traveled or remained a few days in a city; he was satisfied with a cheap furnished room and simple food in any restaurant. The only luxury he indulged—he would have called it a necessity—was the annual visit to the Bayreuth festivals; attending the entire *Ring* and also *Tristan* and *Parsifal* took a few hundred francs from his small allowance.

All this may give the impression that Appia was almost saintly. This was by no means the case. As Abraham Lincoln said, "Folks who have no vices have very few virtues." Smoking, however, was not one of Appia's vices. He was seldom seen to light a cigarette. But drinking was a different matter. As a student and young man he drank quite heavily although probably not more than was customary then among young artists. All his adult life he was accustomed to drink a light table wine. Hard liquor became one of his regular habits later, when, in times of tension, he would overindulge and, worse yet, would pour into his drink or into a glass of water some drops of laudanum, an opiate easily available. This was his custom from around 1900 through the twenties, when he particularly felt the need for a "tranquilizer." He drank excessively at times when he could no longer bear his frustrations, but, medically speaking, he could not have been termed an "alcoholic" or "a sick man." Such drinking bouts lasted only briefly. Fully conscious of his sporadic urge to drink heavily, he would on such occasions send word asking Dr. Forel, his trusted friend and physician, to look after him; or at the onset of a crisis, he would betake himself to Dr. Forel's sanatorium. His inquisitive and analytic mind did not miss an opportunity of probing into the problem of alcoholism. In his essay *Pittoresque (Picturesqueness)* (1922) he described the dilemma of a drunkard: "On the one hand the relapse he secretly desires; on the other, the acceptance almost beyond hope of an ideal he somehow sensed when he signed the promise [of abstinence], but which he has since lost."

His occasional excessive drinking is understandable in view of his inner conflicts, his failures in his profession as well as in his relation to people. He longed for the affection of friends, yet at the same time he coveted solitude. This duality is obvious in his association with men as well as women, and undoubtedly contributed to the intricacies of his sexual relations. Appia did not openly discuss such matters, he did not even touch upon them save incidentally. Still, enough is known from his own remarks and from friends and relatives to infer that he was homosexual. It may be doubted that he was so by nature, for he was virile and, in fact, had a great attraction to women, to whom he was always kind and considerate. It is more likely that he was driven to homosexuality through circumstances in adolescence, among them his parents' attitude, the altogether unwholesome home life. The stuttering he developed as a probable consequence may have made him feel uneasy in the presence of women. To some extent his deep admiration for the Greek civilization was perhaps a contributing factor. There is some ground to assume that for quite a while, he lived, or at any rate had a love affair, with a young girl; and when he was middle-aged, a woman was willing to marry him though she must have realized that the marriage would never be consummated.

Appia was of robust health; he had an iron constitution and was never really ill until his sixties, except for the common childhood diseases. Whenever he complained about not feeling well, of being unable to do anything, his "ailment" apparently was psychological, not physical. In times of stress, when nothing would work out as expected or hoped for, he suffered headaches as many sensitive people do. They disappeared, of course, as soon as conditions changed to his satisfaction. His eyes too were remarkably good until he was about fifty, when glasses were prescribed; even then he rarely wore them in the presence of people. When he had to read something while others were around he preferred to use a magnifier which was always on his desk.

For all his depressions, a basic optimism saved him from complete nervous breakdown. His mood could change quickly from exalted enthusiasm to profound sadness, but as he grew older he did not show the latter to outsiders. And the depressive moods, mainly caused by lack of success, did not deter him from enjoying life, which for him meant nature and simple people. He loved to be outdoors, to hike through the woods and hills wherever he happened to be. His long walks afforded him the best opportunity to dream, meditate, and clarify ideas and problems. Almost every day, weather permitting, he went on a hike for at least a few hours. He loved just to stroll, to admire what nature and small towns offered him; whenever he came to a particularly beautiful spot he sat or lay down. On such walks he talked to common folks, for whom he had sincere sympathy and understanding, and who in turn adored him. How well Appia got along with these people was demonstrated during his long stay in Bière, where he befriended not only the family with whom he boarded, but many villagers. He joined them for talks in an inn or in front of a house and, typical for him, he worked with them in the fields and vineyards during the harvest time.

Appia's Homes

HERETOFORE several places were mentioned where Appia stayed for varying lengths of time. To give a complete listing of all is impossible, at least at this writing, since not enough pertinent data are available. His correspondence and reports from friends and relatives allow one to trace his life but not to document it accurately. Even when residing in a town, he sometimes disappeared for a while. A day-by-day account would indeed contribute nothing to the over-all picture of this restless man. Fundamentally he was a wanderer, a gypsy, or as a cousin described

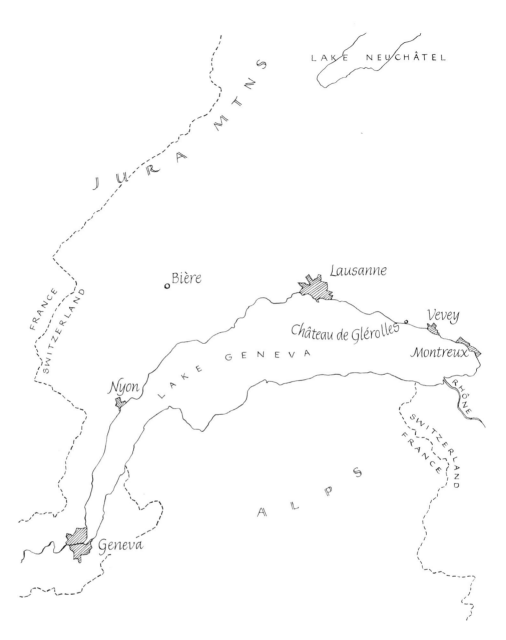

Figure 25. Map of Lake Geneva.

him, "a prince of the vagabonds." His craving for independence, his unconcern for bourgeois customs, and his indifference toward creature comfort made him disregard all accepted norms. He did not care where he lived as long as he could wander in a beautiful countryside and had a room to sleep and work in, undisturbed by visitors except when he was ready to see them. He was by no means a knight-errant fighting opponents in the wide world, but rather a pilgrim or hermit who loved to meditate and theorize.

Thus he lived unencumbered by worldly possessions; he had no real home, and when he moved he carried a suitcase for his belongings and his portable drawing board. His only wish was to be free to move wherever and whenever he felt like going. At his sister's apartment he left, at least temporarily, scores, books, and sketches which he could not take on his many trips. Sometimes a house of a relative or friend served him as storage space. Home was for Appia, in the first place, any town in French Switzerland, specifically in the Canton de Vaud, where he mainly lived after his studies in Germany and to which he traveled back and forth until 1914; after that he rarely left this region.

Except for the limited travels of his study years, Appia did not see much of foreign countries. He visited Italy four times. In the early nineties he spent several weeks on the Riviera, mainly at Bordighera, in his search for a peaceful place where he could write down his thoughts about his newly discovered theories of staging. In 1900 he hiked with Raymond Penel through central Italy to see the art treasures in Rome, Naples, Salermo, Paestum, and on Capri. Four years later he returned to study and enjoy the art of the early Renaissance in Florence and Venice. Lastly he went to Milan in 1923 upon Toscanini's invitation to stage the production of *Tristan* (see Chapter V). He dreamed about going to Greece but never found the opportunity to walk through the temples and amphitheatres whose style was such a great inspiration to him. He thought of, maybe planned, other trips to far-away places but they never materialized. His restlessness prompted him in 1923 to toy temporarily with the idea of migrating to the United States, a change he pondered though not without horror. He seriously discussed this question with his cousin, Mrs. Blanche Bingham, in New York; at the same time he was also communicating with Dr. Raymond Penel, then a practicing physician in Ajaccio on Corsica, inquiring whether he might stay with him at least for a while. This urge to get away occurred at a crucial moment in his life when he was suffering dreadfully from lack of encouragement, let alone success.

At approximately a dozen places Appia lived comparatively long, for several months or even years. For three of these residences detailed information is available: Bière, Glérolles, and Nyon, all in the Canton de Vaud. In Bière-Montbrillant, some eight kilometers north of Lake Geneva, he stayed from 1893 till 1904, which seems a long sojourn unless we remember his intermittent visits to Paris, Munich, Vienna, Bayreuth, and many other places. His quarters were in a small house, typical of that region, owned and lived in by the winegrower Cloux who rented him an upstairs room furnished only with the bare essentials. He took his meals with the Cloux family. His time was divided between work and walks. Shortly before 1900 Appia made an extravagant decision—he acquired a bicycle on which he roamed through the region during the following years.

At the château de Glérolles too Appia spent a considerable length of time. His stay there from 1909 until 1919 was of course interrupted by extended visits to Hellerau, aside from frequent trips to Geneva and periodic moves to hotels and rest homes during the war. The castle, whose origin reaches back to the twelfth century, is located directly on Lake Geneva about six kilometers west of Vevey. Rebuilding and additions modified the original character of the castle; nevertheless it is still very impressive though not as magnificent as the better-known château de Chillon. Glérolles is dominated by a large square tower the foundation of which is a rock jutting out in the lake. Three buildings altogether surround the inner courtyard with its old huge trees. A bridge across the moat connects the castle with the highway beyond; a main railroad passes under this bridge. Appia must have had this castle in mind as a possible retreat years before he actually moved there; indications are that he stayed there briefly in the early 1890's and again in 1905; he had certainly seen it when he attended school in nearby Vevey.

In 1909 he rented two rooms in the large turret; one served as a guest room for friends and hence was rarely used by himself. This room faced the courtyard whereas the other, his large living room, had a breathtaking view across the lake and beyond to a majestic range of the Alps. A few photographs of Greek and Renaissance art graced the walls of this room; otherwise no personal mementoes or pictures of his family or friends. As Mercier describes it, "his working table was placed close to the window so that the light fell in from the left. Here he had his drawing board; here he wrote. Lifting his eyes he could see the mountains and the sky; lowering them he could watch the waves rolling against the walls of the tower." Appia loved this part of the country which had inspired one of his most bewitching designs. Once when returning with Mercier from Vevey, he pointed to a hill between Rivaz and Chexbres, the outline of which had served him as the basic inspiration for his famous setting of the Rock of Valkyries. A winegrower couple, the Ruchonnets, also lived at Glérolles, and Appia had his noon meals with them; in the evening he prepared himself a bite.

In his living room was a piano, and his friends who would visit enjoyed hearing him play and sing his favorite operas. Naturally, on such occasions he did not stutter. He was not an accomplished pianist but he played with dramatic verve, intensity, and extremely precise rhythm. He had a fine, though untrained, voice and his interpretation was fascinating. Such musical sessions went on into darkness, perhaps with a candle burning or the moon shining into the room; sometimes he played until the wee hours.

Glérolles could have been an ideal home for Appia; it was an old, simple building, almost monumental, with a beautiful location and environment, and, further, it offered him the opportunity to be alone or to invite friends if he so wished. Only one factor, but the most decisive one, was missing to make him utterly happy here: regular work for a theatre to demonstrate his reform ideas. Often, when he was unable to see where all his writing and drawing would lead to, he was overcome with a feeling of uselessness.

In 1923, giving up his plans to flee to New York or Corsica, he followed the suggestion of Dr. Forel, and moved into a house on the grounds of the doctor's sanatorium; this facilitated a vigil over Appia's physical and mental health. The sanatorium, La Metairie, under Dr. Forel's direction since 1922, was near Nyon, a short train ride from both Geneva and Lausanne. There, as we already know, Copeau came to see his mentor. From his new home Appia had a grandiose vista: Lake Geneva and the Alps to the South; the Jura mountains to the North. Copeau describes the room which Appia occupied on the second floor of a small garden house. The furniture resembled that of a monk's cell: an iron bedstead, a table made of pine, and a few chairs. On the table sketches and manuscripts were lying around and, of course, writing and drawing material. In addition there were sundry volumes of Molière, Rabelais, and Shakespeare; this was all.[30] For his meals he joined the staff and patients in the main dining room. Apart from these hours he was alone working in his room or roaming the lovely countryside. Sometimes after a long walk he dropped in at the main house to play music with Dr. Forel or to bring flowers to the nurses. He also liked to help decorate rooms or entertain the patients and staff members.[31]

In 1927 Appia moved to La Chaumière, also near Nyon; otherwise his life followed about the same routine. In that year Dr. Forel planned to build a new sanatorium and Appia assisted him in selecting the most suitable and beautiful location, but he did not live long enough thereafter to enjoy the new building. In the peaceful atmosphere of his last retreat he had indeed reached, as Dr. Forel describes it, the absolute "feeling of security, not alone materially but spiritually as well." With his doctor friend, the other physicians, and the patients he felt safe from "hostility or indiscretion, imaginary as these may have been." His stutter was hardly noticed since everyone was accustomed to it. Here he was able to talk, make music, write, and design to his heart's delight. Here at last he found the equanimity that let him enjoy whatever he happened to do. "I think," stated Dr. Forel, "his stay in sanatoriums definitely increased his capacity for work."

Appia's Philosophy

In Dr. Forel's sanatorium Appia had a refuge where he could concentrate without inner stress, with no need to turn to tranquilizers, alcoholic or otherwise. The surrounding nature gave him comfort and strength. His relation to nature was akin to that of Goethe who wrote in *Wahrheit und Dichtung (Truth and Fancy):* "there is no more beautiful devotion to God than that which . . . blooms in communion with nature." This thought may also have been the fountainhead of Appia's philosophy and religion.

To speak of religion in regard to Appia is somewhat risky for, like his political belief, his religious faith did not lend itself to normal definition. His family background explains his profound distaste for narrow-mindedness, bigotry, and the organized church altogether. Yet though no churchgoer, he believed in and trusted God. From the days of his childhood he preserved a simple discipline that penetrated the core of everything. Thus, while he loathed dogmatism and intellectualism in any form, he was always deeply concerned with man's soul. Ostentatious celebrations, such as the religious observances of holidays, meant little to him. On the other hand, words like "God," or "the Lord" were not uttered lightly. His cousin Raymond remembers an experience that illustrates Appia's attitude in this respect. They were walking with a foreign lady through the streets of Paris when the conversation touched upon a religious theme. The lady somehow teased Appia with a reference to "Our Father"; his face turned red with anger.

It is natural that religion as such does not occupy a place in Appia's writings, which deal exclusively with themes on art and above all, the theatre. Still, there are passages or just a word revealing a profoundly religious feeling. In his last book, *L'Oeuvre d'art vivant,* he significantly called for a "cathedral," not simply for a new form of theatre building. And discussing the question of cooperation, he states that all good Christians must be able to work together. After his Paris experiences, when circumstances isolated him from almost everyone and he was near despair, he confessed, "At this moment I feel again a kind of confidence which could well be an act of believing in God." In *Formes nouvelles (New Forms),* written early in the twenties, Appia leaves no doubt that he firmly believes in the "Great Unknown," the guiding spirit and arbiter of human beings. His concept of religion, like his concept of art and life in general, was guided by genuine confidence; underlying his faith was his communion with nature created by Him. If any generalization is feasible, the term "pantheism" may serve to explain his religious belief.

Artistic Likes and Dislikes

BEETHOVEN'S *Missa Solemnis* had fascinated Appia in his youth and he never ceased to admire this great work. But when later he became acquainted with other compositions of this genius he remained unmoved. It cannot be assumed that he did not understand them; he must have had a personal reason for what actually amounted to an aversion, as it is strange that so sensitive a musician should reject Beethoven. Mercier explains this attitude by Appia's distaste for "intellectualism" and his complete surrender to Wagner's sensual music. This may have been one cause. Dr. Forel, as a psychiatrist probing more deeply, wonders "whether there was not a great resemblance in personality and destiny between the two." One might say "he defended himself against his own romanticism, against a kind of rivalry with the other creative genius who like Appia encompassed the range of sorrow and joy in life from one end to the other." Beethoven displayed his emotions while Appia, reticent as he was, concealed his suffering. Both explanations are plausible but not conclusive. Appia himself never referred to his peculiar attitude. When friends brought up this question they received no answer, merely a shrug of the shoulder.

If it is disturbing to learn that he actually disliked Beethoven, it is no surprise that he ignored Mozart, the greatest composer of the rococo. Not even *The Magic Flute* attracted Appia, although the wonderful simplicity of many of its scenes should have aroused his interest. His low regard for Verdi's earlier operas can be understood, but his utter coolness toward *Otello,* that monumental work, remains almost inexplicable. Very few modern composers drew Appia's attention. He heard some of Richard Strauss's symphonic poems and also played them on the piano. Though he had no particular liking for this musical form he thought *Death and Transfiguration* a marvelous composition. Of the operas by Strauss he is said to have known only *Salome* which, understandably, did not induce him to get acquainted with his other operatic compositions or for that matter, with any contemporary operas. He had no use for Puccini at all although he admitted, a bit apologetically, that some passages in *La Bohème* were so irresistible that he sometimes had to play and sing them. In general he ignored the existence of compositions he did not like. When asked to evaluate such a work he would merely answer: "This has no name." His love for Debussy remained a temporary phenomenon and diminished considerably, as we already know, after a performance of *Pelléas et Mélisande* which apparently bored him. He knew the score of *Carmen* by heart from cover to cover. As a young man he studied the operas of Karl Maria von Weber whose *Der Freischuetz* captured his fancy. Rather late he discovered Moussorgsky and became very fond of *Boris Godunov,* especially its dramatic chorus scenes and its sensual orchestration. On the other hand he had a lifelong admiration for Bach whose works he often played, and also for Gluck to whom he had felt closely drawn since his collaboration with Dalcroze in Hellerau. In Gluck he found classical simplicity combined with pure reason, just as he did in Bach. Scanning the stories and characters of Appia's favorite operas one detects that all, except *Carmen,* have superhuman dimensions and a symbolic rather than a realistic basis. In any case, his preferences indicate again the duality of his complex nature: his earthbound sensuality in conflict with his striving for eternal beauty.

His views on painting, sculpture, and architecture were essentially influenced by Greek classicism and some of its Roman followers, the artists of the early Renaissance, and the pre-Raphaelites. Almost everything else was summarily dismissed; he was not even willing to acknowledge Michelangelo, some of whose works he bitterly criticized. Of course he was familiar with the paintings of the impressionists in Paris but neither they nor the German secessionists affected him in any measure. Since Wagner had been interested in Arnold Boecklin's art, Appia went on a few occasions to see his paintings in museums and exhibits, but apparently Boecklin's style did not excite him either.

In the field of literature Appia's choice covered a wide field; French, German, and particularly English authors were on his reading list. Besides Molière and the other French classics he repeatedly read Shakespeare's dramas and the novels by Dickens. His ideal was Goethe, the model for his esthetic views. Friends and relatives are unanimous in their belief that Appia was no avid reader at all, that in fact he read very little. This somehow contradicts his numerous references to authors in his letters, books, and essays. He obviously was no bookworm, not a scholar; but he certainly had a sound knowledge of many subjects, a knowledge impossible to acquire through observations or conversations alone. He was indeed not systematic in his reading; whatever book happened to strike his fancy or was recommended to him by trusted friends he read. Then he could be voracious, digesting for instance within a short space of time volumes of Calderón, Cervantes, Rabelais, Rousseau, Voltaire, in addition to works by Lessing and Tolstoy, and a number of Greek tragedies. It seems certain he read more while under Chamberlain's influence than afterwards. The older he grew, the less he read; yet some of his favorite books were always in his room.

Working Habits

LIKE most creators, Appia had to be alone, secluded, when he designed or wrote. There were no set hours he preferred, although he rarely worked in the morning. He liked to retire in the afternoon or evening after returning from a walk. Then his mind would overflow with ideas and in complete solitude he would organize everything, making one draft after another of a setting or an essay. He was his own

Figure 26.   Appia at his drawing board, ca. 1910. *Jean Mercier.*

severest critic, never satisfied with what he had done toward the ideal solution of his vision. Basically he relied on intuition, yet at the same time he proved to be a very logical thinker in his drawings and writings. Here are his own words about how he proceeded in creating his designs: "Spontaneous to begin with, and directly and somehow chronologically derived from the score, my vision accidentally implied the theories which I discovered only later on." First he sorted out the details of the action; then he searched for the episode he considered most representative of the composer's style. Simultaneously he studied each scene for its "theatrical significance." Delineating his approach he wrote: "It is faith in the unconscious, and strangely enough, that faith has never deceived me." To Donald Oenslager, who visited him in Geneva, he explained his over-all conception thus: "The great man of the theatre must first have the mind and endless imagination," adding that he should know thoroughly every phase of the theatre; and he concluded that the process of studying and creating should go hand in hand.

As stated previously, all his sketches were done with a pencil. His answer to a question about this peculiar habit was, "I design with my eraser" (another example of his strong desire to feel free to alter things as he saw fit). His manuscripts, too, were written with a pencil. In his younger years he used pen and ink, though he began fairly early to write letters to friends with a pencil. Later, when he applied this informality to his semi-official correspondence, he apologized for his impoliteness. An acceptable excuse for using the pencil may have been that in his frequent changes of residence it was easier to carry along a handy, clean, and comfortable tool than a pen and an ink bottle.

His style of writing has puzzled many, irritated others. In criticizing his sometimes "obscure" passages, it could be conceded that his writing lacks the simplicity he so highly treasured in life and in his designs. Nevertheless, it definitely has a very personal character; the involved style may have been caused by the fact that he dealt with a subject then entirely unknown; sometimes he complained how difficult it was clearly to explain those new ideas. This condition was aggravated by a lack of practical experience. Experimentation in theatres might have been of great benefit in clarifying his ideas. An external reason may be detected in the methods of European publishing, especially in his day; editors rarely, if ever, served as advisers to an author and hence manuscripts were usually printed as submitted. A decisive factor was surely within his complex personality, which in his formative years was subject to two strong national influences. As he himself confessed, "My misfortune is that I think in German and write in French." After reading Appia's first writings somebody once remarked that they brought to mind those of Chamberlain—or more politely expressed, those of Schopenhauer or Wagner translated into French. Probably one could also refer to French authors, like Sainte-Beuve and Rousseau, who left their stamp on Appia. It is true that his first works somehow leave the impression that German and French became entangled in his mind; but after 1914 when the predominant German influence had virtually vanished, such a reservation is not appropriate. At any rate, a critique of his style should not be interpreted as meaning that the French of his early books was not satisfactory. If it does not match the best of French writing, it is at least competent and above petty cavil by superficial critics. One comes perhaps nearest to the truth by comparing his style on the whole with the involuted writings of the nineteenth century. Certainly he had mastered his mother tongue, which he spoke perhaps with a slight trace of a French Swiss accent. Keen observers were not even convinced that it was this "trace of an accent" that gave his diction a certain peculiar flavor, they rather ascribe it to his stutter. Evidently he used some typical "Helveticisms" in his vocabulary, and in Paris anyway he was accepted as a Frenchman and not considered a foreigner.

Among Friends

THE listing of names already mentioned as Appia's friends can, without difficulty, be multiplied, but of all his acquaintances, only a few were in close contact with him for a long stretch of time; some saw little of him though letters were regularly exchanged, others met him frequently during a brief period and then disappeared from his life. In addition, the older Appia grew, the less he talked about his past. Actually, the number of those privileged to observe him intimately for twenty or thirty years is infinitesimal.

During most of his life Appia was an ardent correspondent, eager to communicate with friends and collaborators. In the loneliness of his later years he also wrote to authors in whose books he discovered ideas similar or kindred to his own. Moreover, he liked to send a few lines of appreciation to those who favorably reviewed his work. As a young and more gregarious man, he made great efforts to meet artists. Frightened of personal controversies, he went out of his way to accommodate everyone, and sometimes when differences arose between two friends, he acted as mediator and tried to heal any wounds. When his attempts failed he suffered more than the parties involved.

All this changed in the last decades of his life; then he became extremely reluctant to befriend anyone, and he even broke, for no apparent reason, with people he had known for years. No one—not even Dr. Forel—was able to penetrate the hard shell he had protectively built around himself. Conversations were strictly directed to topics which interested him at the moment, thus automatically excluding his past life and work. Nevertheless, he remained always kind and friendly, if reserved, to outsiders. This whole attitude, noticeably after his sad experiences in 1903 and 1904, worsened with the years. After reaching middle age he no longer had any illusions about people, and pitilessly scrutinized all those around him just

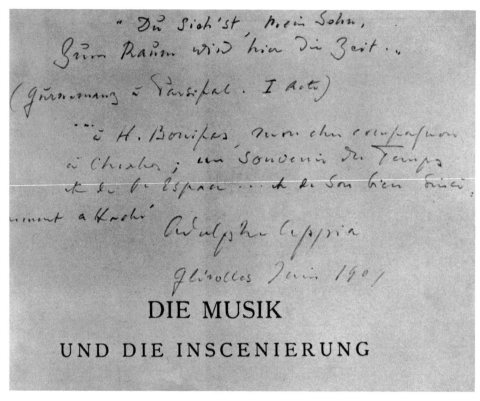

DIE MUSIK

UND DIE INSCENIERUNG

Figure 27. Title page of *Die Musik und die Inscenierung* with a dedication to his friend Bonifas. The quotation from *Parsifal* means: "Thou seest, my son, to space time changeth here." *W. R. Volbach.*

as he did himself. Yet for all his disappointments, he never blamed anyone but himself for his failures. As passionate as he could be in expressing his opinions, as ironical in his criticism, his attacks were never personal but were exclusively based on principles and on artistic ground.

The few who were allowed the benefit of Appia's company felt not only the strong impact of his fascinating art but also of his extraordinary personality. His own tensions notwithstanding, he was perfectly capable of dissipating the tensions of others. Henry C. Bonifas (1887–1952), Professor of Psychology at the University of Geneva, who wrote some pertinent essays about Appia, was a depressed young man when, about 1908, he first met the great artist in Dr. Reymond's sanatorium at Chexbres, located in the hills above Montreux, where Appia was recovering from intense exhaustion. Henry might have become an excellent pianist except that his left arm was an inch shorter than the right due to a fracture he had suffered at the age of thirteen. The two shared many interests, especially music; both were ardent admirers of Bach and Wagner, both regretted that their piano playing was far from perfect. Appia, though, did not care too much for this "corruptive" instrument,[32] feeling it was a poor substitute for an orchestra. They soon noticed that they suffered from similar repressions and inhibitions. Appia's influence on Henry was indirect, functioning through his very nature and genius as revealed in conversations which were "like the continuous building of bridges between different domains." With Appia's marvelous assistance, reports Henry's brother Paul, the young man was soon able to face the world again "without fear, without hate and false arrogance." Henry Bonifas gave up the study of theology and changed to his erstwhile love, music and eurythmics. Appia's encouragement remained his friend's guiding light when he later concentrated on psychology. Appia also came to the aid of Paul Bonifas, after others had tried in vain to straighten him out. The young man, who was to become a noted silversmith, was troubled about his future. Without ever giving direct advice Appia solved his problems with relative ease because, in his clear mind, he saw things nobody had seen before, and what he noticed was essential and to the point. His comments on Paul's designs were "like interpolations of plastic valves into feelings and human interpretation." Of prime importance in those prewar years was Appia's sense of humor, a faculty he lost with the years. Paul Bonifas describes the artist as "affectionate" but also "somewhat distant," like a man willing to help others but unwilling to allow any intrusion into his own affairs. A significant example of Appia's fine gift as a mentor of young people is given by Raymond Penel who gratefully remembers how Appia brought out everything valuable in him at a time when he was rejected by all others as "a bad boy." "To some degree he became my Socrates," adds Dr. Penel, who became a successful physician. Those who knew Appia well emphasize his extraordinary kindness. He went out of his way to help his friends, especially in cases of more serious troubles, yet even their small tribulations found a patient ear. Like an elder brother or an uncle, he took care of their daily life, down to his request that they rest a while after hours of hard work.

Many confirm that anyone who met Appia was immediately fascinated by him. This was not true, however, of the brothers Jean and René Morax, who built the Théâtre du Jorat in Mezières where they offered festivals after 1908, sometimes referred to as the "Bayreuth of the Jura."[33] René was a musician and dramatist, Jean a painter; both moved in artistic circles, particularly in Paris, from where they drew their collaborators. Their festival theatre was a simple frame building, with an equally simple interior, seating about 1100 people on wooden benches. Stage and house were connected by a broad staircase, and the productions were offered with a modicum of scenery, closely following Appia's ideas. Emphasis was on splendid and complicated lighting effects, and the use of movement.[34] In conversations with friends Appia delicately hinted at some sort of collaboration. This may have been wishful thinking, for Mercier who worked at Mezières for a while states definitely that there was no artistic relationship between them; however, he further maintains that the Morax brothers were inspired by Appia's ideas about theatre buildings and staging. They obviously used some of his suggestions but, at the same time, were jealous of him. According to another source, Appia went to see an *Orpheus* performance in 1911 and afterwards talked to René frankly, though tactfully, about all phases of the production, the strong and not so strong ones; he did not miss a single point.[35] This story, if true, and indeed it sounds true, may explain the lack of any further contact.

The man who knew Appia's sealed heart best was his physician, Dr. Oscar Forel (1891–   ). Dr. Forel, son of the famed Dr. August Forel and himself a leading Swiss psychiatrist, met the artist about 1918 in a Berne sanatorium where Appia stayed to recover either from nervous exhaustion or a bout with alcohol. In Berne and later in his own sanatorium he gained a deep insight in the artist's troubled heart, yet he does not pretend to have penetrated his most intimate thoughts. He noticed how at gatherings Appia was always correct, but frequently stood apart to listen and observe. He was considered "jovial and humorous," but the doctor cautions that this may have been "feigned rather than genuine. He laughed and joked with his lips while deep within himself he remained a tragic person." Therefore, even Dr. Forel feels he is not competent to interpret the workings of Appia's mind; he was "impenetrable, secretive, perhaps wary, almost distrustful." This personal analysis did not interfere with Appia's standing among the staff and patients. Again it must be pointed out that his outward joviality as well as his concern for others were of great help to Dr. Forel, for his attitude brought some joy into the miseries of others. It is no surprise to learn that the physician called him the "eternal young man."

His Pupils

APPIA has often been regarded as a great teacher though not in the usual sense of educator. He was too independent and too much of an introvert to function in this way. Students of Dalcroze in Geneva and Hellerau had the opportunity to partake of his enthusiasm and inspiration at informal sessions in the school or in his home. There were, however, meetings with one or never more than a few persons. His speech impediment made it impossible for him to lecture before a group, but he was always ready to explain his ideas to someone who showed talent and serious interest. Best of all he liked to coach a singer in one of his own favorite roles. Then he gave his all. His cousin, Blanche Claparède Bingham, remembered with deep emotion the many hours he spent with her going through every intricate detail of *Carmen*. She was then fourteen years old, but the wonderful interpretation of this demanding role which he imparted to her remained with her all her life.

In addition to Jacques Copeau, the self-styled disciple of Appia, two noted stage directors may truly be called his pupils: Jean Mercier and Oskar Waelterlin. Both were profoundly and decisively influenced; he opened their minds to the new art form of the theatre and taught them how to apply its principles. The two men proceeded very similarly in preparing a production; kindly and cooperative by nature, both knew how to treat sensitive performers; they carried no grudge against those who disagreed with them, yet they insisted on the highest standard, as the master had taught it. Both served their teacher with great distinction.

Jean Mercier (1895–   ) was born in the small town of Ballaigues, Canton de Vaud, near the French border. He was fourteen when he met Appia, by chance, in the sanatorium of Chexbres. Soon thereafter Appia left and settled at Glérolles where young Mercier visited him several times during the following years. In long conversations his interest in the theatre intensified, and Appia was, in fact, responsible for his decision to become a stage director. Mercier enrolled at the University of Geneva and Lausanne, receiving his bachelor's degree at the former and his licentiate at the latter. In 1914 the young actor participated in the *Fête de Juin* and toward the end of the first World War he joined the newly organized company of Georges Pitoëff as his assistant. Mercier remembers that Appia had a brief contact with Pitoëff. He attended some of the latter's productions in Geneva which he praised in general, and he talked to friends about him with high regard. Between 1919 and 1923 Mercier played an important part in Appia's life. In spite of the age difference Appia had infinite confidence in Mercier who sometimes felt that Appia virtually leaned on him, obeying him almost like a child. This absolute trust made it possible for Mercier to mediate in delicate situations between Appia and his brother Paul. In 1919 when Appia was in a state of extreme depression, Paul wanted to have him interned in a rest home near Neuchâtel and asked Mercier to do him the favor of going there to make the necessary arrangements. Mercier first agreed to assume this precarious responsibility but he changed his mind when he visited his older friend. He was so moved when he saw the deeply depressed master that he took him along to Geneva, to his own home, and had Appia live with his family at Clos Belmont where Mrs. Mercier managed a boardinghouse. Some time later Appia rented a room in the neighborhood but took all his meals with his friends; in summer he accompanied them to their châlet at La Comballaz-sur-Aigle. Their generous hospitality coupled with an altogether friendly home atmosphere in the city as well as in the mountains allowed Appia once more to concentrate on his work. His project to finish the manuscript of *L'Oeuvre d'art vivant* was carried through with Mercier helping as an author's adviser and later finding a publisher. During these four years Appia kept his friend informed about everything he was writing or designing.

The pleasant stay with the Merciers was ended by Paul, who was anxious to get his bohemian brother out of Geneva to spare the staid Appia reputation. He insisted on moving him to the sanatorium Waldau near Berne. Since Paul held the purse strings, he won—and Appia had to leave Geneva. Unhappy and feeling "demoralized" in the sanatorium, he begged Mercier to save him. Again Mercier, the benign spirit, came to the rescue and brought him back to his home over the doctors' protest and, of course, over Paul's. At Waldau only one physician approved of Mercier's action, Dr. Forel, then on the staff of the sanatorium, who fully realized that all Appia needed was moral support by benevolent and understanding friends. Mercier, always ready to answer Appia's call for help, did so without ever asking any favor in return. Appreciating his many invaluable services, Appia sometimes called him "my Kurvenal."

Oskar Waelterlin (1895–1961) appeared rather late in Appia's life. After receiving his doctor of philosophy degree in his native Basel he became an actor in the municipal theatre of that city. He soon assumed the duties of dramaturgist and stage director. He had the great luck to be initiated in modern scenic ideas, particularly those of Adolphe Appia, by an older but progressive colleague, Dr. Ernst Lert. It may well have been Lert who advised Waelterlin to see the great reformer. Mercier remembers that he arranged their first meeting, which took place either in his mountain châlet or at Waldau-Berne about 1920. By the fall of that year a plan was inaugurated to stage *The Ring* in Basel with Appia's designs, a plan which did not materialize as the master was not well enough to execute the demanding preparatory work. Waelterlin then decided to direct some productions with Appia as adviser. Wagner's *Siegfried, Tristan, Parsifal, The Mastersingers,* and Shakespeare's *Hamlet* were prepared by relying on the designer's detailed letters and scenarios.[36] It is of interest to discover that the scenic innovations which differed so thoroughly from the conventional staging received high praise. Thus the last setting of *Siegfried* was called "monumental" and giving "the impression of an almost unlimited mountain world," in spite of the comparatively small scenic frame.[37] This objective evaluation of Appia's designs ought to be kept in mind with reference to the production of Wagner's *The Ring* staged in new settings a few years later. Waelterlin met Appia again in 1922 and 1923 at Mercier's summer châlet where, especially on his second visit, the project to present the entire Cycle during a single season was thoroughly discussed although no specific dates were set at the time.

Appia's association with Waelterlin was exclusively professional. Mercier was Appia's friend in whom he had unqualified confidence and on whose assistance he relied when faced with artistic and personal problems. In Waelterlin he found a young stage director who was in a position to materialize on stage his designs and scenarios. It must be added, however, that no selfish motives were involved on Appia's part. Appia was extremely grateful to these two pupils and friends. Both were close to his heart though for different reasons.

A profile of Adolphe Appia, the great artist and man, shows many facets, some of them so contrasting that one can scarcely imagine them combined in one human being. To lump all characteristic features together under a general denominator would therefore be a grave mistake. The proper way seems to be simply to state the fact that his conflicting features or peculiarities existed side by side, some dominating in his youth, others coming to the fore later, and still others so salient when he was old that they made him appear almost like a different man. And most of the time one can detect an undercurrent of traits at war with those on the surface. To understand and explain the tremendous force of this strange man, it is important to remember his deeply rooted optimism. It enabled him to continue his reform in the face of the internal and external obstacles which prevented him from bringing to fruition the work that alone gave his life sense and purpose. Appia was able to justify his optimism by his utmost confidence in his ideas and their future. No disappointment could destroy this trust. His secret strength, as he confided to a relative—not in arrogance, but rather with an undertone of sadness—was the judgment he had made about himself: "I know that I am a genius."

Figure 28. Adolphe Appia, ca. 1923. *Jean Mercier.*

V

An Invitation from Toscanini

Toward the end of 1922 when he was past sixty, fate smiled on Adolphe Appia, offering him an opportunity to join the mainstream of theatrical life. At that time he met through Dalcroze Marchese Emanuele de Rosalès, an Italian sculptor who was not only interested in eurythmics but also in modern scenic art. This artist spread several enticing plans before Appia; he intended to arrange an exhibit of Appia's designs in Milan and in connection with it to prepare a performance of *Echo and Narcissus* with Dalcroze's students, and still more intriguing, to interest Arturo Toscanini, then the artistic director of La Scala, in a production of *Tristan and Isolde* with Appia's designs.[1]

A few months later the maestro actually invited Appia to collaborate in the preparation of a new *mise en scène;* but de Rosalès was not the only one responsible for that invitation. In 1922 the Milanese Conservatory of Music had a strong class in eurythmics and the names of Dalcroze and Appia were highly esteemed. Toscanini, always abreast of developments, was already acquainted with the work of this group when de Rosalès called the maestro's attention to Appia's new art. Walter Toscanini believes that his father had read *L'Art théâtral moderne* (1910) by Jacques Rouché, who had thoroughly discussed Appia's revolutionary conception in his book. Furthermore, he assumes that R. Aloys Mooser, a music critic in Geneva, had talked to his father about Appia. Count Emanuele di Castelbarco, too, must be mentioned in connection with these prearrangements. He was deeply interested and highly versed in poetry and dramatic art, and was the president of La Bottega di Poesia in Milan, headed an art gallery, a bookstore, and a publishing house. Walter Toscanini was active in the latter. Lastly, Dr. Ernst Lert, chosen as stage director for the forthcoming production, may have had at least some influence. During the two decades of his artistic management of La Scala, Toscanini was both musical and stage director. All sketches for the settings had to have his approval and so had the costumes and the light plot. In addition he advised his singers in the art of acting and even corrected their make-up. He was indeed as much concerned with staging as with conducting.

To present Wagner's music drama in a scenic frame contrary to the accepted norm included a risk for all participants even under the protection of the illustrous name of Toscanini. No one "could measure the audacity," wrote Appia about his experience in Milan.[2] Milan was hardly ready for a scenic revolution. A few experiments had been tried after World War I—by Enzo Ferrieti with his Teatro de Convegno, and above all, by Duilio Cambellotti who fully accepted Appia's austere stylization and applied it in the reorganization of the Istituto del Drama Antico.[3] But these attempts were devoted to plays, while the lyric theatre remained untouched by any modern trend. The sponsors of the operatic experiment did everything in their power to prepare the ultraconservative patrons of La Scala for the daring venture. An exhibit of Appia's designs was arranged and attracted many curious visitors. The club Il Covegno, whose director was Walter Toscanini, invited Appia to give a lecture with slide demonstrations. Shunning the limelight as usual, the artist declined to speak, but La Bottega di Poesia published one of his essays, *Art vivant? ou nature morte? (Living Art or Dead Nature?)* written a year earlier for the International Exhibition in Amsterdam. Its new edition created so much interest that it had a second printing in 1924. Il Covegno also issued an Italian version of his essay *La Mise en scène et son avenir (Theatrical Production and Prospects in the Future)*, written in 1920, in addition to a long evaluation by Gio Ponti of Appia's work augmented by several of his designs. Appia's supporters, moreover, led a vigorous campaign which included articles with and without sketches for newspapers in Milan. Toscanini, his son, and those connected with La Bottega di Poesia were extremely busy smoothing the rough road for Appia's scenic reform.

In the summer of 1923 Appia went to Milan to meet Toscanini and talk with some of his staff members. His dislike for technical details and his shyness before strangers prompted him to ask for an assistant. First, he suggested Oskar Waelterlin, but when the young director was unable to obtain a leave of absence from Basel, he recommended his other friend and pupil, Jean Mercier, who in late fall joined him in Milan for about four rehearsal weeks. A star-studded ensemble was brought together by Toscanini—the Russian tenor Stefano Bielina sang Tristan; the Swedish soprano Nanny Larsen was cast as Isolde; and among the Italian singers, Ezio Pinza took on Marke. The program of the production reads that *Tristan* was staged by Appia in cooperation with Lert and da Caramba. A recheck of other available sources, particularly Jean Mercier, permits a more precise statement: Lert served as stage director in full accord with Appia's designs of the settings and costumes. Appia of course devised the lighting. He and Mercier dealt with the technical heads —da Caramba, in charge of costuming; G. B. Santori, who built the scenery in the shop; and Giovanni and Peride Ansalda, the technical supervisors on stage.

During the first piano rehearsals he attended, Appia became reconciled to the Italian translation. His previous abhorrence of a French version had naturally made him wary of the Italian, but twenty years had obviously mellowed him. He confessed to Mercier that the Italian translation—by Verdi's excellent librettist Arrigo Boito—was quite acceptable. When he thus approved of *Tristan* in Italian, he recalled Wagner's own statement that the composition, especially Act II, was inspired by the Italian language.[4]

The *Tristan* Production

THE great day, December 20, 1923, arrived. Appia himself did not attend opening night nor the second performance two days later. The strain of the preparatory work had been too much for him and he remained at his hotel. Besides, he dreaded the moment of finding himself in the center of curiosity, exposed, like a star, to the gaze of the spectators. Therefore, it became Mercier's task to check the stage before curtain time, then to rush to the royal box in the rear of the auditorium where he and the master electrician were in constant contact by telephone with the technicians backstage. During the troublesome technical rehearsals, Mercier was so active that the crew members addressed him as "maestro," a compliment he enjoyed very much.

Appia was not completely happy with Lert's directing. The two men had high regard for one another, but a few times Lert's touchiness about receiving advice caused a tension between them. Since Appia had his own ideas about the staging of *Tristan*, he could not refrain from criticizing some arrangements, specifically those at the end of Act I which he later described in a letter to Waelterlin as "inadequate" and resembling "a glee club." Appia was in a delicate situation regarding Lert because, in his capacity as designer, he had really no right to interfere in the acting other than perhaps to exchange views with the stage director. But Appia always thought of himself as a stage director; and as the designer of a production based on an entirely new approach, he felt justified in making suggestions that might integrate all phases of the production. He deplored Lert's concentration on too many details without "concern for dramatic perspective." In his opinion Lert tried and irritated the singers "with many nonessentials unnoticeable on an immense stage," as he informed Waelterlin. Nevertheless, generally speaking, Appia was extremely grateful for the cooperation and support Lert gave him.

The performance of *Tristan*, at least its musical phase, was a huge success; the patrons acclaimed the singers after each act and jubilantly welcomed Toscanini and Lert after the final curtain. But the artist who had conceived the revolutionary new *mise en scène* was absent. How would the audience have reacted to Appia's appearance? Conversations during the intermissions indicated that the scenic reform had gained few friends. Underneath the surface of enthusiasm for maestro Toscanini, his orchestra, and his singers, one could detect antagonism toward the designer. The Latin temperament under these circumstances might have exploded in condemnation, for Italian audiences have often expressed their indignation in no uncertain terms. Indeed, yells of "Wagner" or "Calvinist" were heard after the performance,[5] and, in fact, derogatory remarks continued even as recently as 1951 when Ugo Ojetti called Appia "an irreconcilable Calvinist."[6]

To be sure the settings of *Tristan* shocked many patrons of La Scala who, used to the convention of sumptuous scenery, missed "seeing something real" on stage. Followers of Bayreuth in particular insisted on a replica or at least a simile of Wagner's settings; they were absolutely opposed to any innovation whatever, let alone such a drastic one as was Appia's. Against these inveterate prejudices even the prestige of Toscanini proved ineffectual. Today, forty years later, we can hardly understand that only a small minority sensed the inner beauty which the unusual settings transmitted, and recognized some ingredients of truly superb quality in this *Tristan*.

In the appendix to *Music and the Art of the Theatre* Appia included a detailed scenario that explains his designs magnificently. Passages in several critiques, Appia's own review of the production, and a letter he wrote Waelterlin prove that the execution of the settings came very close to his wishes, and that basically, the artist had not changed in 1923 the plans he had conceived before 1900. Two of Appia's books and the *Portfolio* of 1929 contain several of his sketches which give a good notion of what the performance in Milan looked like.

In his first analysis Appia had decided that the scenery of *Tristan* could be limited to a bare minimum, since emphasis on the inner development of the two leading characters relegated the external action to a minor role. His aim was then, as he wrote in his scenario, to make "the audience see the drama through the eyes of the hero and heroine." Consequently he planned the three settings of this music drama in such a manner that nothing, nothing whatever, could distract from the inner action. The setting of Act I, the ship carrying Isolde and Tristan, was indeed simple. An enormous tent, or, rather, very long, dark-reddish drapes, divided the ship into two areas. Downstage belonged to Isolde and Brangaene; upstage, visible when the drapes opened, was the domain of Tristan, of Kurvenal, and the crew. The dividing curtain symbolically separated "the outer world from the expression of inner life." In his letter to Waelterlin, Appia added these details: "Tent very little depth—a kind of bas relief: here all was of a beautiful dark red in spite of the great distance. The ship simple, expressive, very close, without mast, some ropes, very large helm." While the tent was closed it was starkly illuminated so that the characters were entirely visible. When the curtain opened, much of this light **was** dimmed to make the tent appear in silhouette. For the cyclorama Appia was able to use the perfected Fortuny system which made it possible for him to "paint with light." Yet he disapproved of a definite color for the light that illuminated the cyclorama. And though Mercier's choice of dark blue for it gave real depth to the setting, Appia declined to be responsible for such an effect. Otherwise the lighting was in accord with his original concept and hence it fully satisfied him.

The artist considered the first act least complex and dealt with it last in his scenario, after devoting much space to the other two settings. For the clandestine meeting of the lovers in Act II, the terrace and garden are described in detail; he pondered carefully all problems posed by the characters' movements and moods, and his wishes were hence the upshot of thorough deliberations. As his sketches for this act were all kept in chiaroscuro—in brighter light only around the terrace where a large torch was attached to the wall—it is possible to compare them with his scenario. Even the shadowy designs indicate that almost the entire stage floor was arranged on many levels, composed of platforms, ramps, and steps. On basis of his description, a floor plan can readily be set up; better than the sketches, it shows the pertinence of his spatial arrangement. Of course there were no "real" trees in his staging, merely reddish-brown drapes shaped to give the impression of trees. Drapes also encircled the wings and the upstage area. The walls of the terrace and the castle were kept in greenish gray; the only truly non-neutral color was in some borders that indicated tree foliage, and it took Mercier no little persuasion to have the master accept this bit of a green hue. Particularly effective was a magic violet light filling the air during the love duet. Appia was very pleased with the over-all impression of the spatial setting and its lighting. Only one platform differed slightly from his design; but he did not think that the change fundamentally affected his concept. A compromise was made in the lighting, which some "influential persons" wanted to be "more realistic." It is charming to read of Appia's naive joy in the skillful construction of the extremely important torch, which in the end was larger than his sketch indicated. "It consisted of three candles cast into a single one with a large wick and the whole encased in a sheath of wood," so he told Waelterlin. From the auditorium the device could not be detected. Isolde extinguished the flame in watersoaked sawdust, which was spread on the steps at the corner of the castle. Mischievously, Appia mentioned that this trick defied the fire department's ordinance.

The execution of Act III met with his complete approval. Again he made a few insignificant concessions. In his judgment this setting, "so very closely integrated with the music, became irresistible." The major part of the stage floor was raised to several levels. The floor dropped from the stage-right platforms which represented the wall; beyond these the sky, but not the sea, could be seen. The floor then rose toward the tree trunk on the opposite side, dropping again toward the wall on the extreme left. Thus, as Appia describes it in his scenario, the spectator had

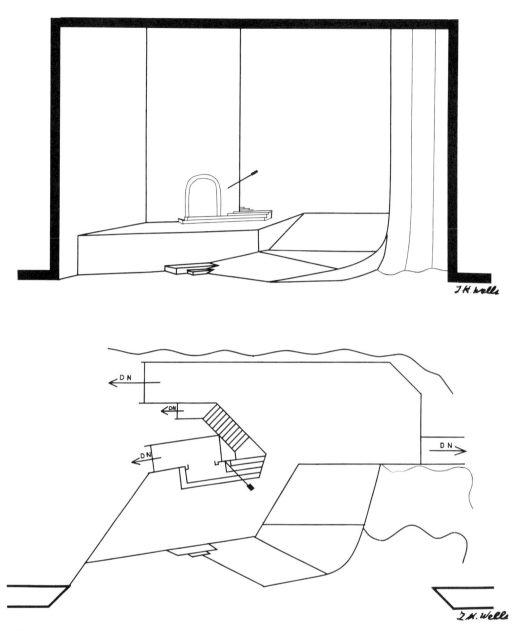

Figure 29. *Tristan and Isolde,* elevation and floorplan of Act II, drawn from Appia's design and description. *Terry H. Wells.*

the impression of "an incline from left to right and the light, falling from the right and increasingly slanting, will eventually strike the base of the buttress." The greatest care was taken in planning the light plot of this act. How at the beginning sunbeams barely touch Tristan's feet, how later the setting sun covers him ever more fully, how the stage darkens toward the end—all these transitions were of the utmost importance, while color played virtually no role in the setting of grayish-brown walls and a plain brown tree trunk. He was especially impressed by the mood of the closing scene. "Isolde, of extraordinary beauty, had enough light until the end," he wrote Waelterlin, "to show the transfiguration in her face—then suddenly when she fell on Tristan, the light faded away unnoticeably into dark night."

The Critical Response

THE printed judgment by the members of the press was divided. While a few ultra-conservative reviewers damned the production outright, others more progressive were at least willing to accept some or all of Appia's ideas, though not their application. The main complaint was directed against the use of so many drapes: drapes around the entire acting area, drapes representing branches and trunks of trees, this was simply too much. Strong misgivings were uttered moreover about the absence of colors in the settings, which led many to find them drab and unimpressive. The view across the sea was missed too. One critic indicated that Appia's designs might be more suitable to a smaller stage than to the huge measurements in Milan. With a proscenium opening 16 meters wide, 10 meters high, and a possible stage depth of 35 meters, one can imagine that the intimate qualities in Appia's concept were lost or anyway not appreciated by the aficionados of opera accustomed to settings overloaded with details.

Not a single aspect of Appia's design was acceptable to the reporter of *Corriere Della Sera;* nevertheless he conceded that the artist, "a scholar and idealist in the metaphysical sense and a poet," had the good idea to overthrow the conventional settings, which for him were merely "a series of colored cardboards."[7] Less detached was the writer who in *Il Popolo d'Italia* condemned "the sacrilegious concept" of this production. He was specifically annoyed by the omission of true colors, although he too admitted that pictorial realism was dead.[8] Words such as "ridiculous," "shameful," "pretentious" appear in the review of *L'Avanti*, evidently written by a member of the editorial staff who made no attempt to understand Appia's esthetics.[9] Carlo Gatti, who in 1926 as author of *Il Teatro alla Scala Rinnovata* included an extended, if not particularly laudatory, review of *Tristan*, served as critic for *Illustrazione Italiana* in 1923. After attending opening night he was puzzled rather than malevolent, finding the scenery so simplified that it "did not allow one's imagination to run freely." Yet he praised among other things the choice of background colors which made the costumes stand out sharply.[10]

Three comprehensive articles appeared in *Il Secolo,* one immediately after the first performance, the other two the following month, surely a token of the significance this newspaper attributed to the scenic experiment which, in the opinion of the first critic, had "the flavor of battle," and hence was "anti-academic and alive." After the opening night Adriano Lualdi pointed out that there existed "discrepancies" in the usage of drapes and a "profound gulf between the spirit and style of Wagner's masterpiece and the spirit and style of the setting," but he did not fail to mention the beautiful impressions provided by the color scheme of Isolde's blue costume against the red drapes in Act I, the light effect in Act II when the singers fused with the setting "in a symphony of blue and silver," and above all the startling effect of Kurvenal's shadow in the last act.[11] In the middle of January the same paper brought another review written by Raffaele Calzini who, having attended *Tristan* twice, confessed that Appia's creations were after all not so "horribly out of place and impossible." On the contrary he acknowledged a definite relation of the singers to the atmosphere surrounding them, but he somehow missed a style unifying all elements of the production. So he wrote: "If Larsen's rhythmic recitation had been matched by all the other artists, by the simplified scenery and costumes, then the pictorial illusion would have been stronger." Signor Calzini was deeply impressed with the violet lighting in Act II as reminiscent of Previati's paintings, furthermore by some groupings which, he thought, resembled those in pictures of Tintoretto, Boecklin, and Rembrandt. He concluded that at any rate *Tristan* was "a very beautiful experiment" and expressed the hope that the cool reception by the patrons and some critics would deter neither Appia nor Gordon Craig from continuing their fight for a scenic reform.[12] The third article was more an esthetic analysis than a critique. In the first paragraph the verb "repels" seemed to introduce the tenor of the whole piece. One reads for instance about the "childish coarseness of some simplified forms" but, fortunately, such blunt statements notwithstanding, the writer made every attempt to acknowledge Appia's fine pioneering ideas and work. He understood the master's intentions quite well, noticing the smooth transition from the auditorium to the stage achieved by the light plot. The scenic style was compared with that of Caravaggio's paintings, the style of Act III with that of Rembrandt's etchings. Some misgivings about the extreme simplification caused the commentator to use the term "cubism" in referring deprecatingly to the many straight surfaces, cylindrical tree trunks, and the straight drapes substituting for branches. And yet, the revolutionary solution in general was welcomed. Impressed by "the poetic light effects, the psychological intimacy and sense of mystery," the writer was moved to grant the production a touch of "sheer genius" and "new grandeur."[13]

The Aftermath

ARTURO TOSCANINI was deeply distressed that his endeavor to modernize the staging at La Scala was appreciated by no more than a handful of connoisseurs. In his son's words Toscanini "was never interested in experimenting with ultra-modern and futuristic nonsense, yet he was always looking for stage improvements and new ideas, and to him the ideas and sketches of Appia must have appealed as a possibility of realizing the eternal love legend of Tristan and Isolde in an atmosphere of dream without dated epoch." In addition to opening night on December 20, the maestro conducted the music drama on December 22, 29, and on January 2, 5, and 13, a total of six performances. There was no *Tristan* for many years afterwards, for the sad experience affected the great conductor so profoundly that during the remaining years of his directorship at La Scala this music drama was never again scheduled.

If Appia was disappointed in his great expectations, even discouraged—and how could he not have been—he did not reveal any depressed mood to his friends. In describing his various experiences later on, he tried to analyze objectively the reasons for the unsuccessful outcome of his scenic reform. He wrote frankly about the passive resistance of some members of the technical staff who opposed his new ideas. Toscanini encouraged him whenever trouble arose: "Speak up, Monsieur Appia!" he admonished him. There were conflicts between the designer and the stage crew when the settings were to be mounted and particularly when the immense drapes had to be hung. As Walter Toscanini remembers this situation, "the stagehands were practical men, who wanted precise directions and orders, and Appia was never able to give such orders, to give exact instructions on how to hang, where to hang, what to do with the lights." He is convinced his father prodded Appia "to spring into action." But this was not Appia's forte, and Mercier, doing his best to arrange all technical details, could not be everywhere; besides, he was not the designer-in-charge. In addition to his frustrating speech defect and his dislike for technical details, Appia's predicament was further aggravated by the prevailing conditions in Italian opera houses where, in his opinion, opera performances were more or less costumed concerts in which music, especially vocal prowess, was all that counted. His experience with indolent technicians must have been agonizing, for several essential questions were not settled until about curtain time. But "how to display impatience or irritation toward gentlemen who, even at the most critical moments, do not drop their exquisite courtesy?"[14] Significant of the atmosphere during the preparatory period at La Scala is an anecdote related by Appia. At the dress rehearsal of a newly mounted production, the technical director came into the darkened house during one of the intermissions and said to Appia so loudly that everyone could hear: "This, Monsieur Appia, is the grandiose style as it should be." This hidebound attitude and the slipshod habit of improvising were hard to bear for an artist who strove for a perfect fusion of all the elements of a production—a goal that required open minds and meticulous preparation.

Apart from these reservations, Appia freely acknowledged whatever cooperation he received. His wholehearted gratitude was accorded Arturo Toscanini whose musical interpretation of Wagner's music drama achieved "the limit of perfection." He was very happy, moreover, about the support he received from Toscanini's son, from a group of new friends whose faith in him never wavered, and above all from Jean Mercier without whose assistance the production might never have been finished. He also greatly appreciated a few kind words indicating that not all staff members of La Scala rejected his scenic ideas. Thus Mercier reported that, in a rehearsal of Mascagni's *Iris*, he overheard a stage director say: "What a dirty thing after *Tristan!*" The best consolation came in an open letter from Senator Enrico Corradini:

> I believe you will welcome my opinion about your *mise en scène* of *Tristan and Isolde.* . . . For the first time the settings conspired with the music and the drama to lift my spirit into the sphere of poetry. And in *Tristan and Isolde*, drama, music, and poetry are mysteries. Your settings express, as it were, the mystery. The scenic picture, as any great art, must be very schematic. It must be transfiguration in order to accomplish the transfiguration of the soul.[15]

Appia expressed his deeply felt thanks with a personal note to the senator.

In Milan Appia encountered the fate of many a reformer whose new ideas were not objectively discussed but were simply ridiculed and slandered. And like pioneers before him, he did not succumb to defeatism. Confident beyond any doubt that his concept of a new scenic form would eventually break through the barrier of inertia, he continued to defend and promote his ideas, even though he had little chance to see them materialize. But in his letter to Waelterlin about his production at La Scala, he wrote, "Not for a million francs would I start it again—with these delightful but inconsistent people who keep you in a state of excrutiating anxiety day after day."

The Rhinegold in Basel

His vow to resist another offer and hence to spare himself another sad experience was forgotten as soon as Appia received a definite invitation from the Municipal Theatre in Basel. The negotiations, discussed in the preceding chapter, had been initiated years before, when Oskar Waelterlin had first met Appia, and they led at last to an agreement in 1924. The offer was most enticing: Wagner's entire *Ring* was to be produced with Appia's settings; according to some reports the artist was to be paid 2,000 francs for his work. Since middling theatres rarely have an item in

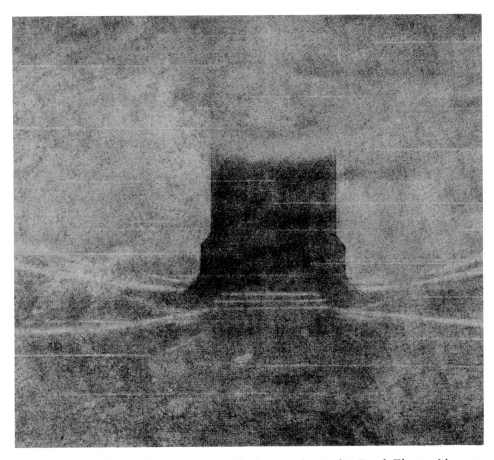

Figure 30. *The Rhinegold,* Scene 1. An early design submitted to Basel. *Theater Museum, Munich.*

their budget for so eminent a guest, the assumption is that some of Appia's friends donated this money to the theatre.

Dr. Lert, who had been instrumental in engaging Appia, had left Basel, but Waelterlin, his successor, was only too glad to materialize the plan. The Swiss city on the Rhine maintained a highly respected theatre though, of course, in size or in artistic and financial means, it could in no way compete with La Scala. Yet there Appia was to find what he missed in Milan, unstinted cooperation. Otto Henning, the managing director, made every effort to keep a high standard with a comparatively small subsidy. In this theatre, rebuilt in 1909 after a destructive fire, patrons were accustomed to see fine productions of plays, operas, and operettas. Since the subscribers of season tickets were entitled to a new production every week, not many rehearsals for each individual production could be allocated on the main stage; a considerable part of the rehearsals had to be scheduled in a large room. Under this condition, evidently not enough hours could be granted to so complex an experiment as Appia's *mise en scène* of *The Ring,* although everything feasible was done to prepare a good performance. The stage had a depth of 16 meters, the proscenium opening was 10 meters wide. A real cyclorama was not installed until 1934; thus for *The Ring* merely a conventional skydrop was available. The lighting system was limited; there were footlights and border lights but only two strong spotlights with so much spill that a "funnel" had to be attached in front of them whenever a narrow beam was desired. Four additional special lamps could be equipped with color filters of yellow, red, and blue. A few arclights in the first balcony were of no use to Appia's lighting plot; however, footlights were needed as the only means to illuminate the downstage area adequately.[16]

Thus Waelterlin had to put up with an imperfect lighting system and with a lack of rehearsals on the main stage, but this handicap was amply offset by his excellent preparation for the staging. He had discussed almost every detail with Appia, who years earlier had given him extensive oral and written instructions for producing *The Ring.* In fact Appia had acted out for him many passages in his restrained style. Although the designer had indeed countless wishes and suggestions, he was always modest and humble, never demanding or arrogant. He attended the stage rehearsals and, on occasion, talked to the singers and also demonstrated his interpretation. Everything worked out to his satisfaction. On November 21, 1924, *The Rhinegold,* the prelude of Wagner's cycle, was presented to the public. Waelterlin was the guiding spirit and intermediary of Appia's conception. Yet the musical and technical achievements of Gottfried Becker, the conductor, and Hermann Jenny-Bergner, the technical director, should by no means be underrated. In that year *The Rhinegold* was performed five times, on November 21, 24, December 7, 17, and 23.

Before opening night the management of the theatre assiduously enlightened the public about things to come. In the weeks preceding the first night, an exhibit

Figure 31. *The Rhinegold*, Scenes 2 and 4. An early design submitted to Basel. *Theater Museum, Munich.*

Figure 32. *The Rhinegold*, Scene 2, as staged in Basel. *Institut fuer Theaterwissenschaft, Cologne.*

Figure 33. The Rhinegold, Scene 3, as staged in Basel. *Institut fuer Theaterwissenschaft, Cologne.*

Figure 34. The Rhinegold, Scene 4, as staged in Basel. *Institut fuer Theaterwissenschaft, Cologne.*

of Appia's designs was shown in a hall of the Gewerbemuseum, stories were released to the newspapers, and Waelterlin explained the new scenic art in two brief articles printed in the theatre's program book. Even a special introductory lecture was arranged on November 16; the announcement stated: "Beckmesser will yell and fill his blackboard with marks, but we trust Hans Sachs and the sound judgment of the people who do not always need sensations such as moving dragons but who respectfully bow before greatness."[17] Evidently both the theatre's manager and Waelterlin anticipated strong opposition from the conservative elements of the audience and thus attempted to mitigate potential trouble.

What the settings of *The Rhinegold* and then *The Valkyrie* really looked like is not so easy to ascertain as it was in the case of *Tristan*. The descriptions in reviews are vague, as they generally are; they do not jibe, moreover, with the photographs and sketches available in the library of the Municipal Theatre. The models of the settings are not accessible to everyone (they are the property of the Theatermuseum des Instituts fuer Theaterwissenschaft der Universitaet Koeln); pictures of the production appeared in the German periodical, *Buehnentechnische Rundschau,* and in a book on the Basel theatre. In addition, there are Appia's new scenarios for *The Ring* which he prepared in 1923–1924. The settings were definitely not based on the designs the artist had devised in the nineties; but it is not completely clear why he relied in Milan on his original ideas and a year later insisted on his new style in Basel. The *mise en scène,* as Appia planned it for Basel, had no resemblance to his previous conception; the last trace of romanticism and symbolism was erased. Appia had reached an extreme point of simplification; the settings were a composite of platforms, various levels, stairs, ramps, a few pillars, drapes covering the wings and occasionally the upstage area, and often a plain blue-gray backdrop; in addition, a traveler cutting off the upstage area provided a more intimate atmosphere for two scenes in *The Valkyrie.* When Lert and Waelterlin began to discuss the plan for a production, Appia apparently first considered using his more conservative sketches, but when in 1924 the production finally materialized, he decided on his new radical solution and then submitted new designs which conformed to the ideas he had developed in his rhythmic spaces for Dalcroze in Hellerau and Geneva. The models Appia made underwent in the final settings some modifications necessitated by the limited measurements of the Basel stage.

The new scenarios, far less elaborate than the first series, strikingly bear witness to his increasing tendency toward simplification. Artistic as well as technical reasons prompted him to devise a unit arrangement of platforms for the four settings of *The Rhinegold,* an arrangement that was less complicated than his original conception. The center piece of the first scene was a rock-like platform with the gold imbedded at the top; this was actually the only set piece added to the basic unit. A scrim in front of the setting gave it an atmosphere of unreality; however no waves were projected on this scrim; this traditional feature was omitted. Alberich had to remain on the stage floor proper during the entire scene except for his climbing to the top of the rock. The Rhine Maidens of course used no swimming apparatus; instead they were to crawl, almost glide, on the floor and across the platforms with slow arm movements to create the general impression. To prepare the three singers for their new task Appia approached Gustav Gueldenstein, a pupil of Dalcroze and director of eurythmic courses in Basel. Since Appia despised imitation, the Rhine Maidens were not permitted to use any gesture which might remind the spectators of swimming.[18] To support their movements, to have them appear and disappear, light came up and faded respectively. No scenic and light effects required by Wagner were used for the transition from one setting to the next; simply the main curtain was drawn during the musical interludes.

In the second setting nothing distracted from the backdrop on which projected clouds and a gauze scrim masked Valhalla, the castle of the gods. In harmony with the music the scrim rose and the clouds faded to free the view of the castle, which dominated the stage from then on and again through the last scene. The spatial arrangement consisted mainly of a large platform across the width of the stage, a few smaller ones, and drapes on both sides. Appia's wish to have the scenic picture focused on Valhalla expressed his thought that the castle symbolized Wotan's dream of ruling the world. In his scenario Appia insisted that the castle "must be painted with utmost care and exactly correspond to the proportions of my design." This was done, and it was painted on a transparent backdrop, lit from behind. In the last scene the conventional rainbow serving as a bridge leading to Valhalla did not appear. Besides, Appia changed the ending: usually Loge remains onstage, but in Basel all characters made their exit and the stage was empty during the final musical passage. The cave of the Nibelung, the third setting, "looked like a slanted pit" with a heavy column supporting the low ceiling. Here Waelterlin altered Appia's plan to use the rock of the first scene as the column and had another set piece made for it. The upstage area was masked by grayish-blue drapes struck by red light from a wing. An interesting innovation was Appia's treatment of the treasure which Alberich had to give Wotan as ransom. Instead of the traditional jewelry and trinkets, the dwarfs carried onstage plain large gold ingots which in the last scene resembled a wall when heaped in front of Freya. Depressing in all its glitter, it created a tragic mood; this was what the designer hoped to accomplish with the simplification which was so eminently successful in Basel.

The costuming was not always felicitously handled, although much thought had been given to this phase. Financial considerations probably prevailed in having Loge wear a modified Mephistopheles costume out of the theatre stock in compliance with Appia's wish to have him dressed in red. As a result of not enough stage rehearsals the giants, Fafner and Fasolt, in simple black garb and death-like masks, ran into trouble with their large spiked clubs, which in the first performance got caught in the drapes, an embarrassing mishap that made many in the audience smile.[19]

As in Milan, Appia shunned the theatre on opening night. Extremely tense and nervous, he remained in his nearby hotel, but shortly before the final curtain Waelterlin, sensing a success, brought, or rather dragged, him from his room over to the stage where the shy artist appeared before a spontaneously applauding audience. The reviews too approved many of Appia's reform ideas. With one exception they were laudatory, if with reservations in several cases. In general, the artistic conception of settings, costumes, properties, and lighting, and in particular Waelterlin's direction, were welcomed. The *Basler Anzeiger* stated that the new scenic version, "basically a substantial simplification," strengthened the fundamental thought of the music drama. This critic was impressed specifically by the setting for the second and fourth scenes, a wide, open place "framed by drapes and stairs with the fantastic and indistinct form of a castle in the background." The writer concluded that Appia's concept allowed "the inner action and the contrasting characters to stand out."[20] Another commentator voiced admiration for Appia's great ideas even though not everything was "perfect."[21] A third reviewer was not happy with the Depth of the Rhine setting, but otherwise, he commended the "exquisite taste and genial creative imagination in the design of every piece of the setting, and also the well-planned light effects. In perfect harmony does one thing fit into another; nowhere is there any weak point, any mistake."[22] Further articles in Basel and other Swiss cities were written in the same vein with epithets such as "greatness" or "triumph" to describe the impact.[23] When Karl Reyle wrote in the *Berner Tagblatt* that "the most important result was a deep and close contact with the audience," Appia was so pleased that someone really understood him and his work that he sent a warm personal note. In a Swiss weekly the simplified settings were considered possibly at variance with Wagner's style yet felicitously successful in tying together the four scenes.[24]

A lonely but shrill voice pierced the general pleasant atmosphere of approval. Not a single good word was said about Appia in the review of the *Basler Volksblatt*. Since this voice was apparently significant and symptomatic of the entire opposition, which later became a power behind the scene, the gist of the commentary is given here:

> The first impression is disappointing. . . . One illusion after another is destroyed, the music characterizes actions that have meaning only for those who are familiar with the score, the eye must become accustomed to performers who merely sing but do nothing else. With the best of our intentions we cannot favor such interpretation of Wagnerian art, even at the risk of being alone in our judgment; however according to many in the audience this may not be the case. This *mise en scène* is a blow to Wagner's artistic wishes. . . . Richard Wagner will turn in his grave!!! You may be sure of that, *Herr* Appia![25]

Figure 35. *The Valkyrie,* Act I, as staged in Basel. *Institut fuer Theaterwissenschaft, Cologne.*

Figure 36. *The Valkyrie,* Act I, as staged in Basel. *Institut fuer Theaterwissenschaft, Cologne.*

Scandal Surrounding *The Valkyrie*

As far as can be ascertained there was only the one wholly adverse critique of *The Rhinegold*. Yet there may have been an agreement, tacit at the time, between the sharp-tongued reviewer and a group whose members became vociferous when *The Valkyrie* was presented in its revolutionary *mise en scène*. Scene rehearsals started early in 1925, and on February 1, this music drama was performed with the same production staff as for *The Rhinegold*. Further performances were scheduled on February 5, 9, 13, and 23. The general mood of the audience and the critics again was appreciative, full of interest and praise for Appia's principles though with some unfavorable critical remarks. This time the opposition, better prepared for opening night than the friends of the artistic endeavor, wildly demonstrated after the final curtain. The disturbance was, however, ignored by most newspapers, except the *Schweizer Arbeiter Zeitung* and the *Basler Volkblatt*, which vituperated the production.

A brief description of the staging, as devised by Appia and executed by Waelterlin and his collaborators, will help explain the ensuing tumult. The interior setting used all of Act I was entirely solid and practicable. In his scenario the master divided the stage into two parts with the large tree trunk in the center: one part was designated for Siegmund and Sieglinde, the other for Hunding, their antagonist. A heavy beam, instead of a border, was laid across the flats. The fire on the hearth lit up the Waelsungens while Hunding remained in darkness on the opposite side of the hall. The over-all lighting was a soft chiaroscuro. Act II bore no resemblance to Wagner's requested rocky landscape; there were high platforms left and right, with lower ones in front of them and a passage, a kind of gorge, between the two summits. The colorful light effects in this act, especially during the fighting scene at the end, must have been impressive. The strongest impact was caused by the dead body of Siegmund lying on a high platform "as though on a catafalque." A traveler behind the first low platform masked the upstage area for the long intimate scene between Brünhilde and Wotan; the same device was used for a similar scene between these two characters in the last act. True to his conviction Appia surrendered every trace of romanticism to the stern atmosphere of the classic tragedy. In the third act the exciting though seemingly pell-mell movement of the Valkyries shifting from one position to another was meticulously planned by Appia, who drew crayon marks on the platforms during the stage rehearsals. The foreground was kept fairly dark so that the summit of the rock, simply a set of platforms rising to a considerable height, would be seen as a silhouette. In the opening scene the Valkyries were barely visible. The magic fire at the end of this act is, in Appia's scenario, interestingly interpreted as "a character." His wish was that when Wotan hit a stone with his spear, a single flame must spring forth, no more; afterwards the fire should merely appear as a reddish glimmer on the backdrop. In the first performance, a few flames were still used, but they were cut out as unnecessary in the following performances.[26]

The principle of this abstraction was largely well received in the newspapers. The *Basler Nachrichten* highly praised the arrangement of the platforms in Act II, but considered the following setting too detailed in its execution and the magic fire somehow debatable. In conclusion "a lack of consistency" was pointed out.[27] The representative of a Berne paper favored the "hard, cubistic arrangement of masses of rocks" in Act II and was generally pleased with the conception as such.[28] A positive report appeared also in the *Schweizer Arbeiter Zeitung*, whose critic was one of the few to mention the thoughtless clash between booing and applauding spectators after the final curtain.[29] A detailed evaluation of the production was offered in the *National Zeitung*, from which we learn that the hearth and tree trunk in Act I were almost invisible. The usefulness of the bare door upstage was questioned and the entire second act was panned. The writer thought the symbol of the magic fire was "well executed at the beginning . . . too meager toward the end." Nevertheless he added that "with the realization of Adolphe Appia's designs and principles, our theatre undertook a very worthy experiment and should even some aspects of this *mise en scène* prove to be no more than that, full recognition must be given for the stimulating courage it thus demonstrated."[30]

In sharp contrast to these voices of approval or at least of acceptance, the obstinate opponent of modern staging from the *Basler Volkblatt* wrote that "it serves no purpose to enumerate once more all objections against this senseless production. . . . No one will ever again dare offer an audience of connoisseurs things like that second act of *The Valkyrie* consisting of boxes and curtains and call it 'a rugged Rock Pass.' . . . Go and see it if you want to get angry!"[31]

"The battle royal after *The Valkyrie*," as Waelterlin called it, became a *cause célèbre* in Basel. It lasted about thirty minutes after the opening-night curtain until the house lights were finally turned off; but the dispute went on in homes, offices, and inns. Even the management of the theatre had to take an official stand, and it released a statement under the title "A Protest in the Municipal Theatre." After a brief, carefully worded account of the event, the writer repudiated the catcalls and other insults heaped on the stage director, and then related how most of the spectators at first did not catch the intention of the gentleman who incited the protest. As soon as the audience grasped what motivated him, those who liked the production rallied to the defense of the performance while others joined the opposition. The management interpreted the rising applause as an expression of protest by a large majority against the impudence of the namecaller, who publicly abused the stage director "thereby degrading his artistic endeavor." The writer commended Waelterlin "who executed his task with full devotion."[32]

The arguments obviously continued behind the scene and soon another statement appeared in a program book. Under the heading " The Appia Productions,"

Figure 37. *The Valkyrie,* Act II, as staged in Basel. *Institut fuer Theaterwissenschaft, Cologne.*

Figure 38. *The Valkyrie,* Act II, as staged in Basel. *Institut fuer Theaterwissenschaft, Cologne.*

the patrons of the theatre were informed that the plan for a new *mise en scène* of the entire *Ring* was abandoned. *Siegfried* and *The Twilight of the Gods* were removed from the schedule. The official excuse was that the repertoire made the execution of the entire *Ring* "inadvisable."[33] It may be taken for granted that this diplomatic retreat deceived nobody. Several factors, however, may have contributed to the decision; for example, a lack of rehearsal time and/or funds, technical difficulties, and hardship for the leading singers. But the suspicion cannot be dismissed that the concerted drive of a small clique had done its work.

Stories about the management's change of mind prompted a lover of opera to write a letter to the managing director of the theatre. It was published together with the official announcement mentioned above. The letter writer quite openly referred to "the opposition of certain circles" who tried everything to prevent any further experimenting with Appia's ideas. Then he spoke of the "tremendous impression" which the performance of *The Valkyrie* had left on him. "As all external matters were banished," he explained,

> one could undisturbed concentrate on the music and meaning of this work. It was gratifying to see this utterly simple setting even further simplified by the closing of a traveler for scenes in which the drama does not develop in external action. To give just one example, how effective was the dialogue between Wotan and Brünhilde in Act III! To me, this scene appeared infinitely more moving than in any previous production.

Even after so many years, the background of that theatre scandal is not entirely clear. We know that the performance of *The Rhinegold* caused no public misgivings apart from the one biting censure. In general Appia's principles were accepted and praised. But between the end of November, 1924, and the first of February, 1925, something was brewing that wrecked all further plans to use Appia's designs. Soon after the dismal event, rumors circulated that members of a local branch of the *Wagner Verein* had communicated with its headquarters, even with the Wagner family at Bayreuth. No proof or witness for such conspiracy has ever been forthcoming. At any rate, it is inconceivable that Siegfried Wagner, the great composer's son, who at that time was the guiding spirit of the Bayreuth Festivals, would have participated in such a conspiracy. He was too fine a gentleman; besides, he himself tried to modernize the festival productions. As a matter of fact, reviewers suggested that his own experiments were related to Appia's ideas but he categorically denied any knowledge of the latter's work.

After all, it takes only a few fanatics supported by some easily swayed, likeminded people to instigate a scandal; or, at least, to create a stir. In Basel, as all signs indicate, two men specifically were responsible for the namecalling after the last act of *The Valkyrie* and the succeeding upheaval in the city. These two, widely taken as the leaders of the traditionalists and opponents of any modernization of the Wagnerian music dramas, were Adolf Zinsstag, a jeweler, who was the pres-

Figure 39. The Valkyrie, Act III, as staged in Basel. *Institut fuer Theaterwissenschaft*, Cologne.

Figure 40. The Valkyrie, Act III, as staged in Basel. *Institut fuer Theaterwissenschaft*, Cologne.

ident of the local *Wagner Verein* and the representative of the Bayreuth Festivals for Switzerland, and Dr. Hermann Stumm, an attorney who allegedly started the whole incident after *The Valkyrie* premiere. In collaboration with the critic of the *Basler Volksblatt* they certainly made so much noise that they won and Appia lost—at least for the moment. Mr. Zinsstag initiated his campaign against the Appia experiment soon after the first *Rhinegold* performance. He sought to have an article appear in a leading local newspaper but found no response. In the end his commentaries were published in the *Rundschau-Bürgerzeitung* on January 23, February 6, and 27. First he defended Wagner's scenic conception while conceding that the new solution of the cave in *The Rhinegold* was acceptable. The next article disclosed his polemic attitude already in its heading that screamed: *"Prostitution of an Art Work at the Basel Municipal Theatre."* It purported to answer an article by Waelterlin in behalf of the theatre's management. The attack then shifted to the finances of the theatre, raising the issue that the new productions contributed to the theatre's deficit.

When the production of *The Valkyrie* thus turned the artistic dispute into a purely emotional one, its opponents began collecting signatures for a protest designed to discredit the management. One hundred and forty-one persons were willing to put their names on a statement; this amounted to a vote of no confidence and consequently to a threat to vote against further subsidies for the theatre. Early in the spring, an editorial in a local newspaper attacked the critic, Dr. Merian, for his article in the internationally recognized *Frankfurter Zeitung* in which he had denounced parochialism in Basel.[34] Thus accusations and counteraccusations confused the basic problem in an emotional explosion. It caused Dr. Rudolf Schwabe, president of the civic association which supported the theatre, to resign in disappointment over the "tragic" incident. This gentleman deeply regretted that a work of art was to bring about such an uproar while insipid operettas and great works poorly prepared in conventional settings were accepted without protest.[35]

Prometheus

THE tempest over Appia's *mise en scène* for *The Ring* must have occupied all the minds interested in dramatic art; so much so that another artistic event at the Municipal Theatre remained almost unnoticed although Appia was also connected with it. Only ten days after the first performance of *The Valkyrie*, Waelterlin presented *Prometheus* by Aeschylus in a new German translation prepared by Max Eduard von Liehburg. The settings and costumes were designed by Appia and the production was first shown on February 11, 1925, and repeated on February 19 and March 9.

Liehburg, later well known as author and translator, had heard about Appia in 1917, when after graduating from high school in Zurich he went to Geneva to study music and take lessons in eurythmics with Dalcroze and his pupil Boepple. In Dalcroze's studio he saw some of Appia's sketches; their clarity and monumentality impressed him so deeply that he examined his work more closely; soon thereafter he met the master. Liehburg's translation of *Prometheus* was published a few years later and the young author was anxious to have it staged in Basel where he then lived and studied. He engaged Appia to design and direct the production, offering him an honorarium of 500 francs. This nearly coincided with the exchange of the final letters between Waelterlin and Appia regarding *The Ring* production in Basel. So Appia went there, taking along not only his sketches for *The Ring* but those for *Prometheus* as well. Details for the production of the Aeschylus tragedy were settled between Appia and Liehburg during long talks at the Hotel Krafft, a favorite meeting place of artists, and in due time the management of the theatre made the arrangements for the rehearsals and the performances.

The outburst against his *Valkyrie* came as a shock to Appia. Friends who visited him during the following days were deeply concerned about his depression. In the midst of the rehearsals for *Prometheus,* Appia left Basel refusing to return to a city where he was unable to breathe. His mood must have changed as soon as letters from Basel arrived. Mr. Henning asked him to send in his sketches and detailed wishes for *Siegfried* and *The Twilight of the Gods.* Then came the catastrophic turn of events. Appia learned about the cancellation of all further plans for *The Ring.* The manager was "deeply disturbed" but his faith in Appia's genius remained untouched.[36]

In the meantime the rehearsals for the premiere of *Prometheus* had to go on. Appia had left a brief scenario when he disappeared from Basel; with these notes Waelterlin, assisted by Liehburg, took over the reins. The setting for the Greek tragedy was entirely different from the sketches Appia had designed for a dance drama of the same title in 1910. Again it became evident that any previous romantic and somewhat impressionistic leanings had given way to the utmost simplification. His erstwhile setting, a formation of rocks, reminded one of the tomb of Druids near Geneva, which Appia must have seen.

The scenario for Basel as preserved—there are only fragmentary notes—delineates his plan for the setting which, with some modifications, was executed according to his wishes. A large platform rose a few feet away from the curtain line. Appia had originally thought of stairs leading into the orchestra pit; this could not be done because of the footlights, and consequently the stairs ended on the stage floor proper. But Appia insisted on the removal of the prompter's box, which by tradition was installed in the center of the footlights. This change resulted in a few "accidents," as the actors were not accustomed to prompting from back-

Figure 41. Prometheus. Theater Museum, Munich.

stage.[37] Center upstage, on the large platform which filled the entire width of the stage, was the huge "rock" on which Prometheus was chained and around which most of the action occurred. The scenario suggests a dramatic effect at the end when, after Prometheus' last words, heavy drapes, invisible behind the teaser, were to drop quickly on the darkening stage. Further specific wishes concerned the incidental music. It was not to be a real composition but rather a tremolo of strings followed by a strong chord of brass instruments in a major key.

Liehburg admired the scenic arrangement and was fully satisfied; not so Appia. He was not happy that the stage could not be enlarged into the orchestra pit and that a compromise had to be made regarding the chorus. Neither he nor Liehburg intended to have women speak the chorus lines and execute the manifold movements. But as not enough men could be mustered for the Okeanides, Mr. Gueldenstein and his advanced group at the conservatory were engaged for this assignment. The performance of the young ladies, a credit to Mr. Gueldenstein and indirectly to Dalcroze, was acclaimed by all who witnessed it, even though the compromise fell short of the ideal envisioned by the director and translator.

The press in general voiced praise except for the usual dissenter, the diehard of the *Basler Volksblatt*, who again rejected the setting because "it sounded strange to hear Prometheus speak the line 'Chained am I here surrounded by rocks . . .' when only legs of brick-red colored drapes could be seen."[38] Typical of all other reviews was the statement that "architecturally everything fits into the space creating a beautiful plastic effect."[39] Even where the question was raised whether Appia had really found the best solution, his "strongly sketched pictorial effect" was fully accepted.[40]

The chorus scenes disappointed the representative of the *Basler Nachrichten*. He found the dance steps of ten delicate girls and their singsong in direct opposition to the forceful speeches of the actors, "the tragic outcry of the tortured, the crying Io," and felt an essential element of Greek drama was thus curtailed. Otherwise he too liked the "beautiful pictures" of the setting and summed up Appia's work in Basel: "In Wagner's operas the theoreticians may find the simple, stylized settings out of place, but here Appia's austerity is in keeping with the simplicity of the ancient scene, even though our stage had to renounce cothurnus, masque, and cultic procession of the chorus, the most typical parts of the ancient theatre."[41]

The success of *Prometheus* was a small consolation for Appia, who had gone to Basel primarily to find acceptance of his scenic reform of Wagner's music dramas. Disillusioned, he returned to Western Switzerland but his innate optimism again got the better of him. He wrote a brief memorandum entitled *La Reforme et le Théâtre de Bâle (The Reform and the Theatre at Basel)* which was published in the *Gazette de Lausanne* on May 3, 1925. With hardly a trace of bitterness, he reported the events in Basel, expressing mainly his gratitude to all those who had collaborated with him in the staging of the first two parts of the *Ring* cycle and who would have supported him in staging the remaining two parts. But in a letter to a young admirer he frankly wrote, "The opposition has won. This is a hard blow for Waelterlin. For me, it is . . . Silence. For the people of Basel . . . ?"[42]

An Analysis

THE productions in Milan and Basel are of eminent interest and importance to both historians and artists. In evaluating Appia's responsibility for the outcome of each, let us state, to begin with, that their failure was apparent rather than real; that in both cities the rejection was by no means unanimous. In Milan, an ultraconservative audience was simply unable to go along with his revolutionary concept, whereas critics gave *Tristan* at least a fair trial if not full approval. In Basel, on the other hand, a small but noisy group of zealots succeeded in having the management cancel their scheduled new production of the remaining two parts of the *Ring* while the average opera lover and the unbiased critics remained powerless. In the perspective of time, success and failure lose much of their weight. What counts is that in these productions with all their shortcomings Appia could execute his scenic vision in a live performance for everyone to see and to judge their value. Today we can add that he has emerged from this trial with flying colors.

At La Scala Appia was theoretically in an exceedingly favorable position with maestro Arturo Toscanini as collaborator and sponsor, and a large splendidly equipped stage plus an experienced technical staff at his disposal. Unfortunately traits of his personality made it impossible for him to cope with the harrassing conditions usually encountered in such an entrenched establishment. But external and internal obstacles notwithstanding, the *mise en scène* came off almost as intended. In the production of *Tristan* Appia adhered to his original concept of the nineties; any changes made from 1896 to 1923 are too minor to mention. Consequently, this production represented less the ideas of the mature artist that those of the incipient artist. This added special flavor to the occasion. For the first time his pioneering theories of, and designs for, a Wagnerian music drama were exposed to the test of reality. In *Tristan* they passed it unequivocally, and although conceived thirty years previously, they made of the *mise en scène* an avant-garde piece of art from which even our contemporary theatre can learn a great deal. The reservation that the settings were too small for the enormous stage of La Scala had some validity in the twenties, when an almost empty stage was unknown apart from a few experimental productions in Central Europe and Russia.

The case of *The Ring* is very different. In Basel Appia did not use his initial version but devised an entirely new one. While in Milan some cavilers erroneously applied the term "cubism" to his *Tristan,* in Basel it is appropriate, though the master himself would have vehemently objected to any classification of style. His sole concern was "simplicity, monumentality" in the classic sense. Unlike in Milan, everyone cooperated in Basel; Waelterlin and the soloists listened eagerly to Appia's suggestions, and no open or hidden opposition came from the technical staff, whose members executed his every wish as best they could with their inadequate equipment. Appia was thus able to demonstrate how even with a modicum of time and means, a demanding opera can be well prepared under the unifying leadership of an inspired artist.

From the historian's viewpoint two issues may be raised: The sketches and models of *The Ring* indicate that the settings positively needed a large frame. Photographs of the productions and reports confirm the impression that a wide and deep stage would have better served Appia's grand concept. The pictures in particular show that the quite limited dimensions of the stage stymied his intentions to some degree. As for the apparent coldness emanating from the numerous cubes and the lack of color, one must remember that without the essential lighting the impression remains necessarily incomplete and incorrect. Witnesses testify that the atmosphere of many scenes was exclusively created through magnificent light effects accomplished even with the limited equipment. No model, no photography can possibly convey the tragic mood Appia achieved with chiaroscuro lighting, his forte.

It should not be our concern to inquire whether Appia found the ultimate solution for *The Ring* with his extreme simplification of the settings and movements in utter disregard for virtually all scenic and lighting effects requested by Wagner himself. Appia did what he considered right, what his artistic instinct dictated to him. Every artist has the privilege of his conviction when he is creating a work. Judgment should not rest on this basis. Appia had taken a logical step from the development of his intitial concept and his experiences in Hellerau. He refuted his own achievements of an earlier period, leaning increasingly toward abstraction in his designs. In his new austere spatial arrangement he overlooked, however, the fact that a Wagnerian music drama still contains romantic elements, unlike an opera by Gluck, whose neo-classic *Orpheus* allowed Appia for the first time to apply rigorously the concept he had developed in his Rhythmic Spaces.

Appia's light plot for *The Ring* in 1924–1925 tells a different story; here he succumbed to a romantic mood using colored filters, such as red, for spotlights, a method which in the twenties had more or less been discarded by most modern stage directors who raised or dimmed repectively the volume of plain spotlights in order to obtain a given mood or a transition. It is thus puzzling to realize that the great designer thoroughly "modernized" his original version of *The Ring* without taking advantage of the big strides that had been made in the field of lighting. He must have seen modern lighting effects in some of Pitoëff's and Copeau's productions. Why did he not progress in a field in which, after all, he was the leader in the 1890's when he first expounded his theories? The question baffles us and we are unable to answer it. We are likewise perplexed about his use of the traveler to provide more intimacy. This was a stunning device in his production of *Orpheus* in Hellerau; but it was unnecessary to repeat it in Basel more than ten years later when the fading of some light sources could have done the trick better and more discreetly. Even the few instruments available in Basel would have sufficed. On the other hand, Appia's predilection for silhouette effects and for keeping one or another character out of lighted areas was virtually unknown at that time, and so was his strategem of having light fall from a wing on a restricted area while the rest of the stage remained dark or only dimly lit. Very few spectators in Milan and Basel were aware that the soft transition from the dark auditorium to the lighted stage was a brilliant stroke imitated later by many stage directors and scene designers.

The lack of action, above all in *The Valkyrie,* irritated some theatregoers accustomed to the traditional gesticulation of the singers. Here the characters made only few but meaningful gestures and movements strictly synchronized with the music. This kind of static staging was without precedent.

Prometheus in Basel received little attention, maybe because Appia's name was almost exclusively identified with Wagner. And yet this Greek tragedy demonstrated that the artist had a wide horizon and great capacities. He was imbued with the classic style and could thus project it in the present. His concentration on the rock as the sole piece onstage seemingly growing out of a large platform was a splendid idea, and his simple, pure conception proved to be tremendously effective. It is regrettable that this artistic event was not given the recognition it deserved; it left no mark beyond that city and little in it.

Unfortunate as was the abrupt halt of the two remaining productions of *The Ring,* the loudly voiced rancor against Appia that caused the cancellation had at least some beneficial result. The publicity which the peculiar scandal received in several leading newspapers in Switzerland and also in Germany spread the word about Appia and his revolutionary work. Soon a professional periodical showed a series of the controversial settings and thus his name became better known among theatre experts, if for the wrong reason. At any rate Appia's sad experience in Basel aroused much interest—or was it only curiosity?—in his designs when they were shown in slides at the Musicological Congress in Leipzig in 1925 and were exhibited in Zurich in 1925 and in Magdeburg in 1927.

VI

Last Works

Dᴜʀɪɴɢ the last decade of his life Appia was a prolific writer. His book *L'Oeuvre d'art vivant*, which appeared in fall, 1921, constitutes his esthetic conclusion about the arts in general rather than about theatrical production. It was followed by a flood of essays until his health made it difficult, almost impossible, for him to use the pencil. As he told Mercier, he wrote and wrote, designed and designed to relieve his tension, to find an outlet. Some forty essays and scenarios were thus begun if not always finished after completion of his book in 1919. Two groups of the essays are of specific interest to a biographer: one containing his personal memoirs and confessions, the other reflecting the philosophy of the mature Appia; they elaborate many of the ideas outlined in his last book. There are also essays expounding theories discussed in previous writings. This last series shows remarkable progress in Appia's ability to express himself, to attack his subject directly. He is less vague and less prone to grope his way by means of examples and allegories, some of which were more confusing than illuminating to the uninitiated reader. His style now becomes more clear and precise than ever before. Several scenarios and introductions to operas and plays conclude this group, except for a few essays which were lost and some which could not be deciphered—his handwriting, always poor, became sometimes illegible during the last years of his life.

L'Oeuvre d'art vivant

L'Oeuvre d'art vivant was the first major work Appia had written after *La Musique et le mise en scène*. When his friends, above all Mercier, sought to find a publisher, brother Paul made it clear that he would not contribute to the fund needed for an agreement with a firm. So his sister Hélène and Mercier guaranteed the

Figure 42. Adolphe Appia, ca. 1923. *Jean Mercier.*

printing expenses when Atar, a publishing house in Geneva and Paris, accepted the manuscript. A small book in comparison with *La Musique et le mise en scène*, it had less than one hundred pages not counting the illustrations and their captions. Five hundred copies were said to be printed; and the publication was well received among experts. Some leading Swiss newspapers reviewed it, as did foreign ones and periodicals. A detailed review appeared in the highly regarded *La Semaine Litteraire*, whose critic inserted the term "miracle" for the manner in which Appia delineated "in the first pages of his book the problem of dramatic art in its profound origins."[1] Some months prior to its appearance Appia sent a copy of his manuscript to Copeau, who enthusiastically endorsed it, calling it "unique"; he indeed intended to recommend it to his friend, the publisher Gallimard. In a long letter to Appia, Copeau described his reaction to the ideas expressed in this volume, revealing again how closely he followed the master's principles. In his opinion Appia's completely original ideas settled the staging problem once and for all, since "the question is no longer one of this perpetual esthetic twaddle about theatre and a new art which does not exist."[2]

With this small volume Appia had clarified his many-faceted vision and arrived at a statement of personal esthetics. "Style is the man himself," he once said. And he had found himself and, thus, his style in writing and designing.

L'Oeuvre d'art vivant is dedicated to two artists: to his onetime collaborator Dalcroze to whom he was deeply grateful for the inspiration and opportunities he gave him—then, surprisingly, "and to you, oh Walt Whitman who will understand me, because you are *living*—always." Appia was not personally acquainted with the American poet but certainly with his works, or at least with some of them. Whitman and Appia had much in common. Throughout their life both hankered for true friendship, yet, in the end, remained very lonely. Both loved nature, independence, and freedom. Both were in search of an ideal in this world, even in the cosmos. Like Appia, Whitman was indifferent to public opinion and to fashions, preferring casual dress. A description of Whitman's habits may as well fit Appia's: "a man who, as long as he had a roof to cover him, a truckle bed to sleep in, a basin and ewer wherewithal to wash, any sort of homely food to eat, and a desk to write upon, could be happy in himself and let the world go on its way unheeded."[3] The dedication is, by the same token, a motto, for Appia quotes: "Camerado! this is no book; who touches this, touches a man. . . ." If we add to "man" the adjective "living," we have a further clue to the dedication as well as to the new book.

How long the master worked on the manuscript before it was ready for publication is not known, but there is good reason to assume that he pondered the outline and basic ideas during the war, perhaps as early as 1915, when he lived in quasi seclusion at Glérolles. In the preface he confessed that his first draft was twice as long as the final version. But he had learned to control himself and to state his thoughts precisely; furthermore, Mercier was not far from him during the final shaping of the manuscript, and Mercier was an excellent editorial adviser. Never satisfied with his own work, Appia rewrote endlessly; formerly this had led to increasingly complicated constructions, but this time, guided by Mercier, he succeeded in being concise.[4]

The ideas in the book are entirely new and different from those he had previously expounded. In the preface Appia states that with this work "were broken, one by one, the precious links binding him to the past which he had thought he would never need to, still less be able to, abandon." He hopes that his book can prepare the reader "for a similar journey" without the "hesitations and anxieties" suffered by the author. To achieve this Appia tries to be "both guide and traveler," admitting that the reader's task would be complex.

The chapter headings pinpoint his new conception. No longer did he linger on the hierarchy (actor, spatial arrangement, light, color) which pervaded so many of his earlier writings. Instead, as he titled them, the chapters deal with "Living Time," "Living Space," "Living Color," and, more importantly, with "Organic Unity," and "Collaboration." The two last chapters carry the mystical headings "The Great Unknown and the Experience in Beauty" and "Bearers of the Flame." Appia still adheres somehow to his basic principles, but the deviations are more striking. In discussing "The Elements" first, he departs from his erstwhile definition of dramatic art, and he omits terms like "a synthesis of all the arts" or "the art form of the future." The former Wagner disciple had outgrown his idol and had discovered his own esthetics which, as he indicates, resembles more that of Emile Faguet, the noted French scholar and interpreter of literature and philosophy. Now Appia simply points out that the art of the theatre is aimed at the eyes, the ears, and the understanding of the audience, in short, at "our whole being." In accord with this approach he seeks to give it harmony; and to obtain this harmony he relies heavily on time and space.

The relationship of time and space had already puzzled Appia early in life; like other great men before him he had grappled with this elusive problem without finding a tangible solution. Doubtlessly he was acquainted with the passages dealing with this question in Wagner's *Oper und Drama*. Yet Appia's curiosity could not have been satisfied with them, for the composer, apart from some abstract statements, concentrated on the term "expression" as the most suitable means to link time with space, a term which for him stands for the power of music. Appia, however, did not search for a mood but for a perceptible element. He did not follow Wagner's theory, but rather Schopenhauer's, whose works he had probably read in his student years in Dresden. As a mature thinker, Appia apparently again took up *The World as Will and Idea,* in which Schopenhauer inserted a significant discussion on time, rhythm, motion, and symmetry in addition to an elaborate chart entitled *Praedicabilia a Priori.* Appia does not literally adopt the German's philosophy; rather he applies it to music, light, and movement—elements fundamental to his thinking. His theme of the living, moving performer returns in the new volume more emphatically than ever before. A brief quotation clarifies his approach beyond the already stated principles: "In space, units of time are expressed by a succession of forms, hence by movement. In time, space is expressed by a succession of words and sounds, that is to say, by varying time-durations prescribing the extent of movement." Appia insists on movement as the unifier of dramatic art which thus creates the ideal form. In relating music, the element of time, to space, movement functions as the main catalyst of the whole.

A definition of these relationships continued to occupy Appia's mind even after *L'Oeuvre d'art vivant*. He took the theme up again in a two-page piece in which he emphasized that "movement brings about the meeting of Space and Time." His reliance on movement became even more pronounced when he wrote that "the art of Movement is . . . the art of balancing in Time-Duration the variable proportions of the two kinds of sensation of Space." These words should especially be remembered in appreciation of his last scenarios and sketches.

Under the heading "Living Time," Appia discusses at length the role of music. Three quotations, used in previous writings, serve to support his concept. From Friedrich Schiller's *On the Aesthetic Education of Man*, letter no. 22, Appia cites, "When music reaches its noblest power it becomes form." To make this statement fit his approach he added the words "in space." The other quotation is from Taine's *Philosophy of Art:* "The aim of a work of art is to reveal some essential, salient character, consequently some important idea, more clearly and more completely than can real objects. It achieves this through a group of parts whose relationships it systematically modifies . . . " From Schopenhauer he borrows again the assertion that "music never expresses the phenomenon but only the inner essence of the phenomenon," which he had quoted previously to justify his nonrealistic style. The chapter "Living Space" is closely linked to the preceding one. He delineates how the body, expressing itself in space through gestures and movements, becomes at the same time both the work of art and its creator. But to this end, the moving body needs the implicit support of inanimate objects, such as a column, whose "quiet immobility" in contrast to the body's movements heightens the effect of the latter. Appia considers it imperative that all inanimate forms "oppose rather than engulf" the human body.

Appia's revolutionary definition of the importance of light is stressed more strongly yet in the chapter "Living Color." The title does not, of course, refer to the use of color in the setting. His statement, "Light is to space what sounds are to time—the perfect expression of life" clarifies his esthetic approach. Emphatically he reiterates his aversion to painted flats and backdrops. Since his aim was to *indicate* rather than to *present*, light colored by means of filters—living color— assumes the task of fulfilling his purpose. As always, he relies on the plain contrast of lighted against darker areas. Even a shadow thrown on a wall suffices to create a telling effect as some of his sketches demonstrate.

In "Organic Unity" Appia turns to the problems related to the playwright. He scorns the dramatist who, writing for the reader rather than the spectator, wastes many pages on prolonged descriptions of the characters. He wants to free him from the superficial fashions and traditions of the theatre and thus to enable him to be a true artist. Considering it sacrilegious to separate the writing of plays from the staging of them, Appia draws the logical conclusion that the playwright should be his own stage director. He thinks it unfeasible to divide the two activities if the ideal unity is to be accomplished. Having been primarily concerned with the performer's role in the production, he warns against a purely visual approach to a scenic reform and he demands that the entire production be under constant scrutiny. Convinced that the author of a drama has still much to learn about the living, moving actor, he advises him to observe students of Dalcroze the better to understand the relationship between space and time.

"Living art implies a collaboration," Appia writes in the following chapter, which more than any other summarizes his experiences at the Dalcroze Institute. Of great significance was the 1914 June Festival in Geneva which impressed him tremendously. Here the audience witnessed historical themes unfold in "a majestic dramatic action," and simultaneously felt the "purely human expression of the action" like "a transfigured realization of the events." His admiration for Dalcroze's work and the perfect rapport of the spectators gave new impetus to his lifelong enthusiasm for the folk pageants he had helped promote in Switzerland. What Appia had vaguely envisioned and touched upon in earlier essays has now taken a distinct form. The potential of an art "lived in common with others" has been revealed to him and he sees now the beneficial effect such an experience can have on the relationship of men. He suggests erecting a building where a multitude of people will assemble to enjoy and serve art together. The "Cathedral of the Future" he calls it in the chapter "The Great Unknown and the Experience in Beauty." In the last chapter, "Bearers of the Flame," he continues in this religious vein, writing, "Every Christian is an artist: he is that because he gives himself, never refusing contact with those he wishes to know and perhaps assist." In conclusion he expects of us and, above all, of the dramatist, "a new attitude." Although this attitude must of course be personal, it "should be shared by all men."

Twenty designs with a general introduction and in many cases specific explanations illustrate *L'Oeuvre d'art vivant*. Those for *The Ring* and *Tristan* had already appeared in his previous book, but also included were three sketches for *Parsifal,* among them the moving and powerful Sacred Forest which at the time became one of the most famous and most imitated scenic pictures. For the first time Appia presented two designs for *Prometheus*, a dance drama planned for Dalcroze. The scenic ingredients are a few steps, tree trunks doubling as pillars, a heavy slab forming a roof, and a few other set pieces; in its simplicity this 1910 draft was extremely impressive; and yet his *mise en scène* of *Prometheus* in Basel showed that he had progressed still further in this direction. The designs for *Prometheus* provide telling examples of his development during the fourteen years that lie between them. The spatial arrangement for *Echo and Narcissus*, as the designer adapted it for a 1920 production in Geneva, is, according to eyewitnesses, essentially as it was in Hellerau, only in smaller scale to accommodate less adequate technical means. Finally there is an exquisite selection of Rhythmic Spaces which Appia prepared for Dalcroze in 1909. With a platform, a few steps, a wall, a pillar he succeeded in creating fantastic combinations. Of course, lighting, the light and shadow effect, is the salient feature in these drawings. Designed in a period of transition, they are an indispensable landmark for the evaluation of Appia's last works. The drawings include one for the *Orpheus* production in Hellerau but, alas, not the monumental staging of the Hades scene which aroused so much enthusiasm there. Instead, Appia chose the Elysian Fields, a fine setting that offered splendid opportunities for the movements of Dalcroze's students but is not among his best designs.

In this his third and last book, Appia regards the visual aspect of a dramatic production exclusively as a means to serve the moving and speaking (singing) performer; for him alone the setting must be built. Actor and scenery must have a common denominator, space; and rhythm expressed through movement must be the element that brings space to life. Basically the idea was not new to Appia, who from the outset professed an intense desire to support the performer in his attempt to compete with the conventional setting for the attention of the audience. But here he went much further. Man, the sole purpose of any dramatic activity, must regain the union of body and soul once considered inseparable but which had gradually disintegrated into nonexistence. He must therefore be freed of all those externals that hamper him in this effort. Yet the deliverance of the individual performer no longer satisfied Appia; he now wished to see him join others in a collective experience which should be extended even to the audience. This vision preoccupied Appia so much during the last decade of his life that it almost became his *idée fixe*; repeatedly he referred to it in *L'Oeuvre d'art vivant* and in subsequent essays. The liberation must begin with the correct training of the body, for, as he reasons, "our body is the expression of space in time and time in space."

In a way *L'Oeuvre d'art vivant* culminates Appia's artistic development. It is therefore regrettable that it has not quite attracted the attention it deserves. Too many theatre people know Appia mainly as the great scenic designer and initiator of modern lighting. But this volume gives him a much higher stature: a philosopher of the stage whose ethic and esthetic principles gave the contemporary theatre new direction and great impetus. Though forceful and more explicit than his former writings the book does not read easily. His tendency toward abstract thinking which alternates with emotional outbursts makes it sometimes unwieldy; besides some passages are still quite ambiguous, lending themselves to different interpretations. In this regard his style resembles that of Friedrich Nietzsche, whose writings too were often poetic and mystic at the expense of clarity.

Personal Writings

APPIA agreed with Goethe that all writing is fundamentally autobiographical. This is particularly true of his later essays, which are interrelated and should be treated as a whole. They may be divided into two groups—one dealing with ideas and intentions; the other with personal experiences underlying his desire to express his conscious, even unconscious, self. All these thoughts are intertwined and it is difficult, in some cases impossible, to separate his artistic principles from those he applied to his daily life. In general the two are one and the same; except for the scenarios and a few essays, all contain personal references. Yet the author seldom openly states "I did, I think" and the like. His observations are usually disguised in a description or a story.

Only once did Appia refer directly to facts related to his life. In 1927 he drafted his *Curriculum Vitae* upon the request of Wilhelm Treichlinger, a journalist from Vienna, who prepared a German encyclopedia of theatre arts to be published in Budapest. Treichlinger never finished his plan, but Appia's *Curriculum Vitae* appeared in a Hungarian translation in 1930, while the original French version was not published until 1962.[5] In this brief outline Appia gives only some essential data on his life and ideas plus a listing of his books and productions. Of interest is his ambiguous passage, "several productions of scenes for different theatres; collaborations and private experiments." The last remark possibly covers plans he had discussed with Copeau (perhaps also with other directors) and the sketches and models he worked on during the twenties.

Far more instructive is an elaborate essay *Expériences de théâtre et recherches personnelles*, finished in 1924. Although distinctly autobiographical it gives little information about the artist's personal life; much, however, can be learned about Appia, the great reformer. Since the material has been amply used in this study we can forgo discussing it further. About twenty years earlier Appia wrote his most intimate confessions, entitled *Introduction à mes notes personnelles*. This causes one to wonder whether he kept a diary to be extended to an autobiography. It is not impossible that such a manuscript exists somewhere, but it is more likely that, if he ever wrote one, either he himself destroyed it, or his niece Geneviève burned it along with the other manuscripts after his death.

Two additional essays may be placed under this category. *L'Intermédiaire* expounds the unique and decisive role played by a teacher or guide in the development of a child and a young man. In Appia's opinion, a person's career takes the right direction if his life is well organized and balanced. Following Goethe's dictum, "Whatever you cannot understand you cannot possess," he emphasizes the importance for someone of the younger generation to be guided by an older man who would be able and willing to do so. He starts his inquiry into the conduct of our life by probing "the accuracy of transmission," because his observations and experiences obviously taught him that "a flaw in transmission" was often the cause of trouble. *L'Intermédiaire* represents the artist's grateful recognition to Fauré and Chamberlain for their magnificent guidance.

In *Après une lecture de* Port-Royal *(Sainte-Beuve)* Appia touchingly grants us insight into his yearning for like-minded companions who would share his devotion to an ideal. He envisions a retreat in the country far away from the hustle and bustle of the big city, like the monastery Port-Royal where "communication of thoughts and feelings" can be achieved partly through art, that is to say, singing; where in "self-effacement" one can gain true freedom. Such dreams should however not lead one to the conclusion that Appia was anxious to join a "collective movement"; on the contrary, his ideal was a group of personalities freely banded together for the purpose of organizing and managing a retreat. Life in such a place would enable everyone "to make a choice, to hold on to it, to examine its content and to adjust himself so well that he has created a new life for himself, a life wisely limited that will suffice him." The basic ideas implied in Sainte-Beuve's *Port-Royal* affected Appia deeply. He did not only write this essay (about 1921) but he obviously tried earnestly to find a group of people willing to live up to that ideal. When he heard—or read—about the Goetheanum in Dornach near Basel, and its founder Dr. Rudolf Steiner, he tried to get in contact with the spiritual leader of the Anthroposophical Society. It is doubtful, though, that he actually met the philosopher. Oskar Waelterlin remembered that Appia went to Dornach in 1922 or '23; another source confirms that Appia was there. If he ever spoke to Steiner it must have been before he was in Basel for his *Ring* production, since the anthroposoph, a sick man at that time, died shortly thereafter. Appia himself never mentioned a visit. Does this perhaps indicate that the Goetheanum did not precisely represent the ideal group he had in mind?

In 1921 Appia wrote an essay peculiar in form and content. He called it a story but it is more appropriately termed a fable. *Formes nouvelles (New Forms)* begins in an unobtrusive manner not foreshadowing a jump into pure fantasy. His statement "Experience serves only one" can well act as the motto to the first part. In this introduction he describes the experience of a sick boy, of people planning a monument, of others convalescing in a sanatorium, of a musician, of a sculptor. They are all anticipating or waiting for something to happen. Is it "victory of spirit over matter?" Then touching upon the issue of being free, Appia adds "free from what?" At this point reality and its problems evaporate into the realm of dreams.

Floating in outer space, as it were, people meet the Great Unknown and are called upon to give an account of what they were doing. All pretend to have done or learned something positive, all except the poet-author who confesses that he knows nothing but is still "searching." "Continue not to know . . . " he is told. On this note the dream and the fable ends.

Known Principles

A few papers expound the principles presented in previous writings. By far the most concise is *Acteur, éspace, lumière, peinture (Actor, Space, Light, Painting)* which, as the title indicates, deals with the hierarchy. Its published version is the abbreviated form of a manuscript which is lost. *L'Art est une attitude* too is clearly composed; it was commissioned as introduction to an American book on "stage decoration." With these two papers Appia evidently tried to address himself to a wider circle of readers. In *Essai sur un problème dangereux (A Dangerous Problem)* he devoted much space to the part played by music; ideas of Plato and Schopenhauer are woven into it, but not completely integrated with other matters. Discussing the subject of reaction and empathy Appia points out that although tragedy on stage may in a way disturb us, we actually enjoy it. Vicariously participating in tragic events that occurred in the past will cause us to shed tears, but the tears bring us wholesome release of our tension. He illustrates his assertion with the famous story of Odysseus who shed tears while listening to the narrative of his own dangerous adventures. Another pertinent point touched upon is the sacrifice of unimportant details as an essential ingredient of any artistic endeavor. To explain his view he introduces an art student, obviously himself, who is unable to grasp the meaning of his professor's advice to "sacrifice." At last he has to listen to the sharp rebuke, "You see poorly, my friend. You do not know how to see. . . . You must subdue nature which you see before you; learn also to see it within yourself." This admonition taught the student how to find the right direction and thus to awaken his true creativity.

A lecture Appia prepared for the pupils of the Dalcroze Institute in Geneva is *La Mise en scène et son avenir (Theatrical Production and Its Prospects for the Future)*. In addition to high praise for the accomplishments of Dalcroze it is mainly a recapitulation of his major theoretical and practical suggestions. But his extended treatment of dialogue in a play makes this paper particularly noteworthy. Carefully Appia delineates how the signs of musical annotation can be adapted to the interpretation of dialogue. Since he usually avoided personal references, it is surprising to find here the names of a few artists for whom he voices admiration, namely Copeau, Craig, Pitoëff, and Stanislavsky. We may take it for granted that Appia did not himself read his paper but had someone else (Henry C. Bonifas?)

deliver it. The essay became widely known after its publication in Italy (1923) and the United States (1932).

Among the other essays of this group one deserves mentioning. In 1925 the designer was asked to participate in a panel at the Musicological Congress in Leipzig. He wrote a paper *Das Problem der Stilbuehne bei den Werken R. Wagners* for which he selected a series of slides to demonstrate his views. Although he attended the meeting he did not deliver the lecture but remained in a corner of the hall. Also on that panel was Dr. Adolf Aber; it is assumed that Dr. George Schuenemann, the chairman, substituted for Appia. No appreciation of this paper is possible as it appeared only in a poorly abbreviated German version; the original has been lost.

New Ideas

THE writings of this series are the creations of a mature artist in full command of his ideas. The times of preparation and formation were long passed. In these mostly unpublished articles Appia presents new ideas or extensions of older principles. This last group can therefore be designated the verification of everything he started in *L'Oeuvre d'art vivant* and the fulfillment of his life.

The best known of the essays is *Art vivant? ou nature morte?* written, as was already stated, for the 1922 Exhibition in Amsterdam and reprinted in Milan a year later. Fitting the occasion, Appia chose as his theme the problem of how to present the art of the theatre to its best advantage. Proceeding from the premise that the diminutive form of models and sketches cannot fully illustrate architecture, he claims that the art of the theatre is subject to the same law of esthetics, even more so. Scores, instruments, copies of plays may be shown in a hall, but they make up minor phases of the entire production. He therefore recommends a radically different solution which would require a building divided in two parts: one, a conventional hall for the exhibit of designs and models, a second suitable to the staging of experimental performances; hence a plain large room with an area left free to mount spatial settings in the manner of his rhythmic spaces. Here movement and action are to be shown, thus providing a true demonstration of the theatre as a living art.

In August, 1923, Appia finished a brief piece called *L'Homme est la mesure de toutes choses (Man is the Measure of All Things)* after a statement by Protagoras. Its subheading says "A Preface to a New Work," and its last paragraph hints at "forthcoming articles." These remarks invite the question of whether the master had the intention to issue a volume of collected essays or perhaps to integrate into a new book the ideas that occupied him at the time. Several of his last writings are evidently planned together for they are interrelated and have in fact a continuity as though they were in preparation for a book. But no one, not even Mercier, has reliable information about such a plan. Mercier merely remembers that Appia was then working on some essays. Since Appia also wrote a four-page *Avertissement pour l'edition de mes "Essais" en I volume (Preface to the Edition of My Essays in One Volume),* there is no doubt about his intention in this respect. The leitmotiv of these essays and also the title of their anthology could well be *The New Presence,* a term he frequently employs. It is not possible to decide which essays he would have selected for his volume. It is easier to determine those he may have excluded, namely his autobiographical writings, the scenarios, the articles about Wagnerian music dramas and about productions, and a few in which he somehow recapitulated his basic principles. The following essays, all an extension of and elaboration on themes partly touched upon in his recent book, were probably intended as the body of that collection: *L'Ancienne attitude, Le Geste de l'art, Le Sujet, Monumentalité, Pittoresque, Mécanisation.* Purely speculative would be the inclusion of *L'Intermédiaire, Essai sur un problème dangereux,* possibly also *Port-Royal,* and others.

In the *Avertissement . . . de mes "Essais"* Appia clarifies the aim of his plan. Though he does not specifically define the term "new presence" he emphasizes that all his further discussions are based on "living art." Again he commends Dalcroze for his successful work in freeing the body from its conventional fetters and, while also acknowledging the merits of Isadora Duncan and other innovators, he leaves no doubt where he stands; he believes that eurythmics, having achieved a high degree of perfection, anticipates the advent of living art, and he predicts that the New Presence will enable man to give himself and give his best.

Appia's ingrained distrust of most artists—and other professionals, for that matter—led him to the conclusion that the peasant, thanks to his close contact and concern with nature, still "embodies activity at its best and preserves its dignity." By the same token he despised the "onlookers," those who merely gaze at a work of art instead of experiencing empathy with it. Such observations are the gist of *L'Ancienne attitude* and *Le Geste de l'art.* Appia passionately felt the world around him and particularly everything related to art; and thus he could not bear people standing vis-à-vis, who remained indolent and indifferent toward a true work of art. His panacea was eurythmics which, in his opinion, could be most helpful to those idlers; he saw eurythmics as "an act of devotion" and art as "the liberating force" which could shake man out of his indolence. Naturally this remained an unfulfilled dream; even in 1963, the late President John F. Kennedy could call Americans "a nation of spectators."

Le Sujet, also written in the early twenties, points to the danger that education can spoil a child's artistic talents and innate sensitivity, a subject touched upon in two articles he wrote at that time for a periodical. Stressing the importance of music as an educational factor, he recommends dancing as the means to acquaint the child with music. But at the same time he cautions against allowing, let alone encouraging, children to "perform" in songs or dances. Such creative activities should be exercised without any audience whatsoever. The innocent joy in doing things solely for their own sake should be retained as long as possible. Appia compares this joy with that of the lonely shepherd singing away in the hills, and of the dancer who can be perfectly happy dancing without an audience. After all, "for the child the subject is he himself, his integral being . . ."and he suggests Dalcroze songs for youth which can easily be mimed as excellent material for this educational purpose.

Three essays, *Monumentalité, Pittoresque,* and *Mécanisation,* are thematically interdependent and must be discussed together. As they are essential to an understanding of Appia's esthetics, it is regrettable that except for the first one, which was published in 1953, they are virtually unknown. The three are related to others aiming at a new attitude, but their scope is much broader. New ground is broken, and Appia shows himself in a different light and style. The first two were finished about 1922; the third probably not until 1926.

The issue in *Monumentalité* is whether an old city such as Florence is to be a museum or a place where people live. Appia takes the visitors to task for their belief that they can grasp the wonders of such a place just because they have read a guidebook or have bought pictures of the old buildings and paintings. Instead of collecting historical facts or picture postal cards and keepsakes the tourist should try to watch, or better yet, to have contact with the inhabitants. Relating thus the old treasures to the living surroundings will give him a sense of the artistic atmosphere.

Great art lives forever; this makes it monumental. To appreciate are one must test its relevance to living man. Monumental work stands that test. As examples Appia cites the Greek amphitheatres and temples, in particular the Parthenon in Athens, and the Gothic cathedrals, as against the generally respected Cathedral Santa Maria dei Fiore in Florence, which he sarcastically calls "a huge cardboard topped by an admirable cupola." The term "monumental" is, in Appia's view, also applicable to the genius of Shakespeare, Goethe, and Wagner. Not unexpectedly, Appia then turns again to his ever-present thought of the theatre. In this case it is the folk festival in Vevey, Canton de Vaud, which he feels deserves to be listed among outstanding monumental achievements. Much space is devoted to a plan for a genuine people's theatre. He touches upon the question of whether it will be attended by everyone, whether the repertoire will be under the guidance of a censor, whether merely simple or also demanding works will be performed.

The building itself would be patterned after the festival house in Hellerau, of course with modifications. The aim of his ideal theatre will be "to stimulate people to meet, and to enjoy a sociable atmosphere." Appia once promised to deal thoroughly with the social aspect of the theatre. It may be assumed that his discussion in *Monumentalité* was the answer to this erstwhile announcement. But the reader will wait in vain for any suggestions concerning matters of management and financing. True to his nature, Appia completely disregarded these practical points. The greater part of the essay is fashioned in dialogue form, a conversation between a fictitious architect of renown and the author. Obviously he chose this classic form in order to dramatize his thesis from all angles. And he made the best use of the opportunity.

In *Pittoresque* he further elaborates his new ideal of enjoying art collectively, even promotes a kind of collective living as he did in *Port-Royal*. Again he refers to the concept of "solidarity" as he found it among the Greeks and until the Medieval era, when the artisan "entered the pernicious path of individualism." He wants now to teach a new generation how to regain the ideal of classicism. Perhaps unwittingly, Appia introduces a moral issue, the obligation to give as well as to take. He expects that as soon as solidarity is regained, the New Presence will be understood. The core of the essay is his definition of picturesqueness as objects that are decadent, deteriorated, dust-laden. And so he condemns the predilection for "antiques" as incompatible with our mode of living. Following up his argument about the approach to monumentality and picturesqueness, he turns to the problem of mechanization in the next essay. He was by no means against tools and machines, if used sensibly for the benefit of mankind, but in the twenties he already had observed an exaggerated reliance on mechanical devices, what we now call a "push-button existence." Naturally, Appia was, in this respect, thinking less of life in general than of art; thus he singled out the movies and the phonograph. Anxious to determine their place in relation to time and space, he found that recordings were limited to the realm of time duration, but did not enter that of space; movies, however, were used "for time in space," which means movement. Appia was fairly lenient toward recorded music; in his opinion it "comes closest to attaining personality." Strange as it may seem, Appia occasionally went to the movies; he evidently was also acquainted with the new invention at that time, the talking movie. In a paper, entitled *L'Art dramatique vivant*, prepared for the 1925 exhibit in Zurich, he writes that the movies are "an incomparable criterion to judge the quality of our taste. . . . " Surely he preferred the living actor on stage; the artistic level of films did not meet his approval, but he realized that in the field of scenic effects, the most elaborate stage productions could not compare with the possibilities of the movies.

A paper, *Conférence américaine (An American Lecture)*, may have been prepared for the theatre exhibition in New York in spring of 1926, to which Appia intended to send a series of his sketches; or it could have been written in 1922–1923, when Craig approached him with the plan of a joint exhibit in New York. Neither materialized. The lecture is really not a finished composition, but rather a draft based on ideas expounded in *L'Oeuvre d'art vivant*; passages are not closely connected and toward the end, a note merely indicates the paragraphs that should be inserted. Clearly this paper was not meant to be delivered by him.

The Last Scenarios and Designs

THE Rhythmic Spaces included in *L'Oeuvre d'art vivant* did not arouse the attention they deserve. Though Appia was highly esteemed by many experts in 1921, he was considered an artist of the nineteenth century, a designer whose ideas had then been prophetic; that was it. Those who had attended a performance of *Orpheus* in Hellerau or had heard about its style should have been prepared for designs different from those he published before 1900 for *The Ring* and *Tristan*. But Appia had no active part in the practical world of the theatre, consequently very few people took note of his development, the change in his esthetic views. His new conception of *The Ring* came therefore as a complete surprise, almost a shock; so did several of the new designs included in the posthumous portfolio. If Appia had been a regular contributor to current productions, his new conception would have been readily understood, but the interim of ten years between his *Orpheus* and the Basel assignments was too long a gap. Besides, no comprehensive collection of his designs was made available until a year after his death.

It is very difficult to do justice to his last artistic accomplishments, because some scenarios are without sketches, some sketches without the interpreting scenarios, and lastly, some scenarios are incomplete. Possibly the master did not finish everything; but it is very likely too that part of the material was lost after his death. Among the late scenarios and sketches are extensive ones for *The Ring* and, for the first time, experiments with *The Mastersingers* and *Lohengrin*; in addition, there is a concentrated effort to solve the staging of Gluck's operas, an effort all the more gratifying as it signifies the master's growing interests beyond Wagner. Fortunately there are also sketches for a series of dramas; however only one is fully treated, Goethe's *Faust, Part One*, perhaps the most admirable of Appia's last scenarios.

The new *Ring*, having been discussed in detail in the preceding chapter, needs no further mention. Very instructive is the scenario of *The Mastersingers* for which, alas, no sketches are available. Although it is possible to visualize floor plan and elevation on hand of his delineation, more information would be desirable, for it was the first comic opera Appia had chosen to interpret; an opera, to boot, in which the external action outweighs the inner drama. Due to the emphasis on action the designer granted this opera some realism; but a realism subject to the music's style, not to the definition of realism as it is generally given in the spoken play. Through lighting Appia expected to create a realistic mood, to give "the impression of reality," not reality itself. In discarding the numerous scenic details which he deemed entirely superfluous, he hoped to deprive the conventional stage of its picturesqueness and in the end to throw it overboard altogether. Thus his setting for the last, the festive, scene of *The Mastersingers* provided, above all, adequate space for the dancers and the "prophetic chorus."

Further details about his plans for staging *The Mastersingers* can be gained from a letter he wrote Oskar Waelterlin; it contains valuable advice for the forthcoming production and was highly appreciated by the director. As one may expect, Appia attached great importance to proper lighting. In Act I, sunbeams were to brighten the interior of the church; Appia recommended a window on stage right through which the beams could fall and strike Walther standing on the opposite side. The underlying idea was to create a brightly lit area stage left around Walther and a chiaroscuro on stage right where the masters would be seated later in the act. Again Appia's delicate handling of various shades of lighted areas is evident. He gave Sachs, the leading role, an opportunity to dominate either area by crossing from one to the other. The artist's concern with dramatic interpretation is apparent in his request to have Walther begin his *"Am stillen Herd . . . "* in an almost conversational tone addressed to the masters rather than to the audience. For Act II he wrote down not only the light plot delineating lighted and shaded areas in front of Sachs' and Pogner's houses, respectively, but he also described a fascinating scenic effect, although he realized that his friend would not have the means on his stage to execute it. His plan was to have the two houses mounted on wagons which would make it possible to move, for intimate scenes, the house of Sachs close to the curtain line, and to roll both houses upstage or to the wings in the last scene of this act in order to gain enough free space for the street fighting of a huge crowd. In addition he recommended that some choristers stand downstage in this last scene with their backs to the audience, thus creating a more natural impression of the lively action, a suggestion virtually unheard of in his day.

Although Appia, under the influence of Dalcroze's broader outlook, eventually became more tolerant of and even interested in other Wagner operas besides the great music dramas, he never felt for them with the passion he had for *The Ring* and *Tristan*. Of course he completely ignored *Rienzi* and those preceding it. To what extent he studied *The Flying Dutchman* and *Tannhäuser* cannot be determined from the few personal remarks on hand. In 1925 and 1926 he concentrated on *Lohengrin*. His approach to this opera is essentially the same as that to the music dramas, or, for that matter, to any opera. The aging master strips *Lohengrin* of the last realistic vestiges. He considers the action as a whole episodic, and Elsa's faith and her final doubt the central theme, to which he adds the appearance of Lohengrin who is sent to redress injustice but leaves "disillusioned by woman's weakness." In his scenario Appia reasons that since the inherent romanticism is sufficiently expressed in the libretto, there is no need for expressing it in the settings. At the same time, he requests that the acting be modified to conform to his scenic conception, i.e. it must express dramatic, not sentimental, feeling.

His staging ideas can readily be visualized from his scenario and the sketches. A sharper contrast to the original production in Bayreuth (1894) can hardly be imagined. Drapes of neutral color, except in the wedding room of Act III which was to breathe a warm atmosphere, a few platforms and steps are his scenic equipment, which for all its scarcity permits an abundance of variations. No two settings are alike, hardly similar; but one must visualize his light plot fully to appreciate his *mise en scène*. Naturally, Appia omitted the swan in Acts I and III, just as he had discarded the animals in *The Ring*. He regards the appearance of the swan as "a gross error dramatically and esthetically" because, having been talked of so thoroughly, the spectators are indeed aware of it anyway. Instead, he requests the use of a trapdoor upstage for Lohengrin's appearance and disappearance. Drapes close and open, and lighting plays a major role. For instance, in Act II, a courtyard, people are visible behind a curtain halfway open; they simulate the celebration underway in the castle upstage.

Besides the scenarios for Wagner, fragments of *Carmen* and *Iphigénie en Tauride* are preserved. About 1920 Appia occupied himself again with the staging of the Bizet opera. No sketch is available, only a few pages of a scenario describing part of Act III for which he recommends an interpretation very different from the conventional productions. His staging ideas are fascinating and indeed deserve to be materialized. Without a sketch, no definite conclusion can be drawn concerning the scenic picture; however there is no doubt that in *Carmen,* too, he dismissed all realism, as we understand this term, mounting his spatial setting in "cubistic" formations. Two of his suggestions are particularly noteworthy—one is to start the action in late afternoon and let darkness fall slowly during the act until at the end "luminous night" covers the stage. The other is to have the smugglers exit in a dance-like walk, an effective solution which was doubtlessly inspired by his collaboration with Dalcroze.

Appia's growing preference for Gluck and his operas is evident in his description of Acts I and II of *Iphigénie en Tauride*—the only passages available for this work. He sees the opera focused on "the struggle of generosity between the two friends," Orestes and Pylades, strangely not on Iphigenia herself whose inner struggle he considers of minor importance. Groupings and ceremonies are carefully pondered and described, although accompanied by the warning that the external actions and costumes must never "distract from the drama's core." The settings are utterly simple. "Under the sign of the perpendicular," Appia devised a large wide platform a few steps above the stage floor proper, filling the whole stage in Act I; from it a few additional steps lead to a temple which is flanked by high tree trunks shaped, of course, by drapes. A simple square block in front of the temple serves as the sacrificial stone. A larger stone is the prominent feature of the following setting; it is placed on the basic platform which now extends even farther downstage. In Act III two small platforms, one on each side, substitute for the large one.

Nineteen twenty-six may be called Appia's Gluck year. No less than four of this master's operas were in the works: *Iphigenia in Aulis, Iphigenia in Tauris, Alcestis* and, in a modified version, *Orpheus and Euridice.* The designs for *Iphigenia in Aulis* betray Appia's propensity for symmetrical form; at any rate its settings are even plainer, less decorated than those of the other *Iphigenia.* Again a wide platform with three steps leading to a higher level fills the stage almost from the curtain line. Another five steps farther upstage lead to a still higher platform. Drapes frame, as often before, the acting area left and right. In Act I a skydrop and in Act II a wide palace front mask the setting upstage; in the opening scene of Act III the sky is visible again but less so because of lowered borders; for the last setting all drapes, save those downstage, are wide open; now a sacrificial stone dominates the high platform. These wonderful, plain spatial settings afford the stage director marvelous opportunities. Lack of a scenario makes almost fruitless any guessing as to how Appia might have planned groups and ceremonies. The new designs for *Orpheus* are not very different from those he prepared for Hellerau; fundamentally his concept remains the same although, in accord with his ultimate style, everything is simplified. Thus the scene in Hades still shows the dominating staircase but the platforms in front of it are less monumental than they were in 1912–1913. On the other hand, Appia now devised high walls surrounding the acting area while once he had relied on drapes. As to Gluck's *Alcestis,* he referred to working on this opera in letters, but details of his solution are not known. The over-all style certainly resembled that of other Gluck's settings.

Between 1921 and 1928 the artist devoted considerable time to the staging problems of drama, a field he had neglected until then except for the scenes of *Manfred* designed for Paris in 1903. He was nearly sixty when, at last, he showed an equal interest in both the musical and the spoken drama. Starting with *L'Oeuvre d'art vivant* we notice his concern embracing far more than operatic productions. Painting, sculpture, architecture, esthetics in general, and first of all the human body in its relation to the arts had come under scrutiny. It is no wonder then that in his specific line, the *mise en scène,* he went farther afield giving more thought to the performer in general, not just to the singing actor, and thus to the productions of plays. To be accurate, Goethe and Shakespeare were always high on his reading list; he returned to them repeatedly and did not often miss an opportunity to see a performance of their dramas.

A thorough analysis of his conception of Shakespeare is not feasible since he left no complete series of sketches and no notes for each drama. Extensive information is at least available about his *Hamlet;* several pages of a scenario were published by a lady who had studied with him; in combination with some sketches they explain his basic approach. Again the style of his Rhythmic Spaces prevails: set pieces placed on a platform in front of a skydrop. His preference for straight vertical and horizontal lines kept him from ever using the modern curved cyclorama. In *Hamlet* he planned the same arrangement for both Act I, Scene 5 and the last scene of the tragedy in order to provoke a parallel between Hamlet's conversation with his father's Ghost and his death scene. In both settings a rather high platform upstage commands attention; here the Ghost disappears and here Hamlet's body is placed at the end. In the last scene this upstage area is masked by drapes until Hamlet dies. When the curtain partly opens, Fortinbras becomes visible. Later the entire backdrop can be seen as Hamlet is carried to the top on a large shield. Typical was Appia's plan to have the light downstage more and more dimmed, thus giving the stage to Hamlet's body, an effect similar to that devised for the dead Siegmund in *The Valkyrie*. Interesting also is a huge octagonal pillar in the two scenes of Act III conceived as a "double symbolism; Hamlet's body versus the pillar is Hamlet's soul versus the whips and scorns of time," and through "its towering protection . . . [becomes] a kind of grim friend that lends strength to Hamlet." Strong light falls from the rear toward the center, "making a path of light." Thus Hamlet notices the entering Ophelia through the shadow she throws. In the following scene the pillar is moved to the right; center upstage three high chairs are now on a dais "in the glare of the fullest light" to put the greatest emphasis on the King's face.[6]

In these years Appia also occupied himself with Shakespeare's *King Lear*, *Macbeth*, and *A Midsummer Night's Dream*; furthermore he made sketches for *The Waves of Love and the Sea* by Grillparzer and three Greek tragedies, *The Choëphore*, *Oedipus*, and *Prometheus*, the latter realized in Basel. As far as they are available, the settings show all the same simplification; only an interior of *Lear* is treated in a slightly different style, with its inclined side walls giving the impression of a setting narrow at the bottom and wide at the top. Again the spectator is struck by the variations Appia was able to conjure up with his few devices and without ever employing a curved line. These sketches alone establish him as a designer-director as effective when planning plays as he was with Wagner's music dramas.

Two of Appia's achievements merit special consideration. One concerns Ibsen's *Little Eyolf* for which he found a scenic solution in 1924. No notes were left to explain the selection of this drama. Obviously he would not have chosen one of the realistic plays, but *The Pretenders* or *Brand* should have engaged him. In any event, Ibsen's love of nature coupled with his penchant for mysticism and morality must have had a strong attraction for Appia. Traces of mysticism surrounding the death of a child indeed are part of *Little Eyolf*, and Alfred's search for truth and recognition that "to live is an art" may have captured Appia's attention. Somehow he may have sensed a kinship with his own life and philosophy, for Alfred gave up his ambition to become a famous author in order to devote himself completely to humanity. The sketches for this drama—Appia regarded them as schematic rough drafts—contain no realistic detail at all. Ibsen required for Act I a "pretty and richly decorated garden room," but Appia had drapes form the walls of the room with openings indicating doors. He was more elaborate, one might say a bit impressionistic, in his plans for the other two acts.

The scenario of *Faust* with a complete set of sketches is one of Appia's most

Figure 43. Faust, draft of the study. *Carl Niessen.*

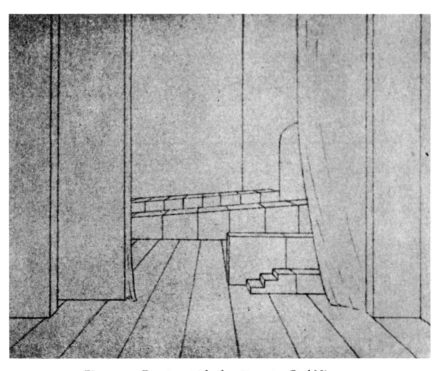

Figure 44. Faust, outside the city gate. *Carl Niessen.*

important accomplishments during these years. There is a symbolic parallel to Goethe's lifelong work on his *Faust*. Appia was almost as much in the grip of this theme as was Goethe himself. The world-spanning drama never ceased to fascinate him. When he organized his memoirs, *Expériences de théâtre et recherches person-nelles*, in the years 1922–1924, he wrote many pages about the production he had witnessed in his youth. And soon thereafter he decided to draft sketches and write an elaborate scenario, a task on which he worked until a year before his death. In the introduction he criticized the staging by Devrient, for whom he had displayed a high regard in his memoirs, and refuted his earlier appraisal of the production which was based on an adapted stage form of the medieval Passion plays (see Chapter I). He was not less dissatisfied with various other staging solutions of *Faust*; among those listed are the *Reliefbuehne*—he probably meant the Kuenstler-theater in Munich—and the so-called Shakespeare Stage at the National Theatre also in Munich, as well as a version he mistakingly called the "Circus Reinhardt." While he was well acquainted with the two types in Munich, his knowledge of any Reinhardt production was purely secondhand. In this case he certainly misunder-stood an oral report or an article. Reinhardt's *Faust* was never moved into the Grosse Schauspielhaus, a former circus. Perhaps Appia remembered the sharp words a critic had heaped upon the work of that famous stage director in general.

A first glance at his manuscript makes Appia's vision of *Faust* immediately clear—one reads, "*Faust, Part One*, 'a dramatic poem'"! Goethe had called it "a tragedy." The scenario and the numerous sketches reveal Appia's preoccupation with Faust's spiritual life; even Faust's relation to Gretchen is window dressing, as are other episodes. The seventeen sketches—they appear in the published Ger-man translation of the scenario—allow the reader to follow Appia's ideas step by step through all scenic changes and every important acting phase. The sketches are not fully drawn, they are, rather, rough drafts; all essential lines are merely indi-cated, and there is no attempt to create an atmosphere through a clarification of brighter and darker areas. It is the method already evident in his designs of the preceding years. The slogan "sacrifice" which Appia had preached for so long is pushed to the extreme in these *Faust* sketches. Indeed no more could be sacrificed.

His scenic solution starts with a neutral frame, a kind of second proscenium blended into the permanent one. This wing, as Appia calls it, separates the Reader from the action of the play, which he never joins. Standing in front of that wing he reads passages assigned by Goethe to several characters such as the Voice of the Lord, the Archangels, the Earth Spirit, and some chorus parts. This solution is part of Appia's concept of *Faust* as a "dramatic poem." The Reader's wing is to be movable, and hence becomes visible only during the Reader's scenes. As a matter of fact, in a few scenes Appia avails himself of two readers, one on each side of the stage. Several feet from the curtain line another frame formed by flats in a neutral color remains throughout the performance, even when wagons are rolled onstage for interior settings, or set pieces are added for the street, the forest, and

Figure 45. Faust, street. *Carl Niessen.*

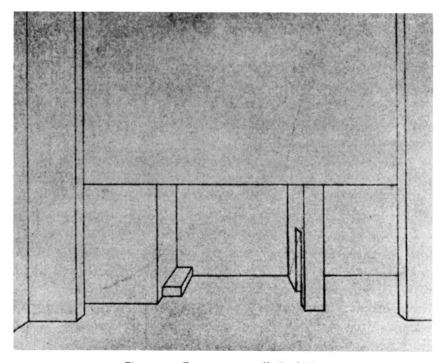

Figure 46. Faust, prison cell. *Carl Niessen.*

the prison scenes. Platforms are sparingly indicated in the sketches, but drapes are used extensively. Again it is amazing to discover how Appia managed to obtain every essential effect with a minimum of means. As is true of his other sketches and scenarios, one must be able to visualize his description of the light plot in order to gain the full impression of his *mise en scène*. Naturally, Appia would not tolerate the appearance of the Archangels or the use of some hocus-pocus by Mephistopheles and the Witch. Anything of that sort was left to imagination, and whenever feasible, the Reader took care of the lines.

Indeed, many brilliant staging details are presented. Students of Appia's art are familiar with some, such as his predilection for silhouette effects, which he achieves by placing a character fairly downstage with a spotlight thrown on him from farther upstage. Of course, the supernatural phenomena are eliminated, as are most of the properties. So, for instance, the furniture in Faust's study consists of a large chair and a lectern on which the magic book and later the Bible are placed. When Faust looks for the poison, he has to disappear briefly backstage to get a cup. Dramatically solved is another scene in the study. Drapes, half covering a window upstage in the first scene, are closed until Mephistopheles, ready to "fly off" with Faust, opens them: no window, only the skydrop is visible, and thus the two characters disappear into a void. A new version is also devised for the scene "Outside the Gate"; a gauze separates the crowd from Faust and his companion. This had the twin purpose of creating greater distance between Faust and the people and, at the same time, giving an unreal touch to the pantomimic action of the crowd behind the gauze. For brief scenes, such as the meeting of Faust and Gretchen, Appia chose what was then called the method "à la Shakespeare," which meant the actors performed before the main curtain. Only the rooms of Gretchen and Marthe were mounted on wagons because "the stage floor proper was too good for them." Interesting is his recommendation for the cathedral to embrace the entire theatre and, therefore, to have the house lights turned on during this scene. The entrance to the church is upstage through a heavy curtain between two pillars, an arrangement he had certainly seen in Austrian and Italian churches. The prison of the last scene is divided into two major areas: a kind of corridor on one side and the cell of Gretchen on the other. A traveler hides Gretchen when Faust and Mephistopheles enter; at the end, when the pair disappear, the traveler masks the other side, showing Gretchen alone in her cell.

In his analysis Appia emphatically defends the view that the first part of *Faust* has only one character, Faust, with Mephistopheles representing his *alter ego*, an interpretation already promoted by scholars of the nineteenth century, especially by Friedrich Theodor Vischer, and still discussed in our day, for instance, by Eugene O'Neill; but rarely implemented in a production. Pursuant to his concept Appia requests that the performers of the two parts "must try to resemble each other in figure, attitude, inflection, and gestures." As he states it, Faust and Mephistopheles must possess an "interchangeable similarity." Appia has complete empathy with Faust's dual personality in which are combined both classical and romantic principles, intellect, and its antithesis, emotion. Many other fascinating observations may be culled from Appia's scenario. It is a pity that he did not have (or did not take?) the time to prepare a scenario for *Faust, Part Two*. We are fortunate though to possess the full treatment of *Part One*; it would be splendid to see it realized on stage. Any director and designer anxious to re-create this masterpiece in a simplified yet dramatic production is well advised to study Appia's conception. Acceptance of his ideas is bound to give an exciting slant to an artistic endeavor.

An Annotation

APPIA, the aging master, was a prolific writer and designer during the last decade of his life. He gives the impression of a man working under pressure from a strong inner urge that did not let him rest. With extreme intensity he took on one task after another, sometimes concentrating on several, as though he had to make up for time lost in his earlier years. While he formerly loved to wander through fields and woods, to lie down and dream, and then, back in his room, to give his dreams form on paper, he now seemed to be in a hurry, to work harder and more steadfastly; he did not give up dreaming and planning, but he wrote faster and sketched more feverishly, spending more hours at his desk. His every effort was focused on finding himself, and a style expressive of himself. For style was to him a manner of seeing, hearing, feeling, and expressing. After years of struggling to free himself from any and all influences of an earlier period, he was at last able to be himself and to draft scenic impressions and express thoughts as he felt them.

The designs created in this period document his new esthetics. He called them "rough drafts" and indeed most of them are simply drafts, their few straight lines indicating rather than marking the drapes, flats, pillars, platforms, stairs, and pieces of furniture needed for the staging of plays and operas. The last trace of impressionism and romanticism is extinguished; instead a unique sense of space, stronger than ever, is evident. Some critics of his *Tristan* and *The Ring* inserted the term "cubism" in an effort to discredit his experiment. They were fundamentally wrong; his work may be slightly related to cubism but it originated from an entirely different source, the classicism of the Greeks and the Renaissance which he interpreted in his own very personal manner. A misunderstanding too was to find a parallel between Appia's final esthetics and expressionism, the predominant movement of the post-war period. His goal was not evolution or modification like that of other reformers, save Gordon Craig of course; his intention was to revolutionize the theatre and even the approach to art in general. He did not remain satisfied with altering existing conditions, certainly not with a mere change of the scenic style, he strove toward an entirely new concept of theatrical experience which rested on the performer as the paramount element of the production. Removal of scenic ballast, emphasis on spatial arrangement and light, ideas he propagated from the very beginning, had only one purpose, i.e. to strengthen the performer's position. This initial conviction is even more pronounced toward the end of his life. He was building a world of harmony, of logic and art, and on this foundation he planned his settings; they had to be simple, formal, and austere.

Among the admirers of his early designs, there were some who did not follow his abstract thinking. But it is one thing to criticize Appia's predilection for well-balanced, symmetrical settings to which even the term "mathematical settings" was heard to be applied. It is quite another thing to do them justice without the benefit of lighting and living performers. His sketches may look monotonous, but the artist made it clear that the living theatre cannot be visualized through a model or a drawing. The spectator who expects no more than an illustration on stage will not accept Appia, but whoever is eager to witness an integrated work of art will agree that Appia has the solution or, more cautiously, one of the solutions. It is on this premise that his last designs must be evaluated; they no longer give an atmosphere, but merely an outline, while the essential ingredient, the living actor and the living light, can ultimately be sensed only in the performance.

Important as the sketches and scenarios are, they are overshadowed by the fecundity of ideas in his writings. These ideas have become the guidelines of our contemporary theatre. In his last essays as well as in *L'Oeuvre d'art vivant* Appia again pondered the problematic relationship of time and space. He somehow felt from the outset that movement was the medium to develop a workable method and he groped his way to find the proper place for it. In his early writings he had vaguely searched for a kind of choreography to help improve the acting of singers. At a crucial time he fortunately met Dalcroze whose views were akin to his own. Their ensuing friendship and collaboration sparked a light in Appia that let him see the right track toward his ideal. Movement was now assigned the task of combining time and space; based on the harmony of these elements he expected to secure a solid foundation for the performing artist.

Another theme that pre-eminently engaged Appia was to show man the way to greater fulfillment in life through active participation in the arts. In the theatre, this meant bringing the spectator and the performer into close contact by removing the strict separation of auditorium and stage. He even substituted "cathedral" for "theatre." The ideal he envisioned is a fruitful communion of laymen and artists, which, so he firmly believed, can be accomplished through mutual respect and love.

The views which the artist perfected during the last ten years of his life show how far he had developed from the complete dependence on the lord of Bayreuth. At last he found himself, the artist who had made the transition from a revolutionary designer to a mature philosopher of the arts.

EPILOGUE

AFTER the great success of *Orpheus and Euridice* in Hellerau there were signs that Appia and Dalcroze might be offered other opportunities, but with the onset of World War I, none materialized, none could be realized. After peace had returned, the first artistic contact led to London. Sturge Moore, who had married a cousin of Appia, was apparently an intermediary in the negotiations for the staging of a play by John Martin-Harvey. Maybe Hugh Barnes, an admirer of Appia, played a part too. But all these efforts did not bring any positive result. When, years later, Appia had the privilege of collaborating with Toscanini at La Scala, he evidently received invitations from other theatres. Once again, he had great hope of preparing *Tristan*, this time for the opera house in Barcelona, as he told Donald Oenslager who talked to him in 1924. This effort must have coincided with a production of *The Ring* planned by the theatre in Toulouse with Appia's designs. But his aversion to the French translation makes it doubtful that he gave much thought to that offer. Of greater interest to him must have been the project promoted by Jacques Rouché to present Gluck's *Alcestis* with Appia in charge of the *mise en scène* in the Paris Opéra, of which Rouché had become the general manager.[1] But by the time this opportunity approached realization, it was too late, for in 1925 and 1926 the ailing master was not able to undertake such a demanding task.

Friends and relatives who met Appia during these years noticed that after a brisk walk, he perspired easily and got out of breath. He dismissed this condition as negligible, but occasionally, in a frank mood, he would concede that his ailment was more serious. He was fully aware of the trouble his heart gave him. In late spring, 1926, he had a particularly severe attack that made it impossible for him even to write a letter. A fortnight thereafter he confessed to a young friend that he would have to change his habits if he wanted to live much longer, adding, however, that he did not particularly care.[2] In this mood he decided to put his worldly affairs in order and he filled a page with his last wishes. The main points of this will were that he should be cremated; that his ashes should be buried under a cedar tree on Dr. Forel's estate, Rives de Prangins, near Nyon, a place he loved so deeply because of its wonderful view; and that his few requests should be executed by three of his friends.[3] These were Dr. Forel; Jean Mercier, the trusted pupil and friend; and Professor Edouard Junod, director of a school for the deaf-mute in Geneva, who through Dalcroze and Bonifas had entered the close circle around Appia. Until the end Appia remained full of optimism, facing death without fear. On February 29, 1928 at Nyon, in his sixty-sixth year, he succumbed to a heart failure without pain as if he had simply returned to Nature. An autopsy was performed by Dr. Ivan Mahain of Geneva, a well-known cardiologist, and, incidentally, a Beethoven scholar. The medical report stated that "calcerous deposits on the nerve center of the heart muscle" caused Appia's death.[4] The brief ceremony in Geneva was attended by his sister, a few relatives, and close friends. Then his ashes were brought to Nyon in accordance with his expressed wish.

The crushing news of the master's death reached Copeau through a telegram. As Mercier remembers, he interrupted his rehearsal to give his actors the sad message with these words: "We have lost one of the greatest theatre men of our era, and our great guide." Deeply moved, all kept silent for several minutes. A few days later Copeau composed a eulogy, one of the most touching tributes a great artist has ever paid his mentor. After briefly pointing out Appia's vast achievements as designer and writer, he elaborated on the master's tremendous importance for the modern theatre, calling him a "musician and architect" who proved that the time values of music can be applied also to the spoken play. He stressed Appia's revolutionary ideas behind his spatial arrangement and lighting and did not fail to mention that leading directors in Germany and Russia had adopted these new principles. The encomium closed with the words: "Yet you will not cease to be among us, lamented, adored, consulted, welcome."[5] (See pp. 206–207)

The three friends charged with the execution of Appia's last will met to plan further steps. At this meeting Dr. Forel suggested that a foundation be set up to protect the artist's estate and to spread his ideas. The first achievement of the Fondation Adolphe Appia was the well-prepared and beautifully published portfolio *Adolphe Appia*, consisting of fifty-six sketches from different periods preceded by an excellent introduction contributed by Henry C. Bonifas. In 1929 the publication appeared with this comment by Dr. Forel: "A year ago Adolphe Appia stopped smiling about the life he loved with a spirit completely overflowing with compassion, and the genius of this artist bursts forth and affects our time."[6] The expensive volume was financed by Hélène with the aid of a few friends. Until her death in 1944 she took care of the numerous manuscripts, sketches, documents, and letters. It is most unfortunate that she did not take precautionary measures to keep this material safe for posterity. Shortly after her death, Geneviève, Paul's retarded daughter, was in a position to get hold of this precious legacy, and one day, she made a big fire in a stove and burned whatever she could discover. Invaluable material was thus irretrievably destroyed.

The Accomplishments of Appia's Pupils

At La Scala Mercier had served as the master's arm, but shortly after his collaboration on the history-making production of *Tristan* he left Switzerland and became a member of Copeau's company, serving it as an actor, director, and manager until 1929. He was then able to see his mentor only during brief vacations and during the company's appearances in Switzerland. In summer, 1930, Mercier sailed for the United States, having been invited to direct and teach at the Cornish Theatre and School in Seattle, Washington. During the succeeding three years, well remembered on the West Coast, he also lectured and directed at the University of Michigan in Ann Arbor and toured with his group from the Northwest to Texas. Upon his return to France he became the director of the Municipal Theatre in Strasbourg until Rouché called him to Paris in 1936 and put him in charge of the *mise en scène* at the Opéra Comique. Mercier held this position until 1965, save for the years of occupation, when he refused to be a collaborator, and directly after the war. During his absence from Paris he was a highly welcome guest director in Basel, Geneva, and Zurich. Before and, even more often, after the war he was invited to stage operas in other cities too, among them Florence, Monaco, Genoa, and Amsterdam. His considerable share in the modern development of operatic art was duly acknowledged by the French Government, which bestowed several high orders upon him and in 1961 made him a *Chevalier de la Légion d'Honneur à titre Civil et Militaire.*

Though mostly known for his sensitive directing of operas, Mercier deserves equally high praise as a director of plays. In all his artistic work he strove without pedantry to realize Appia's theories in the modern theatre. Twice he went even beyond staging opera in his teacher's spirit. In 1947 he had the fascinating designs of *Tristan* executed for a performance in Geneva; to clarify the case he wrote an article expressly for the program book. A few seasons thereafter, he staged *Orpheus* with settings based on Appia's sketches in the same opera house. Both productions were extraordinarily successful. Mercier helped also spread his master's fame with two long essays. Of great value is his *L'Avenir du Théâtre Lyrique,* in which he exposed the current ills of the operatic stage, adding twenty pregnant recommendations for their cure. This essay reads extremely well twenty years after its publication, and many of its suggestions are still valid.[7] Of greater importance yet is another article published only in *Theatre Arts Monthly* in an English translation. It is the most perceptive appreciation of Appia's life and art. One passage in particular ought to be taken to heart: "To be a disciple of Appia is not to copy his designs more or less successfully, to interpret his ideas more or less correctly, but to have, above all else, as he himself has said, an inner attitude toward the work one is creating or performing."[8]

Oskar Waelterlin, Appia's other pupil, also had a distinguished career. From 1925 he served as managing director of the Municipal Theatre in Basel for seven years, seven seasons in which he demonstrated his adherence to the master's reform through his concentration on the training of the performer and the support he gave him with simple spatial settings and living light. Waelterlin became then a highly esteemed stage director in Germany until 1938 when, disgusted with the Nazi cult, he returned to Switzerland to accept the position of managing and artistic director of the Schauspielhaus in Zurich. Until his death in 1961, he led and inspired one of the outstanding companies in the German tongue. During and after World War II his theatre was the center of German drama. When Austria and Germany had recovered from their injuries, Waelterlin was also in great demand as a guest director of both plays and operas in Berlin, Vienna, Hamburg, and Salzburg. Everywhere he was admired for his dramatic sense of style and his discreet art of directing the performers.

In many talks with artists as well as in public appearances Waelterlin spoke up for Appia. He left his finest testimony in an autobiographical book in which he depicted his master's "Calvinistic stubbornness" that made any compromise impossible. With an understanding smile he remembers how Appia suffered unbearable discomfort as he crossed the backstage area in Basel where several wobbly canvas pieces were stored.[9] His memoirs offer much interesting material on how a contemporary director might develop and maintain an artistic repertoire without succumbing to the expediencies of the commercial enterprise. His book contains, furthermore, pertinent details of Appia's ideas for the production of *The Ring*. As he had the priceless opportunity to discuss all problems with the designer and to work with him in Basel, his statements are of particular relevance. It is touching to read that Appia, though bursting with intensity, was always controlled and modest.

Followers

INTERNATIONALLY better known than the two pupils is Jacques Copeau, Appia's disciple. Although Copeau had worked outside the French capital after the middle twenties, his friends and admirers in Paris did not forget him. In fall, 1929, his name was openly suggested as director of the Comédie Française, but these first feelers met no response among the authorities. Unruffled, Copeau and his company continued to tour French and Swiss cities from their headquarters in Burgundy. When, in the thirties, he could spare the time he accepted invitations to direct plays in leading theatres in such cities as Brussels, Florence, and Paris. At last in 1936, a number of his influential friends succeeded in pushing his engagement as one of the directors at the Comédie Française, of which Edouard Bourdet became the administrator.[10] But in this old institution, encumbered with tradition and convention, Copeau served as an advisor rather than a potent participant. It was not until 1940 that he was appointed general manager, but now war conditions indefinitely delayed all plans for drastic reforms, and a year later Copeau resigned in protest against the German occupation.[11] He returned to his beloved Pernand where he remained until his death in 1949.

In his thinking and his deeds Copeau proved himself a true disciple of Appia. He sincerely believed in the principles of his friend and executed them with "an inner attitude" toward the work he had staked out for himself. His productions were a revelation; they demonstrated that the modern theatre does not need elaborate realistic settings or gimmicks for an ensemble of performers well trained and so rehearsed that, supported by simple spatial arrangements, they live their characters and project the inner meaning of the plays. Performances under his directions manifested the validity of Appia's principle that the spoken drama submits to the same laws as the musical drama. In his theatre Copeau showed, moreover, how actors and audience can be brought in close contact through the installation of a forestage. Great value was also set on lighting although not to the extent that Appia himself would have used it. The most essential decision was that all these elements were fused into an integral whole under the guidance of the director's driving idealistic spirit. Indeed Copeau more than anyone else made Appia's dream a reality.

If judged by a direct success with the audience at large, Copeau's career and achievements do not seem very impressive. Yet they are of historical significance, for no one in the modern French theatre deserves deeper gratitude and higher praise; through his writings and his lectures, and above all through his productions and his training of a large number of actors and directors, the long overdue reform was considerably advanced. After his departure from Paris in the early twenties, Copeau's ideals were carried on, though not formally, by the *Cartel des Quartre* consisting of Louis Jouvet, Charles Dullin, Gaston Baty, and Georges Pitoëff.[12] To be sure these four artists did not imitate Copeau. All available evidence shows that Jouvet and Dullin were much closer to his esthetics than the two other gentlemen, who merely adhered to some general principles of the Cartel. Each of the four had an independent mind which excluded all imitation, but this does not mean that they disregarded Copeau's aims.

The offspring of brilliant parents often antagonize their elders in a desperate effort to assert themselves, to find their own individuality. But their heritage is just as often too strong to let them completely deviate, and some parental ideas are preserved. The same is true of immediate spiritual and artistic heirs. No matter how much they try to be independent, to go their own way, they cannot escape the influence of an overpowering personality. Copeau's influence, and through him that of Appia, is noticeable in a younger generation. Besides Jean Mercier and Michel Saint-Denis, Copeau's nephew who is openly working in the spirit of his great uncle, there are, among others, Jean-Louis Barrault; Jean Dasté, Copeau's son-in-law; Jacque Hursman; and Jean Vilar. Their particular style in acting and staging, their consistent emphasis on the performer, on spatial settings, on lighting effects is undeniably Copeau—and Appia. It cannot be overlooked, moreover, that the renaissance of the art of mime may largely be attributed to Copeau's work.

Direct and Indirect Influence

In contrast to the few directors who do not hesitate to acknowledge their debt to Appia as their spiritual father, there are many who have borrowed from him but veil in silence the origin of their scenic concept. During the last years of his life Appia had to discover that in one case or another entire designs of his were used in production nearly unaltered; and friends informed him that his ideas found their way into the movies. Furthermore, he showed Dr. Forel articles in which the problems of a scenic reform were delineated in complete accord with his writings, but without quotation marks or reference to the source. The great artist noticed such plagiarisms free of the least resentment or "hurt vanity," merely with a word of regret about "injured justice," as the physician describes Appia's reaction. He was unable to grasp such unfairness. More explicit was his reference to the unauthorized use of his sketches of *Parsifal*. (It is not known which opera house he referred to.) He did not actually say so but simply mentioned the rather peculiar theft by pointing out that his settings "make sense only in connection with their scenarios." All this saddened him but by the same token he somehow felt the satisfaction that these imitations really spelled victory. For him "the main thing was that the idea was created and is alive."[13] He resigned himself to the fact that he experienced the same fate as his father, who never received full credit for initiating the Red Cross.

The elusive art of the theatre is far more vulnerable to plagiarism than is any other art form. In the first place, unlike the play itself, the production is not protected by a copyright law. Thus a court trial will lead nowhere even if the probability of conscious copying exists. Consequently, unless the complete scenic arrangement, the blocking, and the dramatic interpretation closely resemble the original, one cannot really point an accusing finger to plagiarism. In addition, it is entirely possible that a director or designer adopts an idea he has heard of incidently, but whose author is unknown to him; or an artist may have been so impressed with a new approach that he unwittingly re-creates its image years later.

Finally there is the chance that an idea or a principle may be born in more than one mind simultaneously. Such was the case of Appia and Craig, ten years his junior. Superficially one might surmise that Craig followed Appia with full intent, and some writers maintain this. To the expert however it is evident that the two dominating reformers developed independently of one another.

Valid conclusions about the ancestry of most contemporary designers and directors can hardly be drawn unless they themselves give us definite clues regarding the origin of their esthetics. In this connection Alfred Roller, the leading designer of the state theatres in Vienna from 1903 until the middle thirties, offers a perplexing example. Repeatedly it has been pointed out that his inspiration was spurred by Appia's scenic reform; at least, that his style in general closely resembled that of Appia. The fact that early in the century H. S. Chamberlain resided in Austria is noteworthy; he was acquainted with many artists, and it is feasible that he knew Roller and showed him Appia's sketches. Could Appia on one of his visits with his friend have met Roller? Maybe. A thorough research into Roller's background and development was undertaken in connection with a dissertation but no such contact has been unearthed in all the private material handed to the researcher. Only a single but very reliable source reports that Roller's novel concept of *Tristan* was developed "under the influence of Count [sic] Appia's ideas."[14] The sole witness is the late Bruno Walter, who had worked with Gustav Mahler, then the artistic director of the Viennese Opera House. Roller had been a well-known painter, a member of the Sezession—a group of avant-garde artists in Vienna—when Mahler asked him to collaborate with him. Roller's fondness for impressionism is clearly revealed in his first designs, and there are similarities to Appia's work, but beyond this, Roller definitely follows Appia's tendency toward heroic monumentality, elimination of external details, and emphasis on the essential. The relation of the Viennese opera productions to Appia's concept grew even stronger in the twenties and thirties when Roller worked with the stage director Lothar Wallerstein, who favored not only simplicity in his settings with emphasis on the light plot but who concentrated to a high degree on the acting singer.

Several other examples of a *mise en scène* resembling Appia's sketches can be found rather early. *Tristan,* as devised by Hans Wildermann for Breslau in 1909, is hardly imaginable without this influence (or did it come from Roller?). The same dependence is easily recognizable in some "new" designs for *Parsifal* and *The Valkyrie. Orpheus* as staged in Hellerau had replicas almost at once in productions of this and other operas of Gluck. Dramas too began to appear in this scenic style, though it is difficult, often impossible, to discern whether designers and directors followed Appia or Craig. In all probability, the foremost designer frankly to adopt Appia's lighting concept, immediately after the first World War, was Emil Pirchan at the National Theater in Munich. His scenic treatment of Grillparzer's *Medea* and Grabbe's *Hannibal* did not venture beyond the simplification already practiced at that time. His later collaboration with Leopold Jessner in Berlin in the staging of *Wilhelm Tell* with its spatial arrangement shows an even closer relation to the work of the Swiss genius; and so did his admirable unit settings for *Othello* and *Richard III*. Appia's "cubistic" concept perhaps left its imprint on Pirchan's sketches for Hebbel's *Die Nibelungen*—its scenery consisted basically of a series of large blocks, and it is surprising that Pirchan refers to Craig in his writings rather than to Appia. Many other examples from large and middling theatres in Central Europe can readily be given to demonstrate that Appia had been the god-father of these productions.

The change in the style of staging, so obvious in plays, proceeded at a far more leisurely pace in the operatic field. As mentioned, Gluck benefited from the new trend almost at once, and so did a few Wagnerian works. Contemporary operas by Hindemith, Stravinsky, and others not subjected to tradition were presented in the new spirit. After 1918 scenic reforms were primarily carried out in medium-sized and smaller theatres of Central Europe. The decisive breakthrough came with the opening of the Kroll Opera (one of the State Opera Houses in Berlin) in 1927. This institution became the leader in modern operatic staging; experiments there followed ultramodern movements such as that of the Bauhaus but a few of its artists were positively influenced by Appia's principles. At any rate, the Kroll Opera showed far-reaching simplification of settings with emphasis on lighting. In addition, there was a perceptible attempt to reform the acting, which means that singers were allowed only a modicum of expressive movements and gestures, thus approximating what then was called static or oratorio-like staging.

The revolution on the stage was of course not restricted to Central Europe. Under the impact of expressionism, cubism, constructivism, and the like, each of which lasted but briefly, the style of staging swayed from one to another in many countries. A forward push was made by a few small groups even in Italy, that artistically most conservative country. Without the experiments undertaken by the Teatro de Covegno and Istituto del Dramma Antico the plan for Appia's *Tristan* in Milan would have been almost unthinkable.

During the middle thirties, the scenic concept underwent a transition in Great Britain too; of course not in the typical West End theatre, but under Tyrone Guthrie in the Old Vic and under Ashley Dukes in the Mercury Theatre. Here however the reform followed Craig, the famed native son, rather than Appia, who remained unappreciated except by a few experts. This makes us understand why Hugh Barnes, a musician who lived and worked in Oxford for many years, did not succeed in publishing his translation of Appia's books and his own essay about the artist whom he had met in Switzerland around 1920. The attitude of neglect still lingers in the British Isles.

Across the Atlantic Ocean American artists were strongly attracted by the revolutionary ideas. By 1914, the greatness of Appia had been firmly expressed in the writings of Hiram Moderwell and Carl van Vechten. The legitimate theatre in New York indeed ignored the new trend, but outside the metropolis, Maurice Brown and others understood and supported it. Few Americans visited Europe prior to World War I to study the reform, but after 1918, it became almost customary for aspiring artists to acquaint themselves with the revolutionary work in Europe. Consequently, our leading designers today are thoroughly imbued with Appia's and Craig's concepts. In fact, Craig's name should be mentioned first, for more artists confess a preference for his approach; as examples, R. E. Jones, Norman Bel-Geddes, and Donald Oenslager, though all of them pay high tribute to Appia. Lee Simonson was in the forefront of those who favor Appia; he wrote and spoke extensively about Appia's great influence on him. In his foreword to *Music and the Art of the Theatre* he is willing to designate, historically speaking, everything before Appia as "B.A."[15]

An inquiry into the development in the Soviet Union does not yield a clear-cut picture. Stanislavsky indeed knew about Appia, possibly through Dalcroze and Wolkonsky and definitely through Copeau. Yet except for a single note made in 1918, Appia's name is not mentioned in his writings. It is well known that he applied eurythmics particularly in the training of singers in his Opera Studio. His friend and collaborator, Vladimir Nemirovitch-Dantchenko, relied to an even higher degree on the body training as developed by Dalcroze. The sharply stylized settings of his musical productions such as *Carmencita* and *Lysistrata* tell of a kinship to Appia, but no proof exists of any conscious adaptation. An equally moot question is whether Alexander Tairov was acquainted with the work of the Swiss master, though it may be assumed that Stanislavsky's and Dantchenko's productions provided at least an indirect link.

It is safer to maintain that V. E. Meyerhold accepted Appia's principles in spite of the fact that the Russian director evidently made no direct statements. His 1909 staging of *Tristan* at the Imperial Theatre in St. Petersburg in collaboration with the designer M. Chervachidze shows strong signs of Appia's reform. In much of his work there are clear indications of emphasis on lighting as well as on multiple levels and, an essential factor, on the importance attached to pitch, timbre, and tempo in the dialogue, which induced him to search for a musical notation that could benefit the actor—unequivocally an idea of Appia's. In the opinion of a keen observer from the United States, the theatre of Nicolai Okhlopov adhered in a large measure to Appia's principles of spatial settings and dramatic movements. This visitor, Norris Houghton, believes moreover that V. E. Ryndin was even more affected by these ideas.[16] With reference to current productions in the Polish city Opole, Appia is mentioned together with Craig, Meyerhold, Vakhtangov, and Piscator as sources of inspiration. The director Jercy Grotowsky went to an extreme particularly in his experiment to erase, as it were, the separate acting area and to bring the performers into the midst of his audience.[17]

Altogether in the U.S.S.R. and her neighboring countries, only a few hints of Appia can be detected in productions and writings, but there are many references to eurythmics, which leads to the conclusion that the work of Dalcroze was and is more extensively accepted than that of Appia.

It is not difficult to enumerate dozens of productions indicating a resemblance to Appia's first, and even his late, period. There is no doubt that many, probably most, of the young directors and designers who grew up between the two world wars have been inspired by his scenic ideas. Emphasis must be on the word "scenic," since his writings were not widely read. Therefore any noticeable leaning toward his esthetics can be traced to a single segment of his work, namely his sketches, seen in divers exhibitions and occasionally in magazines and books. Specifically his concept of the art of acting is mostly appreciated indirectly as implicit in Dalcroze's eurythmics.

Jaques-Dalcroze fully deserves the credit given him as the originator of the modern dance movements, an honor he must share with Isadora Duncan. Because some of their followers were engaged in opera houses, their work gave impetus to the reform of musical productions. Outstanding among these was Rudolf Laban, ballet director in Berlin, whose sense of space is certainly related to that of Appia. The new attitude spread from ballet via the opera to the spoken drama, although it must be stated that in many a drama school, eurythmics has been part of the actors' training for years. It is gratifying to discover that several contemporary directors and designers have been stressing the new concept in articles and lectures during the past two decades. Music is the unifying factor for them, and they call for the synchronization of music and action, of tone and word, and for the integration of all visual and aural elements. Although such statements refer to opera, similar goals may be discerned in drama.

Of significant relevance to the question of Appia's influence on the contemporary theatre are the conditions in Bayreuth. After a rather timid reform under the guidance of Siegfried Wagner, the Festivals received a thorough modernization in the thirties thanks to the noted designer Emil Preetorius. In his works for Berlin, Hamburg, and Milan he proved himself a modern artist who believed in scenic simplification, spatial settings, and the power of light. Early in his career he was not acquainted with Appia's designs. In a book on Preetorius, Appia is mentioned but not that he had any influence. However, passages about relating the scenic frame to the lively action, and the importance of the light plot, may be taken as a clue to the ancestry.[18]

The views of Wolfgang and, even more, of the late Wieland Wagner, the perpetrators of the Bayreuth Festivals, are extremely pertinent to this investigation. Their productions decisively demonstrate that they are no longer the guardians of an antiquated tradition but are the propagators of a revolutionary style. In contrast to Cosima Wagner, their grandmother, they are willing to pay homage to

Figure 47. Siegfried, last scene. The rock of the Valkyries in Wieland Wagner's staging for the 1954 Bayreuth Festivals. *Richard Wagner Gedenkstaette, Bayreuth.*

Adolphe Appia who in a program book is mentioned as the godfather of the new esthetics accepted by Wagner's grandsons.[19] In spite of this and other public acknowledgments of a debt to the great designer, those in charge of the Appia Foundation were not satisfied with the tardy recognition. A request from Bayreuth for permission to publish one of Appia's essays in a program book received a negative response. The refusal was apparently not based on sentimental reasons alone; the impression prevailed that the new Bayreuth had little in common with Appia.

To prove some degree of relationship, superficial similarities can quickly be listed: hardly any color is seen in the scenery; the spatial settings are simplified to an extreme; the stage is veiled in mystic penumbra with emphasis on the cyclorama on which a multitude of projected images are thrown. There are however incisive dissimilarities such as the numerous curved lines which he would have opposed. He would have objected even more strongly to the use of an exaggerated sex symbol in the staging of *Tristan*. As to the art of lighting, the Swiss genius thought in terms of contrasts, of bright and dark areas, not in terms of a general semi-darkness which obscures the action considerably. Furthermore, avoiding everything that may approximate picturesqueness, Appia inserted projection sparingly, not elaborately. In the field of acting too a sharp difference of style is recognizable. In many scenes Bayreuth seems to favor a static pictorial arrangement whereas Appia aimed at an active, dramatic interpretation by all singers. Like other contemporary artists, Wagner's heirs pay tribute to Appia's early volume, *La Musique et la mise en scène*, almost to the exclusion of all his later writings and designs. Thus the relation of the Bayreuth Festivals to their spiritual father remains tenuous.

But an objective judgment makes it imperative that one hear the creator of modern Bayreuth himself, Wieland Wagner, who emphasizes that Appia was the first to discover an alternative to

> the thoughtless, naturalistic rendering of Wagner's annotations, but who for decades remained without succession, not the least because of the strict rejection of his ideas by Cosima Wagner and the Bayreuth of her time. In all fairness, though, one must admit that in Appia's day the theatre did not offer the technical possibilities to transfer his ideas onto the stage, and that, consequently, the effect of his magnificent ideas was less practical than theoretical.

Wieland Wagner makes it thus clear that he feels free to adapt Appia's principles in any way he decides under the contemporary esthetic and technical conditions.

With reference to current trends in architecture, Appia's vision of a "cathedral" with all its implications deserves full consideration. Leading architects, designers, and directors have nurtured similar ideas. Each differs from all the others, but all have certain points in common: the elimination of the proscenium frame and, related to it, of the footlights, and if feasible, of the main curtain; the shifting of the acting area closer to the audience and, vice versa, of the spectators to the stage by seating them around a large forestage (hardly practical in opera houses). The ideal theatre of today is indeed based on the creation of a space stage or *Raumbuehne*, uncluttered by non-essentials, dominated by lighting. Appia brought it further along in his drive to bring the audience into intimate contact with the performers and to have the spectators participate in the action. His consistent endeavors to change their role from observer to that of participant are now shared by many eminent theatre people, all of whom agree that a production of a play or an opera can and should intellectually and emotionally become a communal experience.

Projects for a new type of theatre, or at least for a modification of its conventional form, did not suddenly appear in this century. As the history of theatre in the nineteenth century demonstrates, several reformers propagated a variety of forms, few of which lasted for any length of time. About 1900 Adolphe Appia, Gordon Craig, and George Fuchs gave these moods toward change strong impetus; they were assisted by Gémier and Aléxandre Lugné-Poë. The first who saw his dream come true was Fritz Erler, the good spirit of the Kuenstlertheater in Munich, a slightly modernized building that opened in May, 1908. Between the two wars many revolutionary programs and blueprints were submitted by Walter Gropius, Adolf Loos, and Hans Poelzig in Germany; Norman Bel-Geddes in the U.S.A.; by V. E. Meyerhold and others in the U.S.S.R. It cannot be held against these men that their plans remained blueprints; their concepts were too far ahead of the conventional taste of those who were to finance their execution. Undaunted, these artists continued to push for a thorough reform because they deeply sensed that a new style of the *mise en scène* must necessarily include the whole building and its social function as it relates to art. The goal was, and is, to erect a building that is practical and above all that can fuse the spectators and the performers into a single unit, a community.

Appia would have approved many of the new theatres, not in every detail to be sure, but as an expression of the architect's "inner attitude." He would indeed have been pleased to see the proscenium flush with the house proper, affording the performers close communication with the audience and giving the theatre, at least sometimes, the atmosphere of a festival house. Again, it cannot be maintained that Appia's influence alone spurred this change; his last book, *L'Oeuvre d'art vivant*, had no wide circulation and the important essay *Monumentalité* was not even published until after World War II. Still it can by no means be denied that his contribution was considerable, for some basic principles of the modern trend can be traced to some of his early essays and especially to the Festival House in Hellerau, the first realization of his plan to unite spectators and performers under the same roof.

When the ruins of the last war gave many cities in Europe the opportunity to rebuild the old theatres or to erect entirely new ones, projects formerly ignored were re-examined and adapted. "Space stage," "open stage," "thrust stage," "communion between actors and audience" became fashionable terms and the remodeled and new theatres proved the practicability of the ideals considered unrealistic by the preceding generation. In the United States a few large universities have assigned at least one of their available halls to the new kind, equipping a big room that has no obvious stage area with a series of easily movable platforms of different sizes. The open stage has also invaded New York, the fortress of tradition, and has been adopted in several countries. In any case, the traditional form of the proscenium stage came to an end; today it is unthinkable to build a playhouse in the old manner. The minimum change includes a wide apron. Opera houses, too, have at least the proscenium frame now flush with the side walls; sometimes there are complicated devices for jutting an apron into the orchestra pit. Even concert halls were drawn into the movement. Thus the Philharmonie in Berlin, opened in 1963, proves that orchestra and audience need not face each other. Here the patrons are seated all around the orchestra without detriment to the acoustics, and hence to the artistic enjoyment.

Appia's prophetic demands were not so crazy after all.

A Last Word

YET, though his ideals have spread throughout the world of the theatre and are widely, if not universally, accepted and applied, their creator is still not always honored as he should be. Full credit is duly given him for the revolution he caused through his designs and writings before 1900. But the oversight, the neglect, of his later works result in a lopsided appreciation. The creations and ideas of his middle and later periods are not known by many, although their principles have permeated the movements of our time.

The sad conclusion is that although Appia directly affected the contemporary development, the influence he indirectly exercised was greater, and this in turn deprived him of the fame due him. It is particularly sad that this general default stems from a misunderstanding and misinterpretation based on ignorance. As a result, this monograph could carry the subtitle *The Tragedy of a Genius*. Once more the question can be raised as to whether we are just and fair to the great man. After a survey of all available material the answer is, "Yes, to some degree. Recognition is given but with reservations." No book on theatre history, on directing, designing, and lighting published during the past decades overlooks the master. Every author refers to him and, depending on his personal preference, gives more space either to Appia or to Craig. New editions of encyclopedias also grant Appia at least a paragraph, often a column and more. The first all-inclusive step to honor Appia was taken in the United States with the translation and publication of *The*

Work of Living Art in 1960 and *Music and the Art of the Theatre* in 1962, the centenary of his birth. The remaining writings are under consideration. Switzerland started to pay homage to her great son with the first publication of *La Musique et la mise en scène* in the original version. A more extensive acquaintance with his work will surely lead to a more intensive appreciation of its importance. Therefore it is most desirable to see all Appia's works made available in several languages.

Appia was, no doubt, one of the two dominating theatre artists and certainly the greatest theoretician of the modern theatre. His logic in expounding his theories was coupled with a tremendous imagination which saved him from ever becoming pedantic. His deep feelings never allowed sentimentality to intrude into his work. He started as an amateur in his chosen field and became its master mind. He was an artist who confined his early development to a single object, yet was lucky enough to throw off his self-imposed fetters in middle age. He was, first of all, a prophet not just in the limited sphere of the *mise en scène* but, designated by fate, in all aspects of theatre arts.

During his life span Appia met many people but very few came really close to him. Too long he was shackled to Chamberlain; fortunately for him and us, he found Dalcroze, who contributed much to his maturing until at last he became entirely independent, listening only to his inner voice. During this last period he befriended Mercier and Waelterlin, his two pupils, to whom he was strongly attached and sincerely grateful for what they gave and meant to him. He treasured the faithfulness of his sister Hélène, the loyal friendship of Copeau, Dalcroze, Dr. Forel, Bonifas, and some others as well as a few of his cousins. They all thought of him as a kind, selfless, and considerate man whom they unhesitatingly called a genius. The memory they preserved of him was not an impersonal matter related to Art, it remained dedicated to the man himself.

Appia, like most outstanding creators, was of a complex nature, yet simple at heart. In his character sensual and ascetic traits are strangely blended. A grave conflict between reality and ideality caused him much hurt and frustration. Totally devoted to the theatre, he was not able to live with it. He longed to have many friends but shrank from meeting people. He extolled communal living and communal experience of the arts, but lived almost as a recluse, rebelling against the most rudimentary rules of sociability. He saw the future, yet was unwilling and unable to cope with the conditions of his own time; and so he is the prophet of our Living Theatre, whom his peers did not recognize for many years. As few before him, Appia had a profound conception of the wholeness of art and a sincere trust in mankind.

Figure 48. Death mask of Adolphe Appia. *Fondation Adolphe Appia.*

L'art et l'œuvre d'Adolphe Appia

Adolphe Appia, dont nous annoncions, voici quelques jours, la mort, fut l'un des maîtres sinon le maître, le créateur de la réforme moderne de la mise en scène. Nul n'était plus qualifié que M. Jacques Copeau, son disciple et un disciple devenu à son tour un modèle, pour adresser à Appia le dernier adieu du Théâtre.
Voici l'article que M. Jacques Copeau a adressé à Comœdia, de sa solitude bourguignonne de Pernand-Vergelesses :

Adolphe Appia est mort, le 29 février, dans une maison de santé, voisine de Nyon (Suisse), où des soins nécessaires le retenaient depuis assez longtemps déjà. Il était dans sa soixante-sixième année.

Plusieurs fois, nous avions craint pour lui. Mais, après chaque alerte, nous reprenions confiance dans les ressources de sa constitution exceptionnelle. La clarté de son regard, l'aisance de toute sa personne, l'animation de son esprit, son enthousiasme toujours alerte et sa grâce inimitable, tout en lui, jusqu'aux derniers jours, respirait la vie et l'amour de la vie. « Votre jeune homme... » C'est ainsi qu'il signait l'une des dernières lettres qu'il m'adressa. Et je recueille, au bas de la dernière, cet adieu : « A tous, mon plus beau salut ; à vous, mon vieux cœur... » Son vieux cœur a cessé brusquement de battre. Il n'est plus maintenant qu'un peu de cendre. Cher Appia !

Je ne songe pas aujourd'hui à retracer l'œuvre et la vie du grand artiste qui fut mon maître et mon ami. Son nom, s'il n'est familier chez nous qu'à quelques initiés, est célèbre dans le monde entier. Sa personnalité, son action créatrice sont inscrites dans l'histoire du théâtre des trente dernières années. Elles n'y sont pas toujours inscrites en clair, car Appia eut plus d'imitateurs que de disciples.

Il vivait à l'écart, modeste et laborieux, rêvant, dessinant, écrivant, un peu farouche aux inconnus, mais prodiguant à ceux qu'il aimait les trésors de son imagination. Trois livres : *La Mise en Scène du drame wagnérien, Die Musik und die Inszenierung* et *L'Œuvre d'Art Vivant*, quelques essais, une centaine de dessins magnifiques, un petit nombre de réalisations comme *Manfred, Tristan, L'Or du Rhin, La Walkyrie*, et ses travaux à Hellerau avec Jaque-Dalcroze suffisent à Appia pour dominer l'art du metteur en scène de son temps.

Toutes les expositions du théâtre moderne, et récemment encore celle de Magdebourg, ont mis au premier plan et en pleine lumière l'œuvre du maître. A Amsterdam, en 1923, la salle d'honneur lui était réservée. On reconnaissait aisément, en visitant les autres salles, que tout ce qu'on a fait après lui, procède de lui, plus ou moins déformé.

C'est lui, avec Gordon Craig, qui nous a ouvert les voies nouvelles. C'est lui qui nous a ramenés à la grandeur, et aux principes éternels.

Appia était musicien et architecte. Il nous a appris que la durée musicale, qui enveloppe, commande et règle l'action dramatique, engendre du même coup l'espace où celle-ci se développe. Pour lui, l'art de la mise en scène, dans sa pure acception, n'est pas autre chose que la configuration d'un texte ou d'une musique, rendue sensible par l'action vivante du corps humain et par sa réaction aux résistances que lui opposent les plans et les volumes construits.

D'où le bannissement, sur la scène, de toute décoration inanimée, de toute toile peinte, et le rôle primordial de cet élément actif qu'est la lumière.

Quand on a dit cela, on a tout dit, ou à peu près. On tient une réforme *radicale* — Appia employait volontiers ce mot — dont les conséquences, en se développant, vont des escaliers de Reinhardt au constructivisme des Russes. On est en possession d'une donnée scénique. On est tranquille. On peut travailler sur le drame et l'acteur, au lieu de tourner éternellement autour de formules décoratives plus ou moins originales, de procédés de présentation plus ou moins inédits, dont la recherche nous fait perdre de vue l'objectif essentiel.

La donnée d'Appia : une action en rapport avec une architecture devrait suffire à faire des chefs-d'œuvre, si les metteurs en scène savaient ce que c'est qu'un drame, si les auteurs dramatiques savaient ce que c'est qu'une scène...

**

Cher Appia, nous allions nous retrouver bientôt, comme chaque année. Et je ne vous verrai plus. Nous n'aurons plus de ces interminables entretiens qui nous laissaient épuisés d'enthousiasme et d'amitié. Vous ne viendrez plus accueillir ma petite troupe sur le quai de la gare, à Genève, ni dans ma loge, avant le spectacle, pour vérifier le détail de mon costume. Vous ne vous tiendrez plus, drapé dans votre redingote ibsénienne, debout contre la baignoire d'avant-scène, au théâtre de Lausanne, et toisant de haut le public, comme si vous montiez la garde à la porte du spectacle que vos amis allaient donner. Vous ne nous jouerez plus la pièce après que nous l'avions jouée, retrouvant nos moindres gestes et toutes nos intonations, jouissant avec un rire d'enfant des plus subtiles intentions, et nous éclairant bien souvent un point de notre art qui nous restait obscur.

Je ne verrai plus, Appia, votre grande tête blanche s'agiter à la portière du wagon qui nous ramenait en France, puis de loin s'incliner encore, avec cette exquise courtoisie qui était la fleur de votre noblesse naturelle... Mais vous ne cesserez pas d'être parmi nous, regretté, vénéré, consulté, écouté.

— Jacques COPEAU.

Pernand, 6 mars 1928.

Jacques Copeau's eulogy to Adolphe Appia, reproduced from *Comoedia*, March 12, 1928.

The Art and the Work of Adolphe Appia

Adolphe Appia, whose death we announced several days ago, was one of the masters if not *the* master, the creator of the modern reform in the *mise en scène*. No one could be better qualified than M. Jacques Copeau—his disciple, and a disciple who himself became a model—to address to Appia the last farewell of the Theatre.

Here is the article that M. Copeau sent to *Comoedia* from the Burgundian solitude of Pernand-Vergelesses:

ADOLPHE APPIA died on February 29, in a nursing home near Nyon (Switzerland), where necessary treatments had kept him for a considerable time. He was in his sixty-sixth year.

Several times we had feared for him. But, after each alarm, we recovered confidence in the resources of his exceptional constitution. The clarity of his vision, the easy assurance of his whole personality, the animation of his spirit, his always ready enthusiasm and inimitable grace—everything in him, up to those last days, spoke of life and the love of life. "Your young man . . ." That is how he signed one of the last letters he sent me. And I recall, at the end of his last letter, this farewell: "To all, my best greetings; to you, my old heart . . ." His old heart abruptly ceased to beat. Now he is only a few ashes. Dear Appia!

Today, I do not dream of retracing the work and the life of the great artist who was my master and my friend. His name, if it is not familiar except to a few initiates among us, is celebrated throughout the entire world. His personality, his creative action, are written in the history of the theatre of these last thirty years. But they are not always written clear, for Appia had more imitators than disciples.

He lived alone, modest and hard-working, dreaming, designing, writing—a little harsh toward outsiders, but to those he loved pouring out the treasures of his imagination. Three books—*La Mise en scène du drame wagnérien, Die Musik und die Inszenierung,* and *L'Oeuvre d'art vivant;* some essays; a hundred magnificent designs; a small number of productions such as *Manfred, Tristan, Rhinegold, Valkyrie;* and his work at Hellerau with Jaques-Dalcroze—these were enough for Appia to dominate the art of the *mise en scène* in his time.

All the expositions of modern theatre, and again recently that at Magdeburg, have shown the work of the master downstage and in the limelight. At Amsterdam, in 1923, the place of honor was reserved for him. Visiting the other rooms, one could easily see that whatever others did after him proceeded, more or less distorted, from his work.

It was he, along with Gordon Craig, who opened for us a new vision. It was he who led us to grandeur and to eternal principles.

Appia was musician and architect. He taught us that the musical duration, which envelops, commands, and shapes the dramatic action, at the same time engenders the space in which it develops. For him, the art of stage production in its pure sense was nothing other than the embodiment of a text or a musical composition, made sensible by the living action of the human body and its reaction to the spaces and masses set against it.

Hence the banishment from the stage of all inanimate decoration, of painted scenery, and the basic role of that active element which is light.

When one has said that, one has said it all or nearly all. One has a *radical* reform—Appia used that word willingly—whose consequences, as they developed, stretch from the stairways of Reinhardt to the constructivism of the Russians. One is in possession of a scenic point of view. One is at ease. One can work on the drama and the actor instead of always revolving around more or less original decorative formulae, more or less "unpublished" staging methods the seeking of which makes us lose sight of the essential objective.

The viewpoint of Appia: An action in rapport with an architecture should be enough for us to create a masterpiece—if stage directors know what a drama is, if dramatic writers know what a stage is . . .

Dear Appia, we will [not] soon meet again, as we have done each year. And I shall not see you more. We shall have no more of those endless talks that left us exhausted with enthusiasm and friendship. You will come no more to welcome my little troupe on the Geneva station platform, nor to my dressing room before a performance to verify a detail of my costume. No more will you stand, draped in your Ibsenesque greatcoat, against the stage boxes at the Lausanne theatre, sizing up the audience from above, as if you stood guard at the doorway of the spectacle your friends were about to present. No more will you act out the play after we have acted it, recapturing our least gestures and all our intonations, enjoying with a childlike laugh our most subtle intentions, and often enough clarifying a point of our art that for us had remained obscure.

I shall see no more, Appia, your great white head nodding at the door of the car that took us back to France, then bowing again with that exquisite courtesy that was the flower of your natural nobility. . . . Yet you will not cease to be among us, lamented, adored, consulted, welcome.

—Jacques Copeau

Pernand, March 6, 1928

NOTES

PROLOGUE

1. Wolzogen, *Aus Schinkels Nachlass*, p. 209.
2. Vernon, *Modern Stage Production*, pp. 41–42.
3. Winter, *Shakespeare on the Stage*, pp. 83–86.
4. Hagemann, *Die Kunst der Bühne*, pp. 81–82.
5. Fuchs, *Revolution in the Theatre*, p. 39.
6. Macgowan, *The Theatre of Tomorrow*, pp. 15–16.

CHAPTER I

1. Bonifas, *Adolphe Appia*, Introduction.
2. Sievers, Trapp, Schum, *250 Jahre Braunschweigisches Staatstheater*, p. 142.
3. Odier, "Adolphe Appia," *Le Rythme*, no. 25 (March, 1929).
4. Keyserling, *Reise durch die Zeit*, p. 132.
5. *Ibid.*, p. 177.
6. Stadler, "*Die Musik und die Inscenierung*," *Der Bund* (August 31, 1962).
7. Chamberlain, *Richard Wagner*, pp. 215, 317.
8. Chamberlain, *Lebenswege Meines Denkens*, p. 241.
9. Chamberlain, *Richard Wagner*, p. 196.
10. *Ibid.*, pp. 207, 211.
11. Pretsch, *Cosima Wagner und Chamberlain in Briefwechsel*, p. 398.
12. Chamberlain, *Drei Bühnendichtungen*, Preface.
13. H., "*Der Weinbauer*," *Neue Zürcher Zeitung* (April 10, 1896).
14. Chamberlain, *Drei Bühnendichtungen*, Preface.
15. Keyserling, *op. cit.*, p. 117.

CHAPTER II

1. Wagner, "Die Kunst und die Religion," *Gesammelte Schriften*, Vol. III, p. 15.
2. Skraup, *Der Fall Bayreuth* (1962).
3. Jean Thorel, a few years older than Appia, was a highly respected jour-

nalist writing for *Le Figaro;* he also became known as translator of some of Gerhart Hauptmann's dramas.

4. *Journal de Genève* (July 9, 1899).

5. Vogt, "Neue Buehnenkunst," *Allgemeine Musikzeitung,* Vol. 35, no. 15 (1908).

6. Simonson, *The Stage Is Set,* p. 354.

7. Reyle, "Als der 'Appia Ring' Zersprang," *National Zeitung* (November 18, 1961).

8. Unsigned, "Lohengrin," *Journal de Genève* (February 15, 1899).

9. Horowicz, *Le Théâtre d'Opéra* (1946), p. 217.

10. Reyle, *op. cit.*

11. Pretsch, *Cosima Wagner und Chamberlain in Briefwechsel.* The succeeding references are taken from the same source, pp. 51, 171, 174, 396, 405, 464–465, 638.

12. Aber, "Das Problem der Stilbühne bei den Werken R. Wagners," *Musikwissenschaftlicher Kongress der deutschen Musikgesellschaft* (1925), p. 313.

13. Appia, "Der Saal des Prinzregenten-Theaters," *Die Gesellschaft,* Vol. III (1902), p. 198.

CHAPTER III

1. Rolland, *Musicians of Today,* p. 253.

2. Bruneau, *La Vie et Les Oeuvres de Gabriel Fauré,* p. 26.

3. Keyserling, "Die erste Verwirklichung von Appias Ideen zur Reform der Bühne," *Allgemeine Zeitung* (April 6, 1903); Valjean, "Une Tentative de reforme scénique," *La Semaine Litteraire* (May 23, 1903); Ferrière, "La Reforme scénique d'Adolphe Appia," *La Suisse* (May 29, 1903).

4. Jaques-Dalcroze, *Rhythm, Music and Education,* p. VIII.

5. *Ibid.,* pp. 153–155.

6. Storck, *Emile Jaques-Dalcroze,* pp. 28–29.

7. Driver, *A Pathway to Dalcroze Eurythmics,* p. 1.

8. Jaques-Dalcroze, *op. cit.,* p. 150.

9. Storck, *op. cit.,* p. 37.

10. Jaques-Dalcroze, "La Technique corporelle et les movements continus," *Le Rythm* (June, 1926), no. 23.

11. Brunct-Lecomte, *Jaques-Dalcroze,* p. 122.

12. Storck, *op. cit.,* p. 89.

13. Salzmann, "Hellerau." *Der Rhythmus,* Vol. II, part 1, p. 71.

14. Seidl, *Die Hellerauer Schulfeste . . . ,* pp. 39–40.

15. Bonifas, "A Propos des Fêtes d'Hellerau," *La Semaine Litteraire,* Vol. XXVIII, no. 1,018.

16. Dent, (ed.) *Bernard Shaw and Mrs. Patrick Campbell, Their Correspondence,* p. 139.

17. Wolkonsky, "Meine Erinnerungen." *In Memoriam Hellerau,* pp. 28–29.

18. *Ibid.,* pp. 26–27.

19. *Berichte der Dalcroze Schule,* no. 3 (August-September, 1913).

20. Wolkonsky, *op. cit.,* p. 24.

21. Feudel, *Rhythmisch-Musikalische Erziehung,* pp. 129–130.

22. Brandenburg, *Der Moderne Tanz,* p. 123.

23. Storck, *op. cit.*, p. 82.

24. *Dresdener Anzeiger* (June 29, 1913).

25. *Ibid.* (October 20, 1913).

26. Feraud, "Paul Claudel Verkündigung," *Wiener Fremdenblatt* (October 9, 1913).

27. Jaques-Dalcroze, *Rhythm, Music and Education*, p. 169.

28. Blanchart, *Firmin Gémier*, pp. 249–250.

29. *Journal de Genève* (July 5, 7, 1914); *La Tribune de Genève* (July 5, 6, 1914).

30. Wolkonsky, *op. cit.*, pp. 13–14.

31. Jaques-Dalcroze, *Souvenirs, Notes et Critiques*, p. 41.

CHAPTER IV

1. Copeau, "Un Essai de Rénovation Dramatique," *Nouvelle Revue Française* (Sept. 1, 1913).

2. Lettres de Jacques Copeau à Louis Jouvet, *Cahiers de la Compagnie Madelaine Renaud et Jean-Louis Barrault*, Vol. I, no. 2.

3. Copeau, "Adolphe Appia et l'art de la scène," *Cahiers de la Compagnie Madelaine Renaud et Jean-Louis Barrault*, Vol. XIII, no. 10.

4. Copeau, "Visites à Gordon Craig, Jaques-Dalcroze et Adolphe Appia," *La Revue d'Histoire du Théâtre* (October, 1963).

5. Mercier, "Adolphe Appia. The Rebirth of Dramatic Art," *Theatre Arts Monthly*, Vol. XVI, no. 8 (1932).

6. Kurtz, *Jacques Copeau, Biographie d'un Théâtre*, p. 62.

7. Borgal, *Jacques Copeau*, p. 140.

8. Hamilton, *The Theory of the Theater . . .*, p. 376.

9. Knapp, *Louis Jouvet, Man of the Theatre*, p. 60.

10. Copeau, *Souvenirs du Vieux Colombier*, p. 41.

11. Borgal, *op. cit.*, p. 198.

12. Saint-Denis, "Le Cinquentenaire du Vieux Colombier," *Premières Mondiales*, Vol. XIV, no. 38 (October, 1963).

13. Copeau, "Accord Jacques Copeau-Louis Jouvet," *Comoedia* (September 17, 1924).

14. Copeau, "Adolphe Appia et l'art de la scène."

15. Reyle, "Eine Kuenstlerfreundschaft im Dienste des Theaters," *Tages-Anzeiger für Stadt und Kanton Zürich*, no. 205 (September 1, 1962).

16. Reyle, "Briefe von Adolphe Appia," *Neue Zürcher Zeitung* (April 17, 1966).

17. Bablet, *Edward Gordon Craig*, pp. 213–214; Craig, *On the Art of Theatre*, p. VIII.

18. Mercier, *op. cit.*

19. Letter from Gordon Craig to William Rothenstein (December 25, 1914). Harvard Library.

20. Bablet, *op. cit.*

21. *Radio Talks. Edward Gordon Craig*, Diary (1960).

22. *Gordon Craig et le Renouvellement du Théâtre*, p. 65.

23. Vernon, *Modern Stage Production*, p. 96.

24. Mercier, *op. cit.*

25. Bablet, *op. cit.*

26. Craig, *Fourteen Notes*, p. 10, 11.

27. *Journal de Genève* (October 8, 1914).

28. Chamberlain, *Briefe, 1882–1924*, Vol. I, p. 268.

29. Reyle, *op. cit.*

30. Copeau, "Adolphe Appia et l'art de la scène."

31. Reyle, "Adolphe Appia als Kuenstler und Mensch," *Opernwelt*, Vol. III (1962), no. 7–8.

32. Odier, "Adolphe Appia," *Le Rythm*, no. 25 (March, 1929).

33. Nicollier, *René Morax*, p. 38.

34. *Ibid.*, p. 45.

35. Odier, *op. cit.*

36. Stadler, "Adolphe Appia and Oskar Waelterlin," *Neue Zürcher Zeitung* (May 26, 1963).

37. L.t.h. (Dr. Luethy?), *National Zeitung* (September 23, 1920).

CHAPTER V

1. Stadler, "Adolphe Appia und Oskar Waelterlin," *Neue Zürcher Zeitung* (May 26, 1963); Radice, "Appia alla Scala quarant' anni dopo," *Corriere Della Sera* (October 22, 1963).

2. Appia, "Preparation de *Tristan* à La Scala," *Journal de Genève* (January 22, 1924).

3. Povoledo, "Stage Design in Italy," *World Theatre*, Vol. XI, no. 2 (1963).

4. Reyle, "Als der 'Appia *Ring*' Zersprang," *National Zeitung* (November 18, 1961).

5. Odier, "Adolphe Appia," *Le Rythm*, no. 25 (1929).

6. Ojetti, *Cose Viste* (1951).

7. G., C. "La Prima di *Tristano e Isotta*," *Corriere Della Sera* (December 21, 1923).

8. Toni, "*Tristano e Isotta*," *Il Popolo d'Italia* (December 21, 1923).

9. "*Tristano e Isotta*," *L'Avanti* (December 21, 1923).

10. Gatti, "*Tristano* à La Scala," *Illustrazione Italiana* (December 30, 1923).

11. Lualdi, "*Tristano e Isotta*," *Il Secolo* (December 21, 1923).

12. "*Tristano e Isotta*," *Il Secolo* (January 11, 1924).

13. Thorez, "Scenarii," *Il Secolo* (January 29, 1924).

14. Appia, "Preparation de *Tristan à La Scala*"; Appia, "*Tristan e Isotta* à La Scala," *La Semaine Litteraire*, Vol. XXXXII, no. 1566 (1924).

15. Corradini, "Una Lettera di Enrico Corradini ad Adolfo Appia," *Il Secolo* (January 19, 1924).

16. Reyle, "Adolphe Appias Basler 'Ring'," *Basler Nachrichten* (September 2, 1962).

17. Program Book, no. 11, Municipal Theatre in Basel (1924–1925).

18. Reyle, "Briefe von Adolphe Appia," *Neue Zuercher Zeitung* (April 17, 1966).

19. Reyle, "Adolphe Appias Basler 'Ring'," *op. cit.*

20. Huis, "*Das Rheingold*," *Basler Anzeiger* (November 22, 1924).

21. [Merian], "*Das Rheingold*," *Basler Nachrichten* (November 22, 1924).

22. er. "*Das Rheingold*" *National Zeitung* (November 22, 1924).

23. "*Das Rheingold* in Basel," *Schweizer Vorwaerts* (November 25, 1924);

"Das Rheingold à Bâle" Gazette de Lausanne (November 28, 1924).

24. Bonifas, "Richard Wagner à Bâle et la mise-en-scène d'Adolphe Appia," *La Semaine Litteraire* (November 29, 1924).

25. Cron, "*Das Rheingold,*" *Basler Volksblatt* (November 23, 1924).

26. Reyle, "Adolphe Appias Basler 'Ring'."

27. Merian, "*Die Walkuere,*" *Basler Nachrichten* (February 2, 1925).

28. Reyle, "*Die Walkuere* in Basel," *Berner Tageblatt* (February 5, 1925).

29. "*Die Walkuere* in Basel," *Schweizer Arbeiter Zeitung* (February 6, 1925).

30. "*Die Walkuere,*" *National Zeitung* (February 2, 1963).

31. Cron, "*Die Walkuere,*" *Basler Volksblatt* (February 2, 1925).

32. Program Book, no. 24.

33. *Ibid.,* no. 28.

34. *Rundschau Bürgerzeitung* (April 9, 1925).

35. Reyle, "Adolphe Appias Basler 'Ring'."

36. Reyle, "Briefe von Adolphe Appia."

37. *Ibid.*

38. "*Prometheus,*" *Basler Volksblatt* (February 12, 1925).

39. Huis, "*Prometheus,*" *Basler Anzeiger* (February 13, 1925).

40. Gessler, "*Prometheus,*" *National Zeitung* (February 12, 1925).

41. "*Prometheus,*" *Basler Nachrichten* (February 12, 1925).

42. Reyle, "Als der 'Appia *Ring*' Zersprang."

CHAPTER VI

1. Chenevière, *La Semaine Litteraire* (December 24, 1921).

2. Letter from Jacques Copeau to Adolphe Appia (February 8, 1921), *Théâtre Populaire,* no. 5 (January/February, 1954).

3. Allen, *Walt Whitman as Man and Legend,* p. 11.

4. Appia did not desist from correcting even the published copies he gave to friends. As Karl Reyle and André Veinstein informed me, he inserted these corrections in the French edition: p. 10, tenth last line—*grave et toujours* douloureuse (instead of *tragique*); p. 13, seventh line—*sous le* (instead of *la*) vocable; p. 110, seventeenth line—*ainsi que nous la connaissons* instead of *ainsi qu'il la fait*); picture of Walhalla—in parentheses—*c'est Froh qui trace l'arc-en-ciel;* picture of *Echo and Narcisse*—*trois* (instead of *cinque*) naiades.

5. Dénes, "*Adolphe Appia vu par lui-même,*" *Musées de Genève,* no. 29 (October, 1962).

6. Van Wyck, "Designing 'Hamlet' with Appia," *Theatre Arts Monthly,* Vol. IX, no. 1 (January, 1925).

EPILOGUE

1. Stadler, "Adolphe Appia und Oscar Waelterlin."

2. Reyle, "Briefe von Adolphe Appia."

3. Copeau, "Adolphe Appia et l'art de la scène."

4. Reyle, "Eine Künstlerfreundschaft im Dienst des Theaters."

5. Copeau, "L'Art et l'oeuvre d'Adolphe Appia," *Comoedia* (March 12, 1928).

6. Forel, "A la memoire d'Adolphe Appia," *Journal de Genève* (March 1, 1929).

7. Mercier, "L'Avenir du Théâtre Lyrique," *Gazette de Lausanne* (February 2, 1945).

8. Mercier, "Adolphe Appia. The Rebirth of Dramatic Art."

9. Waelterlin, *Bekenntnis zum Theater*, p. 95.

10. Borgal, *Metteurs en scène*, pp. 48–51; Knapp, *Louis Jouvet, Man of the Theatre*, p. 176.

11. Kurtz, "Homage Paid to Copeau," *New York Times* (November 17, 1963).

12. Elder, "The Cartel of Four," *Theatre Annual*, Vol. I, 1942, p. 29.

13. Reyle, "Adolphe Appia als Kuenstler und Mensch," *Maske und Kothurn*, Vol. VIII, no. 3–4 (1962).

14. Walter, *Thema und Variationen, Erinnerungen und Gedanken*, p. 187.

15. Appia, *Music and the Art of the Theatre*, p. XII.

16. Houghton, *Moscow Rehearsals*, pp. 168, 191.

17. Barba, "Theatre Laboratory 13 Rzedow," *Tulane Drama Review*, Vol. IX, no. 3 (1965).

18. Ruediger, *Emil Preetorius. Das Szenische Werk*, pp. 7–16.

19. Herzfeld, "Buehnenbild und Bildende Kunst," *Program*, Goetterdaemmerung, p. 34 (1955).

APPIA'S WRITINGS

T HE year in which Appia wrote a particular piece is given directly after its title. The German title appears in the few cases in which an essay has been published only in Germany and the manuscript has been lost. English titles are added to all essays.

BOOKS

La Mise en scène du drame wagnérien. 1892–1894.
(The Staging of the Wagnerian Music Drama).
 Paris: Léon Challey. 1895.
La Musique et la mise en scène. 1894–1896.
 Berne: Theaterkultur Verlag. Schweizer Theater Jahrbuch. No. 38–39. 1963.
 Die Musik und die Inscenierung. Munich: Bruckmann. 1899.
 Music and the Art of the Theatre. Coral Gables, Fla.: University of Miami Press. 1962.
L'Oeuvre d'art vivant. 1916–1920.
 Geneva-Paris: Edition Atar. 1921.
 The Work of Living Art. Coral Gables, Fla.: University of Miami Press. 1960.

ESSAYS, ARTICLES, SCENARIOS

Das Rheingold. Scenario. c. 1891. (lost).
Die Walkuere. Scenario. c. 1891–1892.
Siegfried. Scenario. 1892.
Die Goetterdaemmerung. Scenario. 1892.
Notes de mise en scène pour l'Anneau de Nibelungen. 1891–1892.
(Comments on the Staging of The Ring of the Nibelung).
 Revue d'Histoire du Théâtre. No. 1–2. 1954.
Parsifal. Scenario. c. 1896.

Der Tuermer. Vol. XVI, No. 5. October, 1912.
Neue Zürcher Zeitung. April 24, 1964.

Die Inscenierung von Tristan und Isolde.
(The Staging of Tristan and Isolde).
  (from Appendix, *La Musique et la mise en scène*).
  Theatre Workshop. Vol. I. No. 3. 1937.
  The Art of Scenic Design. Lee Simonson. New York: Harper & Row, Publishers, Inc. 1950.
  Theatre and Drama in the Making. John Gassner and Ralph Allen (eds.). Boston: Houghton Mifflin Company. 1964.
  Wagner on Music and Drama. Albert Goldman and Evert Sprinchorn (eds.). New York: E. P. Dutton & Co., Inc. 1964.

Comment reformer notre mise en scène. c. 1900.
(Ideas on a Reform of our Mise en Scène).
  La Revue des Revues. Vol. I. No. 9. 1904.
  Directing the Play. Toby Cole and Helen Krich Chinoy (eds.). Indianapolis: The Bobbs-Merrill Company, Inc. 1953.

Der Saal des Prinzregenten-Theaters.
(The Auditorium of the Prinzregenten-Theater).
  Die Gesellschaft. Vol. XVIII. No. 3. 1902.

Manfred. Scenario. 1903.

Introduction à mes notes personnelles. 1905.
(Introduction to my Personal Notes).

Retour à musique.
(Return to Music).
  Journal de Genève. August 20, 1906.

Notes sur le théâtre.
(Comments on the Theatre).
  La Vie Musicale. Vol. I. No. 6. 1909.

Response au questionnaire.
(Answer to the Questionnaire).
  L'Essor, July 11, 1908.

Style et solidarité.
(Style and Solidarity).
  Le Rythme. Vol. I. No. 6. 1909.
  Der Rhythmus. Vol. I. No. 6. 1909.

La Gymnastique rythmique et le théâtre.
(Eurythmics and the Theatre).
  Les Feuillets. No. 14. 1912.
  Der Rhythmus. Ein Jahrbuch. Vol. I. Jena. 1911.

L'Origine et les débuts de la gymnastique rythmique.
(The Origin and Beginnings of Eurythmics).
  Les Feuillets. No. 5. 1911.
  Der Rhythmus. Ein Jahrbuch. Vol. I. Jena. 1911.

La Gymnastique rythmique et la lumière.
(Eurythmics and the Light).

Le Rythme. No. 34. 1932.

Du Costume pour la gymnastique rythmique.
(*About the Costume for Eurythmics*).
    Die Schulfeste der Bildungsanstalt Jaques-Dalcroze. Jena. 1912.

Die Inszenierung als Ausdrucksmittel.
(*The Mise en Scène as Means of Expression*).
    Moderne Theaterkunst. Geleitworte. Katalog. Mannheim. 1913.

Die Musik und das Buehnenbild.
(*Music and the Setting*).
    Theaterkunst Ausstellung. Katalog. Zurich. 1914.

En écoutant l'orgue à Saint-Pierre.
(*While Listening to the Organ in Saint-Pierre*).
    Journal de Genève. October 8, 1914.

Fêtes de l'Institut Jaques-Dalcroze.
(*Festivals of the Jaques-Dalcroze Institute*).
    Program. Dalcroze Institute. 1917.

Préface à l'édition anglaise de Musik und Inscenierung. 1918.
(*Preface to the English Edition of* Musik und Inscenierung).

Acteur, éspace, lumière, peinture.
(*Actor, Space, Light, Painting*).
    Journal de Genève (Abbreviated). January 22, 1954.
    Théâtre Populaire (Abbreviated). No. 5. January–February, 1954.

Carmen. Scenario, fragment. c. 1920.

Reflexions sur l'éspace et le temps.
(*Reflections on Space and Time*).
    Aujourd'hui. Vol. III. No. 17. 1958.

L'Art est une attitude. c. 1920.
(*Art is an Attitude*).
    20th Century Stage Decoration. Walter Rene Fuerst and Samuel J. Hume. London: Alfred A. Knopf, Inc. 1928.

L'Ancienne attitude. c. 1920.
(*The Former Attitude*).

La Mise en scène et son avenir. c. 1921.
(*Theatrical Production and Its Prospects in the Future*).
    Il Covegno. Vol. II. No. 4–6. 1923.
    Theatre Arts Monthly (Abbreviated). Vol. XVI. No. 8. 1932.
    Theatre Arts Anthology (Abbreviated). New York: Theatre Arts Books. 1950.
    Cahiers de la Compagnie Madeleine Renaud—Jean-Louis Barrault. No. 10. 1955.

Essai sur un problème dangereux. 1921.
(*A Dangerous Problem*).

Formes nouvelles. 1921.
(*New Forms*).

Le Geste de l'art. 1921.
(*The Gesture of Art*).

Après une lecture de Port-Royal *(Sainte-Beuve)*. 1921.
(After Reading Port-Royal *by Sainte-Beuve)*.
Art Vivant? ou nature morte? c. 1922.
(Living Art or Dead Nature?).
      Wendigen. No. 9–10. 1922.
      Bottega di Poesia. Milan. 1923.
      Theatre Annual. Vol. II. 1943.
      Players Magazine. Vol. 33. No. 4. 1962.
Le Sujet. 1922.
(The Theme).
L'Intermédiaire. 1922.
(The Intermediary).
Monumentalité. 1922.
(Monumentality).
      Revue d'Esthétique. October–December, 1953.
Pittoresque. c. 1922.
(Picturesqueness).
L'Enfant et l'art dramatique.
(The Child and Dramatic Art).
      Pour l'Ere Nouvelle. January, 1923.
A Propos de l'enfant et l'art dramatique.
      Pour l'Ere Nouvelle. April, 1923.
L'Homme est la mesure de toutes choses. August, 1923.
(Man Is the Measure of All Things).
      La Revue Théâtrale. Vol. VIII. No. 25. 1954.
      The Work of Living Art, see Books.
Les Maîtres Chanteurs. Scenario. c. 1922.
(The Mastersingers).
Tristan et Iseult. *Brève analyse du drame.* 1923.
Introduction aux representations de Tristan et Isolde *à la Scala de Milan. Direction A. Toscanini*. 1923.
(Introduction to the Performances of Tristan and Isolde *under the Direction of A. Toscanini at la Scala in Milan)*.
La Preparation de 'Tristan' à la Scala.
      Journal de Genève. January 22, 1924.
Tristano e Isotta *à la Scala*.
      La Semaine Litteraire. January 24, 1924.
Das Rheingold. Scenario. 1924.
Die Walkuere. Scenario. 1924.
Siegfried. Scenario. 1924. (lost)
Die Goetterdaemmerung. Scenario. 1923–1924.
Mise en scène pour Promethée. Scenario, fragment. 1924.
La Reforme et le théâtre de Bale.
(The Reform and the Theatre at Basel).

(Appia also used the title *A propos d'art scénique*). *Gazette de Lausanne*. May 3, 1925.

Expériences de théâtre et recherches personnelles. 1922–1924.
(Theatrical Experiences and Personal Investigations).

L'Art dramatique vivant. 1925.
(The Art of the Living Theatre).

Richard Wagner et la mise en scène.
(Richard Wagner and Theatrical Production).

Das Problem der Stilbuehne bei den Werken Richard Wagners.
(The Problem of Stylized Settings for Richard Wagner's Works).
> *Musikwissenschaftlicher Kongress zu Leipzig, 1925*.
> (Abbreviated). Leipzig: Breitkopf und Haertel. 1925.

Iphigenie en Tauride, Scenario, fragment. 1926.

Lohengrin. Scenario. 1926.

Macbeth. Scenario. (lost).

Fiction. c. 1926.

Mécanisation. c. 1926.
(Mechanization).

Conférence américaine. A draft, not finished. 1926.
(A Lecture for America).

Avertissement pour l'édition de mes "Essais" en I volume. 1926.
(Preface to the Edition of My Essays in One Volume).

Goethes Faust. Erster Teil. 1927–1928.
(Goethe's Faust. Part One).
> Bonn: Fritz Klopp Verlag. 1929.
> *Theatre Arts Monthly* (abbreviated). Vol. XVI. No. 8. 1932.

Curriculum Vitae d'Adolphe Appia par lui-même. 1927.
(Adolphe Appia's Curriculum Vitae written by himself).
> *Szineseti Lexicon*. Budapest. 1930.
> *Musées de Genève*. No. 29. October, 1962.

Quelques Pensées et citations.
(Some Thoughts and Quotes).
> *Le Rythme*. No. 37. August, 1934.

BIBLIOGRAPHY

BOOKS

Adami, G. *One Century of Design at La Scala.* Milan: G. Ricordi. 1940.

Allen, Gay Wilson. *Walt Whitman as Man, Poet, and Legend.* Carbondale, Ill.: Southern Illinois University Press. 1961.

Anderson, John. *The American Theatre.* New York: The Dial Press, Inc. 1938.

Apollonio, Mario. *La Regia.* Milan: Radio Italiana. 1960.

Aykroyd, Phyllis. *The Dramatic Arts of La Companies des Quinze.* London: Partridge, Ltd. 1935.

Bab, Julius. *Das Theater der Gegenwart.* Leipzig: J. J. Weber. 1928.

Bablet, Denis. *Edward Gordon Craig.* Paris: L'Arche Edition. 1962. New York: Theatre Arts Books. 1967.

————. *Esthétique générale du décor de théâtre de 1870 à 1914.* Paris: Centre Nationale de la Recherche Scientifique. 1965.

Bellonci, Goffredo (introd.). *Adolphe Appia.* Mostra della Scenografia di Adolphe Appia organizzato del Centro di Ricerche Teatrali. Rome: Centro di Ricerche Teatrali. 1951.

Bentley, Eric. *In Search of Theatre.* New York: Alfred A. Knopf, Inc. 1953.

Berchtold, Alfred. *La Suisse Romande au Cap XXème Siècle.* Lausanne: Payot. 1963.

Blanchart, Paul. *Histoire de la mise en scène.* Paris: Presses Universitaires de France. 1948.

————. *Firmin Gémier.* Paris: L'Arche Edition. 1954.

Blattler, Ugo (ed.). *Adolphe Appia e La Scena Costruita.* Rome: Fratelli Bocia. 1944.

Bonifas, Henry C. (introd.). *Adolphe Appia.* Zurich: Orell-Fuessli. 1929.

Borgal, Clement. *Jacques Copeau.* Paris: L'Arche Edition. 1960.

————. *Metteurs en scène.* Paris: Fernand Lanore. 1963.

Brandenburg, Hans. *Der Moderne Tanz.* Munich: George Mueller. 1921.

Brocket, Oscar G. *The Theatre, An Introduction.* New York: Holt, Rinehart and Winston, Inc. 1964.

Bruneau, Alfred. *La Vie et les oeuvres de Gabriel Fauré.* Paris: Charpentier et Fasquelle. 1925.

Brunet-Lecomte, Hélène. *Jaques-Dalcroze.* Geneva: Jeheber. 1950.

Buliga, Helen. *A Study of Adolphe Appia and his Influence. Master Thesis. Manuscript.* Detroit: Wayne University. 1949.

Carter, Huntly. *The New Spirit in Drama and Art.* London: Frank Palmer. 1912.

———. *The New Spirit in the European Theatre. 1914–24.* New York: George H. Doran Co. (Doubleday & Company, Inc.). 1926.

Chamberlain, Houston Stewart. *Richard Wagner.* Munich: Verlagsanstalt fuer Kunst und Wissenschaft. 1896.

———. *Drei Bühnendichtungen.* Munich: F. Bruckmann. 1902.

———. *Die Grundlagen des Neunzehnten Jahrhunderts.* Munich: F. Bruckmann. 1906.

———. *Lebenswege Meines Denkens.* Munich: F. Bruckmann. 1919.

———. *Briefe, 1882–1924.* 2 Vol. Munich: F. Bruckmann. 1928.

Copeau, Jacques. *Souvenirs du Vieux Colombier.* Paris: Nouvelles Editions Latines. 1931.

———. *Le Théâtre Populaire.* Paris: Presses Universitaires de France. 1942.

———. *Les Fourberies de Scapin de Moliere.* Paris: Edition du Deuil. 1951.

Jacques Copeau et le Vieux Colombier. Paris: Bibliothèque Nationale. 1963.

Craig, Edward Gordon. *On the Art of the Theatre.* London: W. Heinemann. 1912.

———. *Towards a New Theatre.* London-Toronto: J. M. Dent & Sons, Ltd. 1913.

———. *Fourteen Notes.* Seattle: University of Washington Book Store. 1931.

———. *Radio Talks.* London: Discurion. 1960.

———. *The Theatre Advancing.* New York: Benjamin Blom, Inc. 1964.

Gordon Craig et le Rénouvellement du Théâtre. Paris: Bibliothèque Nationale. 1962.

D'Amico, Silvio (ed.). *Enciclopedia della Spettacolo.* Rome: Casa editrice Le Machere. 1954.

Delpit, Louise. *Paris-Théâtre Contemporain.* Northampton, Mass.: Smith College. 1925.

Dent, Alan (ed.). *Bernard Shaw and Mrs. Patrick Campbell, Their Correspondence.* New York: Alfred A. Knopf, Inc. 1952.

De Zoete, Beryl. *The Thunder and the Freshness.* New York: Theatre Arts Books. 1963.

Driver, Ethel. *A Pathway to Dalcroze Eurythmics.* New York: Thomas Nelson and Sons. 1957.

Dussane, Béatrix. *Dieux des Planches.* Paris: Flammarion. 1964.

Ellis, H. Ashton. *Richard Wagner's Prose Works.* London: Kegan Paul, Trench, Truebner and Co. 1892–1900.

Evreinov, Nicolas. *Histoire du Théâtre Russe.* Paris: Editions du Chêne. 1947.

Feudel, Elfriede. *Rhythmisch-Musikalische Erziehung.* Wolfenbuettel: Moeseler Verlag. 1956.

Fischel, Oskar. *Das Moderne Buehnenbild.* Berlin: E. Wasmuth. 1923.

Fort, Paul. *Mes Memoires. 1872–1944.* Paris: Flammarion. 1944.

Freedley, George. *A History of the Theatre.* New York: Crown Publishers. 1941.

Fuchs, George. *Revolution in the Theatre.* Ithaca, N.Y.: Cornell University Press. 1959.

Fuerst, Walter Rene, and Hume, Samuel Y. *Twentieth Century Stage Decoration.* London: Alfred A. Knopf, Inc. 1928.

Gassner, John. *Form and Idea in Modern Theatre.* New York: The Dryden Press. (Holt, Rinehart and Winston, Inc.). 1956.

————. *Directions in Modern Theatre and Drama.* New York: Holt, Rinehart and Winston, Inc. 1965.

Gatti, Carlo. *Il Teatro alla Scala Rinnovato.* Milan: Fratelli Treves. 1926.

Goldman, Albert, and Sprinchorn, Evert (eds.). *Wagner on Music and Drama.* New York: E. P. Dutton & Co., Inc. 1964.

Gollancz, Victor. *The "Ring" at Bayreuth.* New York: E. P. Dutton & Co., Inc. 1965.

Gorelik, Mordecai. *New Theatres for Old.* New York: E. P. Dutton & Co., Inc. 1962.

Gregor, Joseph. *Kulturgeschichte der Oper.* Vienna: Gallus Verlag. 1950.

————. *Grosse Regisseure der Modernen Buehne.* Vienna: Austrian Committee of UNESCO. 1958.

Grimel, Pierre (ed.). *Dictionaire des Biographies.* Paris: P.U.F. 1958.

Groscher, Robert. *Paul Claudel.* Hellerau: Verlag Hegner. 1930.

Guerrieri, Gerardo. *Da Appia a Craig. La Regia Teatrale a cura di Silvio D'Amico.* Rome: Belardetti editore. 1967.

Gvozdev, A. A. *Western European Theatre at the Turn of the 19th–20th Century.* Leningrad-Moscow: 1939.

Hagemann, Carl. *Die Kunst der Bühne.* Stuttgart: Deutsche Verlagsanstalt. 1922.

Hainaux, René (ed.). *Stage Design Throughout the World Since 1935.* New York: Theatre Arts Books. 1956.

————. *Stage Design Throughout the World Since 1950.* New York: Theatre Arts Books. 1963.

Hamilton, Clayton. *The Theory of the Theatre and Other Principles of Dramatic Criticism.* New York: Henry Holt and Company, Inc. (Holt, Rinehart and Winston, Inc.). 1910.

Hart, Jean. *Les Théâtres du Cartel.* Geneva: Skira. 1934.

Hartnoll, Phyllis (ed.). *The Oxford Companion to the Theatre.* London: Oxford University Press. 1958.

Hewitt, Barnard. *Theatre U.S.A.* New York: McGraw-Hill Book Company. 1959.

Horowicz, Bronislaw. *Le Théâtre d'Opéra.* Paris: Edition de Flore. 1946.

Houghton, Norris. *Moscow Rehearsals.* New York: Harcourt, Brace and Company. 1936.

Hughes, Glenn. *The Story of the Theatre.* New York: Samuel French. 1928.

Jaques-Dalcroze, Emile. *Rhythm, Music and Education.* London: Chatto & Windus Ltd. 1921.

————. *Rhythmic Movement.* London: Novello and Co. 1921.

————. *Souvenirs, notes et critiques.* Neuchâtel-Paris: Attinger. 1942.

Jones, Robert E. *The Dramatic Imagination.* New York: Duell, Sloan & Pearce. 1941.

Joseph, Stephen (ed.). *Actor and Architect.* Toronto: University of Toronto Press. 1964.

Keyserling, Hermann. *Reise durch die Zeit.* Vaduz: Liechtenstein Verlag. 1948.

Kindermann, Heinz. *Buehne und Zuschauerraum.* Vienna: Hermann Boehlens. 1963.

Kitzwegerer, Lisa. *Alfred Roller als Buehnenbildner*. Dissertation. Manuscript. Vienna: Universitaet Wien. 1959.

Knapp, Bettina L. *Louis Jouvet, Man of the Theatre*. New York: Columbia University Press. 1957.

Kosch, Wilhelm (ed.). *Deutsches Theater Lexikon*. Klagenfurt-Vienna: Kleinmayer Verlag. 1951.

Kunz-Aubert, Ulysse. *Le Théâtre à Genève*. Geneva: Perrat-Gentil. 1963.

Kurtz, Maurice. *Jacques Copeau, Biographie d'un Théâtre*. Paris: Nagel. 1950.

Langner, Lawrence. *The Magic Circle*. New York: E. P. Dutton & Co., Inc. 1951.

Le Maître, Jules. *Theatrical Impressions*. London: H. Jenkins Ltd. 1924.

Lert, Ernst. *Mozart auf dem Theater*. Berlin: Schuster und Loeffler. 1921.

Levik, Serge Y. *Notes of an Opera Singer*. Moscow: Art. 1955.

Lifar, Serge. *La Danse*. Paris: Gauthier-Villars. 1965.

Lindlar, Heinrich. *77 Premieren*. Rodenkirchen, Rhineland: P. J. Tonger. 1965.

Lintilhac, Eugène-François. *Histoire Générale du Théâtre en France*. Paris: Flammarion. 1904–1911.

Littmann, Max. *Das Muenchner Kuenstlertheater*. Munich: L. Webner. 1908.

Macgowan, Kenneth. *The Theatre of Tomorrow*. New York: Boni & Liveright. (Liveright Publishing Corporation). 1921.

————. and Jones, Robert E. *Continental Stagecraft*. New York: Harcourt, Brace and Company, Inc. (Harcourt, Brace & World, Inc.). 1922.

————. and Melnitz, William. *The Living Stage*. Englewood Cliffs, N.J.: Prentice-Hall, Inc. 1955.

Marotti, Ferruccio. *Edward Gordon Craig*. Bologna: Cappelli. 1961.

————. *Appia e Craig: La Origini della Scena Moderna*. Venice: Estrato de la Biennale di Venezia. 1963.

Martersteig, Max. *Das Deutsche Theater im Neunzehnten Jahrhundert*. Leipzig: Breitkopf und Haertel. 1924.

Martin, Frank A. (introd.). *Emile Jaques-Dalcroze*. Neuchâtel: Editions de la Baconnière. 1965.

Matthews, Brander. *The Theatres of Paris*. London: Low, Marston, Searle and Rivington. 1880.

Melchinger, Siegfried, and von Einem, Gottfried. *Caspar Neher*. Velber-Hannover: Friedrich Verlag. 1966.

Mell, Max. *Alfred Roller*. Vienna: Wiener Literarische Anstalt. 1922.

Moderwell, Hiram. *The Theatre of Today*. New York and London: John Lane, The Bodley Head, Ltd. 1914.

Moreau, Pierre (introd.). *Claudel, Homme de Théâtre*. Cahiers Paul Claudel. Paris: Gallimard. 1964.

Moussinac, Léon. *The New Movement in the Theatre*. London: B. T. Batsford Ltd. 1931.

Nicoll, Allardyce. *The English Theatre*. London: Thomas Nelson & Sons. 1936.

————. *The Development of the Theatre*. London: George G. Harrap & Co., Ltd. 1937.

Nicollier, Jean. *René Morax*. Geneva: Editions du Panorama. 1958.

Oenslager, Donald. *Scenery Then and Now*. New York: W. W. Norton & Company, Inc. 1936.

Ojetti, Ugo. *Cose Viste*. Florence: Sansoni. 1951.

Otto, Teo. *Meine Szene*. Cologne: Kiepenheuer und Witsch. 1966.

Parker, John (ed.). *Who Is Who in the Theatre*. London: Sir Isaac Pitman & Sons, Ltd. 1912–1938.

Pendleton, Ralph (ed.). *The Theatre of Robert Edmond Jones*. Middletown, Conn.: Wesleyan University Press. 1957.

Perfall, Karl von. *Ein Beitrag zur Geschichte der Koeniglichen Theater in Muenchen*. Munich: Piloty & Lohle. 1894.

Pirchan, Emil. *Zweitausend Jahre Buehnenbild*. Vienna: Bellaria Verlag. 1949.

Pitoëff, Georges. *Nôtre Théâtre*. Paris: Messages. 1949.

Pluess, Eduard, in collaboration with Elles, Iris. *Kuenstlerlexikon der Schweiz, 20. Jahrhundert*. Frauenfeld: Verlag Huber & Company, A. G. 1959.

Pretsch, Paul (ed.). *Cosima Wagner und Chamberlain im Briefwechsel*. Leipzig: Ph. Reklam. 1934.

Rhodes, Salomon. *The Contemporary French Theatre*. New York: F. S. Crofts & Company. (Appleton-Century-Crofts). 1942.

Roberts, Vera. *On Stage*. New York: Harper & Row, Publishers. 1962.

Rolland, Romain. *Musicians of Today*. New York: Henry Holt and Company, Inc. (Holt, Rinehart and Winston, Inc.). 1915.

Rouché, Jacques. *L'Art Théâtrale Moderne*. Paris: Edouard Cornely et Cie. 1910.

Rowell, George. *The Victorian Theatre*. London: Oxford University Press. 1956.

Ruediger, Wilhelm. *Emil Preetorius. Das Szenische Werk*. Berlin-Vienna: Albert Limbach. 1944.

Sadler, M. E. (introd.). *The Eurythmics of Jaques-Dalcroze*. London: Constable & Company, Ltd. 1920.

Saint-Denis, Michel. *Theatre. The Rediscovery of Style*. New York: Theatre Arts Books. 1960.

Schubarth, Ottmar. *Das Bühnenbild*. Munich: G. D. W. Callway. 1955.

Seidl, Arthur. *Die Hellerauer Schulfeste und die Bildungsanstalt Jaques-Dalcroze*. Regensburg: Gustav Bosse. 1912.

Seltzer, Daniel (ed.). *The Modern Theatre*. Boston: Little, Brown & Company. 1967.

Shaw, George B. *Dramatic Opinions and Essays*. New York: Brentano's. 1906.

Sievers, Heinrich; Trapp, Albert; and Schum, Alexander. *250 Jahre Braunschweigisches Staatstheater*. Brunswick: E. Appelhaus & Company. 1941.

Simonson, Lee. *The Stage Is Set*. New York: Dover Publications. 1946.

––––––. (ed.).*The International Exhibition of Theatre Arts*. Toronto: George S. McLeod Ltd. 1934.

Skelton, Geoffrey. *Wagner at Bayreuth. Experiment and Tradition*. New York: George Braziller, Inc. 1965.

Skraup, Siegmund (et al.). *Der Fall Bayreuth*. Basel: Basilius Press. 1962.

Speaight, Robert. *William Poel and the Elizabethan Revival*. London: William Heinemann, Ltd. 1954.

Stadler, Edmund. *Adolphe Appia und Richard Wagner*. Zurich: Katalog der Richard Wagner Ausstellung. 1951.

––––––. *Das Schweizerische Buehnenbild von Appia bis Heute*. Zurich: Theaterkultur Verlag. 1954.

––––––. *Le Festspiel Suisse, Adolphe Appia et Emile Jaques-Dalcroze*. Paris: International Federation for Theatre Research. 1961.

————. *Mostra dell'Opera di Adolphe Appia.* Venice: Catalogo Ufficiale La Biennale di Venezia. 1963.

————. *Adolphe Appia.* Florence: La Strozzina. 1963.

Stamm, Rudolf. *Geschichte des Englischen Theaters.* Bern: A. Francke. 1951.

Stern, Ernst. *Buehnenbildner bei Max Reinhardt.* Berlin: Henschel Verlag. 1955.

Storck, Karl. *Emile Jaques-Dalcroze.* Stuttgart: Greiner & Pfeiffer. 1912.

Stuckenschmidt, H. H. *Oper in dieser Zeit.* Velber-Hannover: Friedrich Verlag. 1964.

Van Vechten, Carl. *Music and Bad Manners.* New York: Alfred A. Knopf, Inc. 1916.

————. *Interpreters and Interpretations.* New York: Alfred A. Knopf, Inc. 1917.

Van Volkenburg Brown, Ellen, and Beck, Edward (eds.). *Nellie Cornish. Her Autobiography.* Seattle: University of Washington Press. 1964.

Veinstein, André. *La Mise en scène théâtrale et sa condition esthétique.* Paris: Flammarion. 1955.

————. *Du Théâtre Libre au Théâtre Louis Jouvet.* Paris: Editions Billandot. 1955.

Vernon, Frank. *Modern Stage Production.* London: The Stage Office. 1923.

Victor, Erlich. *Russian Formalism. History-Doctrine.* The Hague: Mouton and Company. 1955.

Volbach, Walther R. *Problems of Opera Production.* Hamden, Conn.: Archon Book, The Shoestring Press, Inc. 1967.

Waelterlin, Oskar. *Bekenntnis zum Theater.* Zurich: Oprecht Verlag. 1960.

Wagner, Richard. *Gesammelte Schriften.* 8 vol. Leipzig: Breitkopf und Haertel. 1912–1914.

Walter, Bruno. *Thema und Variationen. Erinnerungen und Gedanken.* Frankfurt a. M.: S. Fischer Verlag. 1963.

Winds, Adolf. *Geschichte der Regie.* Berlin: Deutsche Verlags-Anstalt. 1925.

Winter, William. *Shakespeare on the Stage.* New York: Moffat, Yard and Company. 1915.

Wolkonsky, Serge. "Meine Erinnerungen." *In Memoriam Hellerau.* Freiburg, Breisgau: Rombach and Company. 1960.

Wolzogen, A. von (ed.). *Aus Schinkels Nachlass.* Berlin: Oberhofbuchdruckerei. 1862–1864.

Zuckerman, Elliot. *The First Hundred Years of Wagner's* Tristan. New York: Columbia University Press. 1964.

ARTICLES AND ESSAYS,

NEWSPAPERS, PERIODICALS, AND MANUSCRIPTS

Berichte der Dalcroze Schule, No. 3, August-September, 1913.

"Das Claudel Programm Buch," Hellerau, 1913.

"Echos de Partout-Tristan à la Scala," *La Semaine Litteraire*, October 6, 1923.

"La Fête de Juin," *Journal de Genève*, July 5, 7, 1914.

"La Fête de Juin," *Tribune de Genève*, July 5, 6, 1914.

"50th Anniversary of the Théâtre du Vieux Colombier, French News," *French Information Service*, no. 2, December, 1963.

"Hellerau Schulfest," *Dresdener Anzeiger*, June 29, 1912.

"*Lohengrin,*" *Journal de Genève,* February 15, 1899.

"The Moscow Art Theatre Musical Studio of Vladimir Nemirovitch-Dantchenko," *Souvenir* (Oliver A. Sayler, ed.), New York, 1925.

"Obscure Pioneer of the Newest Art in the Theatre," *Current Opinion,* August, 1916.

"*L'Oeuvre d'Art Vivant,*" *Tribune de Genève,* January 2, 1922.

"Programm Hefte," Stadttheater Basel, 1924–1925.

"*Prometheus,*" *Basler Nachrichten,* February 12, 1925.

"*Prometheus,*" *Basler Volksblatt,* February 12, 1925.

"*Das Rheingold,*" *National Zeitung,* November 22, 1924.

"*Das Rheingold,*" *Schweizer Vorwaerts,* November 25, 1924.

"*Das Rheingold à Bâle,*" *Gazette de Lausanne,* November 28, 1924.

"Stadttheater" (editorial), *Rundschau-Buergerzeitung,* April 9, 1925.

"The Staging of Wagner's *Tristan and Isolde* by A. Appia in Milan," *The Weekly of Academic Theatres,* Leningrad, 1924.

"*Tristan*" (editorial), *L'Avanti,* December 21, 1923.

"*Tristan*" (editorial), *Il Secolo,* January 11, 1924.

"Die Verkuendigung," *Dresdener Anzeiger,* October 20, 1913.

"*Die Walkuere,*" *Schweizer Arbeiter Zeitung,* February 6, 1925.

Aber, Adolf. "Das Problem der Stilbühne bei den Werken R. Wagners," *Musikwissenschaft. Kongress der deutschen Musikgesellschaft,* Leipzig: Breitkopf und Haertel, 1925.

Albright, H. Darkes. "Appia Fifty Years After," *The Quarterly Journal of Speech,* Vol. 35, nos. 2/3, 1949.

Appia, Henri. "Notes sur Adolphe Appia," Manuscript.

Bab, Julius. "Dalcroze," *Die Schaubuehne,* no. 19, 1912.

Bablet, Denis. "Adolphe Appia of Geneva, Great Friend and Collaborator of Emile Jaques-Dalcroze," *Le Rythme,* April, 1963.

————. "Technique, éspace, lumière," *Le Théâtre,* January 15, 1964.

————. "Adolphe Appia, la musique et la mise en scène," *Le Mesure de France,* February, 1964.

Babenchikov, M. "From Appia and Craig to the Theatre of the Future," *New Studio,* Moscow, 1912.

Barnes, Hugh. "The Life and Work of Adolphe Appia," Manuscript.

Barba, Eugenio. "Theatre Laboratory 13 Rzedow," *Tulane Drama Review,* Vol. IX, no. 3, 1965.

Beck, Gordon, "Adolphe Appia. His Life and Work," *Players Magazine,* Vol. 33, no. 4, 1962.

Bekker, Paul. "Die Opernszene," *Frankfurter Zeitung,* August 22, 1913.

Bentley, Eric. "Copeau and the Chimera," *Theatre Arts Monthly,* Vol. 32, no. 1, 1950.

Berthoud, D. "*L'Oeuvre d' art vivant,*" Suisse Liberale, February 2, 1922.

Bie, Oscar. "Zur Inszenierung *der Walkuere* in Basel," *National Zeitung,* no. 56, 1925.

Bonifas, Henry C. "A Propos des Fêtes d'Hellerau," *La Semaine Litteraire,* June 29, 1913.

————. "A Propos des Fêtes d'Hellerau," *La Semaine Litteraire,* July 5, 1913.

————. "La Gymnastique Rythmique," *L'Essor*, September 25, 1915.

————. "La Rénovation scénique et les travaux d'Adolphe Appia," *Ecrits Nouveaux*, June, 1918.

————. "Le Temps viendra," (no data available).

————. "Richard Wagner à Bâle et la mise en scène d'Adolphe Appia," *La Semaine Litteraire*, November 29, 1924.

————. "Adolphe Appia," Eulogy, Manuscript.

————. "Adolphe Appia," *Le Rythm*, no. 23, June, 1928.

Bonifas, Paul A. "Quelques Souvenirs à propos Adolphe Appia et Henry Charles Bonifas," 1961. Manuscript.

Bridel, Gaston. "Sur Adolphe Appia," *Gazette de Lausanne*, March, 1928.

C. G. "La Prima di *Tristano e Isotta*," *Corriere Della Sera*, December 21, 1923.

Chenevière, Jacques. "*L'Oeuvre d'art vivant*," *La Semaine Litteraire*, December 24, 1921.

Cheseaux, René. "Adolphe Appia et l'art dramatique de demain," *Pages d'Art*, Vol. III, no. 10, 1917.

————. "*L'Oeuvre d'art vivant*," *Gazette de Lausanne*, March 27, 1922.

————. "*Tristan et Iseut* à Milan," *Gazette de Lausanne*, January 20, 1924.

Claudel, Paul. "Le Théâtre d'Hellerau." *La Nouvelle Revue Française.* September, 1913.

Clurman, Harold. "Conversations with Two Masters." *Theatre Arts Monthly*, Vol. XIX, no. 11, November, 1935.

Combe, Ed. "L'Art de la mise en scène," *Wissen und Leben*, October 10, 1914.

Conrad, Herbert. "Mit Appia nichts zu schaffen . . . ," *Bayreuther Tageblatt, Festspielnachrichten*, July 26, 29, 1966.

Copeau, Jacques. "L'Art théâtral moderne." *La Nouvelle Revue Française*, January, 1911.

————. "Le Théâtre du Vieux Colombier," *Le Théâtre*, September, 1913. *Educational Theatre Journal*, Vol. XIX, no. 4, 1967.

————. "Un Essai de rénovation dramatique," *La Nouvelle Revue Française*, September, 1913.

————. "Le Réouverture du Vieux Colombier," *La Nouvelle Revue Française*, November, 1919.

————. "Accord Jacques Copeau-Louis Jouvet," *Comoedia*, September 17, 1924.

————. "L'Art et l'oeuvre d'Adolphe Appia," *Comoedia*, March 12, 1928.

————. "Lettres de Jacques Copeau à Louis Jouvet," *Cahiers de la Compagnie Madeleine Renaud et Jean-Louis Barrault*, Vol. I, no. 2, 1950.

————. "Lettres de Jacques Copeau à Adolphe Appia," *Théâtre Populaire*, no. 5, January-February, 1954.

————. "Adolphe Appia et l'art de la scène," *Cahier de la Compagnie Madeleine Renaud et Jean-Louis Barrault*, Vol. XIII, no. 10, 1955.

————. "Visites à Gordon Craig, Jaques-Dalcroze et Adolphe Appia, 1915," *La Revue d'Histoire du Théâtre*, October, 1963.

Corradini, Enrico. "Una Lettera di Enrico Corradini ad Adolfo Appia," *Il Secolo*. January 19, 1924.

Crommelin, Armand. "Hellerau," *Bayreuther Blaetter*, Vol. VII, no. 192.

Cron, Joseph. "*Das Rheingold*," *Basler Volksblatt*, November 23, 1924.

————. "*Die Walkuere*," *Basler Volksblatt*, February 2, 1925.

Curjel, Hans. "Moderne Buehnenbild Typen," *Das Werk*, Vol. 31, no. 2, 1944.

Dalcroze, Gabriel. "Appia et Jaques-Dalcroze," *Journal de Genève*, June 20, 1962.

Dénes, Tibor. "Georges Pitoëff à Genève," *Tribune de Genève*, September 9, 1961.

————. "La correspondence de Georges Pitoëff et de Matthias Morhardt," *La Revue d'Histoire du Théâtre*, December, 1961.

————. "Nous honorons Appia, pionnier du théâtre actuel," *Journal de Genève*, May 26, 1962.

————. "Adolphe Appia jusqu'à nos jours," *Journal de Genève*, October 20, 1962.

————. "*Adolphe Appia vu par lui-même*," *Musées de Genève*, no. 29, October, 1962.

————. "Bilan d'une amitié fameuse," *Journal de Genève*, July 3, 1965.

Dutour, Alfred. "*La musique et la mise en scène*," *Journal de Genève*, July 9, 1899.

Ed. "*L'Oeuvre d'art vivant*," *Tribune de Genève*, January 2, 1922.

Elder, Judith. "The Cartel of Four," *Theatre Annual*, Vol. I, 1942.

Engel, Fritz. "Paul Claudels 'Verkuendigung'," *Das Theater*, Vol. V, no. 4, 1913.

F. "M. Denis Bablet évoque l'oeuvre et l'action d'Adolphe Appia," *Journal de Genève*, April 27, 1964

F. "*L'Oeuvre d'art vivant*," *Journal de Genève*, December 21, 1921.

Feraud, Ernest. "Paul Claudel, Verkündigung," *Wiener Fremdenblatt*, October 6, 1913.

Ferrière, A. "La reforme scénique d'Adolphe Appia," *La Suisse*, May 29, 1903.

————. "Les dessins d'Adolphe Appia." *Journal de Genève*, May 18, 1929.

Fischel, Oskar. "Adolphe Appias Werk," *Das National Theater*. Vol. III, no. 2, 1931.

Forel, Oscar. "A la memoire d'Adolphe Appia," *Journal de Genève*, March 1, 1929.

————. "Appia reformateur de la mise en scène," *Gazette de Lausanne*, October 10, 1962.

————. "Adolphe Appia," Memorandum, Manuscript.

G.M. "*L'Oeuvre d'art vivant*," (no date available; *La Semaine Litteraire*.)

Gatti, Carlo. "*Tristan* à La Scala," *Illustrazione Italiana*, December 30, 1923.

Gessler, Dr. "*Prometheus*," *National Zeitung*, February 12, 1925.

Granville-Barker, Harley. "Letter to Jacques Copeau," *Theatre Arts Monthly*, Vol. XIII, no. 10, April, 1929.

Guiral, M. "Return of Jacques Copeau," *Living Age*, no. 346, April, 1934.

H.S. "Der Weinbauer," *Neue Zürcher Zeitung*, April 10, 1896.

Haj. "Adolphe Appia. Eine Gedenkausstellung," *Neue Zürcher Zeitung*, October 16, 1962.

Herzog, Friedrich H. "Adolphe Appia in Basel," *Das Theater,* Vol. VI, no. 9, 1925.

Hewitt, Barnard. "Gordon Craig and Post-Impressionism," "*The Quarterly of Speech,*" Vol. 30, no. 1, 1944.

Hille, Gertrude. "Adolphe Appia und sein Werk," *Neue Zürcher Zeitung*, June 7, 1929.

Huis, Franz. "*Das Rheingold*," *Basler Anzeiger*, November 22, 1924.

————. "*Die Walkuere*," *Basler Anzeiger*, February 3, 1925.

————. "*Prometheus*," *Basler Anzeiger*, February 12, 1925.

Ingham, Percy. "The Jaques-Dalcroze Method," *The Eurythmics of Jaques-Dalcroze*. London: Constable & Company Ltd., 1912.

Jacobi, Johannes. "Neu-Bayreuth und die Vorgaenger," *Die Zeit*, November 30, 1962.

Jaques-Dalcroze, Emile. "La Technique corporelle et les movements continus," *Le Rythme*, no. 23, 1928.

Jordan, Margarethe. "Adolphe Appia tel que je l'ai connu," Manuscript.

Kaucher, Dorothy. "Adolphe Appia's Theories of Production," *The Quarterly Journal of Speech*, Vol. XIV, no. 3, 1928.

Kernodle, George. "Wagner, Appia, and the Idea of Musical Design," *Educational Theatre Journal*, Vol. XVI, no. 3, 1954.

Keyserling, Hermann von. "Die Erste Verwirklichung von Appias Ideen zur Reform der Bühne," *Allgemeine Zeitung*, April 6, 1903.

Kurtz, Maurice. "Homage Paid to Copeau," *The New York Times*, November 17, 1963.

L.t.h. (Dr. Luethy?) "*Siegfried*," *National Zeitung*, September 23, 1920.

Lert, Ernst. "Staging *The Ring of the Nibelung*," *The Wagner Quarterly*, Vol. I, no. 1, 1937.

————. "Some Pertinent Remarks on the Psychology of Conducting," *The Wagner Quarterly*, Vol. I, no. 4, 1937.

Lualdi, Adriano. "*Tristano e Isotta*," *Il Secolo*, December 21, 1923.

Marotti, Ferruccio. "Il Teatro Moderno Nella Conzezione e Nell' Opera di Adolphe Appia," *Critica d'Arte*, Vol. XI, September/October, 1964.

Marsop, Paul. "Bayreuth, die Zeitenwende und das Reich," *Die Musik*, Vol. XVII, no. 1, 1925.

Matter, Jean. "Le 'Parsifal' d'Adolphe Appia au Grand Théâtre de Genève," *Gazette de Lausanne*, May 9–10, 1964.

Mauricheau-Beaupré. "Adolphe Appia," *Polybiblion*, 1929.

Melchinger, Siegfried. "Adolphe Appia, der Utopische Prophet," *Stuttgarter Zeitung*, October 20, 1962.

Mercier, Jean. "Adolphe Appia. The Rebirth of Dramatic Art," *Theatre Arts Monthly*, Vol. XVI, no. 8, 1932.

————. "L'Avenir du Théâtre Lyrique," *Gazette de Lausanne*, February 2, 1945.

————. "Adolphe Appia," Memorandum, Manuscript.

Merian, Wilhelm. "*Siegfried*," *Basler Nachrichten*, September 24, 1920.

————. "*Das Rheingold*," *Basler Nachrichten*, November 22, 1924.

————. "*Die Walkuere*," *Basler Nachrichten*, February 2, 1925.

Meyerhold, Vsevelod. "Meyerhold Orders Music," *Theatre Arts Monthly*, Vol. 20, no. 9, September, 1936.

Mitchell, Lee. "Appia's Influence on Modern Stage Artists," Manuscript.

N.R. "Zum Gedaechnis eines grossen Buehnenbildners. Appia Ausstellung in der Landesbibliothek," *Der Bund*, September, 1962.

Odier, Henri. "Adolphe Appia," *Le Mondain*, December 8, 1928.

————. "Adolphe Appia," *Le Rythme*, no. 25, March, 1929.

Paumgartner, Bernard. "Festspielregie in der Mozartstadt Salzburg," *Maske und Kothurn*, Vol. VIII, no. 2, 1962.

P.G. "Une exposition. Adolphe Appia à la Bibliothèque Nationale," *Journal de Genève*, October 12, 1962.

P.R. "L'Oeuvre d'art vivant," *St. Galler Tagblatt*, February 24, 1922.

Poertner, Paul. "Adolphe Appia—Wegbereiter des modernen Theaters," *Neue Zürcher Zeitung*, July 21, 1959.

Poesio, Paolo Emilio. "In una mostra a Venezia due profeti del Teatro Moderno,"

La Nazione, September 12, 1963.

Ponti, Gioro. "Il Teatro di Appia—L'Opera d'Arte Vivente," *Il Covegno,* Vol. IV, no. 1, 1923.

————. "Il Teatro di Appia," *Domus,* 1929.

Povoledo, Elena. "Stage Design in Italy," *World Theatre,* Vol. XI, no. 2, 1962.

Radice. "Appia alla Scala quarant' anni dopo," *Corriere Della Sera,* October 22, 1963.

R.E. "*Das Rheingold,*" *National Zeitung,* November 22, 1924.

————. "*Die Walkuere,*" *National Zeitung,* February 2, 1925.

Raff [Raffaele Calzini?]. "Il caso Appia," *Il Secolo,* January 11, 1924.

Rauscher, Ulrich. "Hellerau," *Die Schaubuehne,* Vol. IX, no. 41, 1913.

Reyle, Karl. "*Das Rheingold* in Basel," *Berner Tagblatt,* December 6, 1924.

————. "*Die Walkuere* in Basel," *Berner Tagblatt,* February 5, 1925.

————. "Erinnerungen an Adolphe Appia," *Der Bund,* February 3, 1961.

————. "Als der 'Appia *Ring*' Zersprang," *National Zeitung,* November 18, 1961.

————. "Adolphe Appia-Wegbereiter der Modernen Inszenierung," *National Zeitung,* August 25, 1962.

————. "Adolphe Appia," *Neue Zürcher Zeitung,* August 26, 1962.

————. "Adolphe Appia and the New Stage," *The American-German Review,* August-September, 1962.

————. "Eine Kuenstlerfreundschaft im Dienste des Theaters," *Tagesanzeiger fuer Stadt und Kanton Zürich,* September 1, 1962.

————. "Ein Reformator der europaeischen Buehnenkunst," *Oltner Tagblatt,* September 1, 1962.

————. "Adolphe Appias Basler 'Ring'," *Basler Nachrichten,* September 2, 1962.

————. "Adolphe Appia als Kuenstler und Mensch," *Opernwelt,* Vol. III, no. 7–8, 1962.

————. "Adolphe Appia als Kuenstler und Mensch," *Maske und Kothurn,* Vol. VIII, no. 3–4, 1962.

————. "Besuch bei Edward Gordon Craig," *Neue Zürcher Zeitung,* January 13, 1963.

————. "Adolphe Appia und Jacques Copeau—eine Kuenstlerfreundschaft," *St. Galler Tagblatt,* September 1, 1963.

————. "'Parsifal' nach Adolphe Appias Ideen," *Tages-Anzeiger,* May 4, 1964.

————. "Appias 'Parsifal' in Genf," *Der Bund,* April 26, 1964.

————. "Briefe von Adolphe Appia," *Neue Zürcher Zeitung,* April 17, 1966.

————. "Edward Gordon Craig," *Neue Zürcher Zeitung,* August 14, 1966.

————. "Adolphe Appia und Edward Gordon Craig," *Basler Nachrichten,* August 28, 1966.

Roeder, Ralph. "Copeau 1921," *Theatre Arts Monthly,* Vol. V, 1921.

Rogers, Clark M. "Appia's Theory of Acting, Eurythmics for the Stage," *Educational Theatre Journal,* Vol. XIX, no. 4, 1967

Rotzler, Willy. "Ahnherr der abstrakten Buehne," *Die Weltwoche,* October 26, 1962.

B., S. "*L'Oeuvre d'art vivant,*" *Journal de Genève,* December 21, 1921.

Saint-Denis, Michel, "Le Cinquentenaire du Vieux Colombier," *Premières Modiales,* Vol. XIV, no. 38, 1963.

Salzman, A. von. "Hellerau," *Der Rhythmus,* Vol. II, 1912.

Sarton, Mary. "Copeau in Florence," *Theater Arts Monthly,* Vol. XIX, no. 9, Sep-
    tember, 1935.
Saylor, Oliver M. "The Moscow Art Theatre Goes in for Opera," *Vanity Fair,* June,
    1925.
————. "The Moscow Art Theatre Musical Studio and Its Work," *Theatre,* Sep-
    tember, 1925.
————. "Ultra-Modern Art in Relation to the Theatre," *Arts and Decoration,*
    December, 1925.
Scharrer, Eduard. "Adolphe Appia im Muenchner Theater Museum," *Rheinisch-
    Westfaelische Zeitung,* August 30, 1929.
Scheffler, K. "Buehnenkunst," *Kunst und Kuenstler,* Vol. V, no. 6, 1907.
Schultze-Malkowsky, E. "Neue Illustrationen zu Wagners 'Parsifal'," *Dekorative
    Kunst,* Vol. IX, 1906.
Seelmann-Eggebert, Ulrich. "Wegbereiter des Modernen Buehnenbildes," *Badische
    Neuste Nachrichten,* November 15, 1963.
Sembranti, Paolo. "Appia e Gordon Craig in vetrina sulla Laguna," *Nazione Sera,*
    September 12, 1963.
Simonson, Lee. "Appia's Contribution to the Modern Stage," *Theatre Arts Month-
    ly,* Vol. XVI, no. 8, 1932.
————. "Principles of Appia Applied to Wagner," *The Wagner Quarterly,* Vol. I,
    no. 2, 1937.
Stadler, Edmund. "Adolphe Appia," *Maske und Kothurn,* Vol. V, no. 2, 1959.
————. "Die Musik und die Inscenierung," *Der Bund,* August 31, 1962.
————. "René Morax," *Neue Zürcher Zeitung,* January 11, 1963.
————. "Adolphe Appia und Oscar Waelterlin," *Neue Zürcher Zeitung,* May 26,
    1963.
————. "Le Festspiel Suisse, Adolphe Appia et Emile Jaques-Dalcroze," *Revue
    d'Histoire du Théâtre,* July, 1963.
————. "Adolphe Appia und Emile Jaques-Dalcroze," *Maske und Kothurn,* Vol.
    X, no. 3–4, 1964.
Storck, W. F. "Die Kuenstlerische Inszenierung des 'Parsifal'," *Die Szene,* June,
    1914.
Toni, Alceo. "*Tristano e Isotta*," *Il Popolo d'Italia,* December 21, 1923.
Thoriz, Enrico. "Scenarii," *Il Secolo,* January 29, 1924.
Valjean, Pierre. "Une Tentative de reforme scènique," *La Semaine Litteraire,* May
    23, 1903.
Van Vechten, Carl. "Adolphe Appia and Gordon Craig," *Forum,* Vol. 54, October,
    1915.
Van Wyck, Jessica Davis. "Working with Appia," *Theatre Arts Monthly,* Vol. VIII,
    no. 12, 1924.
————. "Designing 'Hamlet' with Appia," *Theatre Arts Monthly,* Vol. IX, no. 1,
    1925.
Veinstein, André. "Rédecouvrons Adolphe Appia," *Cahier de la Compagnie Made-
    leine Renaud et Jean-Louis Barrault,* Vol. XIII, no. 10, 1955.
————. "Rédecouvrons Adolphe Appia," *Heptagone,* Vol. I, no. 2, 1958.
Vogt, Karl. "Neue Buehnenkunst," *Allgemeine Musik-Zeitung,* Vol. 35, no. 15,
    1908.
Volbach, Walther R. "Appia's Productions and Contemporary Reaction," *Educa-*

tional Theatre Journal, Vol. XIII, no. 1, 1961.

————. "Beginnings of a Genius," *Players Magazine,* Vol. 33, no. 4, 1962.

————. "Profile of a Genius," *Educational Theatre Journal,* Vol. XV, no. 1, 1963.

————. "Jacques Copeau, Appia's Finest Disciple," *Educational Theatre Journal,* Vol. XVII, no. 3, 1965.

————. "Adolphe Appia und Houston Stewart Chamberlain," *Die Musikforschung,* Vol. XVIII, no. 4, 1965.

————. "The Collaboration of Adolphe Appia and Emile Jaques-Dalcroze," *Paul A. Pisk. Essays in his Honor.* Austin: College of Fine Arts, The University of Texas, 1966.

————. "Time and Space on the Stage," *Educational Theatre Journal,* Vol. XIX, no. 2, 1967.

Waelterlin, Oskar. "Adolphe Appia und die Inszenierung von Wagners 'Ring'," *National Zeitung,* no. 540, November, 1924.

————. "*Das Rheingold* am Stadttheater Basel," *National Zeitung,* no. 552, November, 1924.

————. "*Die Walkuere* am Stadttheater," *National Zeitung,* no. 55, February, 1925.

————. "*Prometheus* am Stadttheater," *National Zeitung,* no. 73, March, 1925.

Wagner, Friedlind. "De Bayreuth à Paris," *Nouvelles Litteraires,* October, 1955.

Wolkonsky, Serge. "Conference sur Appia," *Apollon,* Vol. III, no. 6, 1912.

Wolzogen, Hans von. "La Mise en scène du drame wagnérien," *Bayreuther Blaetter,* no. 4–5, 1895.

Zeiss, Karl. "Die Neue Szene," *Jugend,* no. 3, 1923.

Zinsstag, Adolphe. "Zur Neu-Inszenierung des Nibelungenringes," *Rundschau-Buergerzeitung,* January 23, 1925.

————. "Die Prostitution eines Kunstwerkes am Basler Stadttheater," *Rundschau-Buergerzeitung,* February 6, 1925.

————. "Via Appia," *Rundschau-Buergerzeitung,* February 27, 1925.

————. "Kunstfeindliches aus Basel," *Rundschau-Buergerzeitung,* April 9, 1925.

INDEX